Praise for Mitch Weiss and Holbrook Mohr

"A tour de force of investigative journalism and storytelling. This is the kind of book that inspires the next generation of journalists and reminds working reporters why they do the job."

—**Kevin Maurer, #1** *New York Times* **bestselling coauthor of** *No Easy Day*

"In light of current events, I can't imagine a more important book than *Broken Faith* by outstanding investigative journalists Mitch Weiss and Holbrook Mohr. Their chilling description of North Carolina's Word of Faith Fellowship and professed Christianity gone horribly awry is unsettlingly parallel to events involving Peoples Temple and its demagogic leader, Jim Jones. Much credit is due to the courageous former Word of Faith members who share their shattering stories in *Broken Faith*. If you care at all about religious abuse and the destructive means by which charismatic leaders exert despotic control of their well-meaning followers' lives, *read this book*."

—**Jeff Guinn,** *New York Times* **bestselling author of** *Manson* **and** *The Road to Jonestown*

"Fascinating and deeply researched... Compelling in its evidence, this shocking narrative examines the bonds of family, the limits of endurance, and how far people will go to save their souls."

—*Booklist*, **starred review**

"A compelling examination of a Christianist cabal whose crimes are evident but whose power seems, for the moment, unbreakable."

"A fast-paced, harrowing exposé... Transfixing.

BROKEN FAITH

Also by Mitch Weiss

Countdown 1945: The Extraordinary Story of the Atomic Bomb and the 116 Days That Changed the World (cowritten with Chris Wallace)

The Heart of Hell: The Untold Story of Courage and Sacrifice in the Shadow of Iwo Jima

The Yankee Comandante: The Untold Story of Courage, Passion, and One American's Fight to Liberate Cuba (cowritten with Michael Sallah)

Hunting Che: How a U.S. Special Forces Team Helped Capture the World's Most Famous Revolutionary (cowritten with Kevin Maurer)

No Way Out: A Story of Valor in the Mountains of Afghanistan (cowritten with Kevin Maurer)

Tiger Force: A True Story of Men and War (cowritten with Michael Sallah)

BROKEN FAITH

INSIDE ONE OF AMERICA'S MOST DANGEROUS CULTS

MITCH WEISS AND HOLBROOK MOHR

HANOVER
SQUARE
PRESS

**HANOVER
SQUARE
PRESS™**

Recycling programs
for this product may
not exist in your area.

ISBN-13: 978-1-335-26675-0

Broken Faith: Inside One of America's Most Dangerous Cults

First published in 2020. This edition published in 2021.

Hanover Square Press
22 Adelaide St. West, 40th Floor
Toronto, Ontario M5H 4E3, Canada
HanoverSqPress.com
BookClubbish.com

Printed in Italy by Grafica Veneta

To our families

CAST OF CHARACTERS

THE CHURCH

Jane Whaley: The unquestioned leader of the Word of Faith Fellowship, Whaley believes she's a prophet who holds the key to eternal salvation. A former math teacher, Whaley and her top ministers control all aspects of congregants' lives, from where they live to when they can get married and have sex.

Sam Whaley: The cofounder of the Word of Faith Fellowship, Whaley was a former used car salesman from Florence, South Carolina, who faded into the background once his wife took control of the church.

Brooke Covington: The daughter of wealthy Kansas farmers, she was an early disciple and is now one of Jane Whaley's closest confidantes. She was one of five people charged with kidnapping and assault in the beating of Matthew Fenner, a congregant who says he was attacked to expel his "homosexual demons."

Kent Covington: After spending eight months in a North Carolina prison in the 1970s, he found his way to the Word of Faith Fellowship. He married Brooke Covington and rose in the church hierarchy.

Mark Doyle: His journey to the Word of Faith Fellowship began after hearing God's voice at an AC/DC concert. A stickler for the rules, Doyle was a minister assigned to keep children in line and in the fold.

Mark Morris: An attorney and minister, Morris was in charge of the dreaded Lower Building—a structure that former congregants say was used as a de facto prison.

Ray Farmer: A minister, business owner, and the head of the church's security team, Farmer may be the most feared member of the Word of Faith Fellowship behind Jane Whaley. Former members say he has elaborate surveillance equipment and carries assault-style weapons in the back of his SUV.

Joshua Farmer: Ray Farmer's son, Josh Farmer, is an attorney who owns several businesses. His trucking company is one of a handful in the world certified to transport deadly potassium cyanide, which is used in the mining industry.

THE VICTIMS

Rick Cooper: After serving on a United States Navy nuclear submarine, Rick joined the Word of Faith Fellowship in 1993 to attend Bible school. He had hoped to eventually start his own church. But he would later regret uprooting his family from Darien, Georgia, to Spindale, North Carolina.

Suzanne Cooper: The matriarch of the Cooper family, she led two of her sisters into the church. Hoping to stay in Jane Whaley's good graces, she turned against one of those sisters in a bitter custody dispute with Kent and Brooke Covington.

John David Cooper: One of Rick and Suzanne's nine children, he was only eighteen months old when his family joined the church. But after nearly two decades of abuse, he became the first of the Coopers to flee.

Jeffrey Cooper: One of John David Cooper's brothers, he became an attorney and accountant. He attended key meetings with other church lawyers as they discussed how to undermine police and child welfare investigations.

Benjamin Cooper: Another of John David Cooper's brothers, he's an attorney and business owner who has dedicated his life to exposing the church in an attempt to save the children left behind.

Shana Muse: One of Suzanne Cooper's three sisters, Muse turned to the Word of Faith Fellowship for help after drugs led to trouble with the law. When she tried to leave, a church couple wrested away her four children.

Wanda Henderson: The mother of Suzanne Cooper and Shana Muse, Henderson was never a member of the church. She watched helplessly as three daughters and more than a dozen grandchildren suffered under Jane Whaley's spell. Affectionately known as "Mama-Gail," she never gave up on her family.

Sarah Anderson: Shana Muse's oldest daughter, Sarah and her siblings were sent to live with Kent and Brooke Covington when their mother tried to leave the church. Those ministers convinced Anderson that her mother was "wicked."

Danielle Cordes: Suzanne Cooper's niece, Danielle suffered brutal abuse at the hands of church leaders. During a child abuse investigation when she was ten years old, Danielle always wore her favorite dress for interviews with social workers. Like an orphan auditioning for a family, she had hoped they'd take her with them.

Michael Lowry: Born into the church, he was abused from a young age. After being held twice in the Lower Building, he escaped and told police about widespread abuse inside the church. He also told them he was brutally beaten because he was gay.

Matthew Fenner: When he was nineteen, he was attacked by congregants because they wanted to beat the "homosexual demons" out of him. He spent two years trying to get police to investigate the case, finally leading to charges being filed against five church members, including Brooke Covington and Sarah Anderson.

Jamey Anderson: Escaping the church at the age of eighteen after years of isolation and physical beatings, Jamey eventually put himself through law school and helped others flee the church.

THE ADVOCATES

Robynn Spence: As soon as she was elected Rutherford County Clerk of Courts, she tried to curb the Word of Faith Fellowship's influence inside the courthouse. She refused to renew the contracts of two employees with ties to the Word of Faith Fellowship. Spence also helped members leaving the church. But Spence died in 2014, about a year and a half after a man told her he was hired by a Word of Faith member to kill her because of her opposition to the church.

Nancy Burnette: A former court-appointed advocate, known as a guardian ad litem, Burnette had never heard of the Word of Faith Fellowship until two foster children under her care were sent to live with a couple in the congregation. After visits to the church school and worship services, Burnette opposed placing the foster children with the couple. Instead of taking action, her boss removed her from the case. She has dedicated her life to helping people escape the church.

John Huddle: He left his wife and children behind when he escaped the church in 2008. After surviving a heart attack and cancer, he became one of Word of Faith Fellowship's most outspoken critics, creating a blog to expose the church to the world.

LAW ENFORCEMENT

Prosecutor Brad Greenway: As district attorney, he chose not to pursue a number of child abuse and criminal investigations against the church.

Sheriff Chris Francis: Francis delayed investigating complaints related to the church. He also refused to help Robynn Spence when she was concerned the church was out to harm her.

TABLE OF CONTENTS

Beware of false prophets, who come to you dressed as sheep, but inside they are devouring wolves.

—Matthew 7:15

INTRODUCTION

This is the troubling story of the Word of Faith Fellowship and the lives destroyed by the secretive church in the foothills of North Carolina's Blue Ridge Mountains. The events depicted in this book come from extensive interviews with more than one hundred former members of the sect, their relatives, advocates, current and retired law enforcement officials, and others. We spent years researching and reporting this story, reviewing thousands of pages of documents ranging from child custody cases to police reports. We reviewed more than one hundred hours of video and audio recordings, many of which were secretly recorded by former congregants. We listened to dozens of tape-recorded sermons by Jane Whaley and other key church leaders from the mid-1990s.

Much of the documentation chronicling the earliest allegations of abuse in the church is based on a damning, 315-page report prepared by the North Carolina State Bureau of Investigation in 1995. Never publicly released, most of the information in the report is being revealed for the first time.

Information on Word of Faith Fellowship leader Jane

Whaley and other ministers is based on dozens of interviews, legal documents, bankruptcy filings, court cases, published material, and a 208-page sworn deposition of Whaley on April 27, 2017. Part of a contentious child custody case, Whaley's deposition has never been released to the public.

Biographical information on many of the current members and church leaders is based on their own words. Shortly after the *Associated Press* published its first in a series of articles about the Word of Faith Fellowship in February 2017, some congregants posted videos online to challenge what the church called "media lies."

And beginning in December 2017, the Word of Faith Fellowship purchased airtime on WCAB, a Rutherfordton, North Carolina–based radio station, every Monday, Wednesday, and Friday. Nearly two hundred members of the Word of Faith Fellowship have used the broadcast to deny allegations made against their church, criticize former members and their advocates, or give glowing "testimonies" about their experiences in the congregation. Videos of the radio programs have been posted on YouTube.com under a channel titled "WFF Speaks Out" as well as on the church's website.

Church leaders categorically deny that any abuse takes place at the Word of Faith Fellowship. The survivors stand by their stories.

PART ONE

IN THE BEGINNING

PROLOGUE

THE ESCAPE

John David Cooper bounded out the front door with a trash bag in his arms. This had to be the last of it. He was out of breath and out of time. He and his wife, Jessica, had been stuffing their clothes and belongings into their Corolla for what seemed like hours, but really it had been ten minutes. Jessica was headed back inside. John stopped her.

"We gotta leave," he said.

"But we still have more things."

"We can get them later."

She shook her head. She knew that wasn't true. Once they left, that was it. But if they stayed they'd lose even more.

"One more trip, just to make sure. I won't take long," she said. She broke into a run, down the hallway and into the bedroom. John sighed. *Stay calm*, he thought. He checked his watch.

The Wednesday night church service had just started. In only a matter of minutes they'd realize John and Jessica weren't there.

"C'mon!" he muttered.

The tree-lined street was utterly quiet, the picture of American middle-class prosperity. John and Jessica shared a tidy home with Jessica's parents and sister, in a neighborhood of respectable one-and two-story dwellings filled with other Word of Faith Fellowship members. Everyone kept an eye on their neighbors. No one went anywhere or talked to anyone new without someone taking note. Anything odd was immediately reported to a church leader. Anyone who looked the other way, or kept a secret, might well face the wrath of Jane Whaley. She was God's anointed, a prophet, the spiritual leader of Word of Faith Fellowship.

John and Jessica had planned this day for months, down to the very last detail. It had to be on a Wednesday or Sunday night, when everybody was in church for the 6:30 p.m. service. The house was ten minutes from the church's thirty-five-acre compound. They'd told Jessica's mom and dad, Randy and Cynthia Fields, they were heading out to gas up the car before church, just in case they wondered why they were leaving early. They left the house at 6:10 p.m.

At the BP station, they filled the tank. At 6:25 p.m. they returned to the house, parked at the side door, and started loading up their things. At 6:30 p.m. on Wednesday, everyone—including any stragglers—would be in the sanctuary, starting the first praise choruses. They had only ten minutes to grab everything and get out. Once church members realized they weren't there, the Word of Faith security team would come looking for them.

John could hear dresser drawers opening and closing. "Come on, Jessica," he shouted. The car was stuffed. He opened a rear door and jammed his bag inside. Jessica came through the door dragging a final bag, probably the biggest one of all.

"I don't know how we're going to find room," John said.

"Just throw it in," she said.

"Where?"

"I don't know. Just take it!" Her voice wavered.

John shoved the bag into the pile and slammed the door. He was sweating, his blue button-down shirt plastered to his back. He fumbled in his pocket for the car keys. He felt like a bank robber, loaded with loot and ready to make his getaway. Except he wasn't stealing anything. All they had were their personal belongings. They had to escape this miserable place.

John jammed the key into the ignition, and the car roared to life. Jessica jumped into the passenger seat.

He took a deep breath. Jessica was trembling.

"You OK?" he asked.

She nodded. "Yes. Let's go."

John was eighteen months old when his parents joined Word of Faith Fellowship, an independent evangelical Christian church in tiny Spindale, North Carolina. Throughout his life he had been choked, punched, and beaten to expel the demons they said possessed his soul. He had been publicly humiliated by Jane Whaley from the pulpit and harangued for long hours by ministers and congregants in a discipline they called "blasting." He was isolated from the outside world, forbidden television, radio, newspapers, and movies. He'd lived for long stretches in ministers' homes, separated from his parents and most of his eight siblings.

For years, John Cooper did not know this wasn't normal. Everyone else in his world had been abused in the same ways.

Life inside the church was brutal, but running away was risky, too. Where would he go? Anyone who left Word of Faith would likely never see his friends or family again, as such "attackers" were cut out of the lives of the faithful.

After today John would be dead to his family. He had been

bracing himself for that reality. He wasn't sure Jessica was ready for that. She was close to her family, especially her mother.

Jessica probably still believed that Whaley was a prophet. They'd been taught that anyone who left the church would face the wrath of God. They'd die a slow death from cancer, or be killed in a car accident, or be struck by lightning. Their souls would be damned for eternity.

John had stopped believing that nonsense a long time ago. But Jessica? She had been talking more and more about what might happen to them if Whaley really did have mystical powers. It had to be nerves, he thought. Jane Whaley was a fraud. That would come clear to Jessica once they were on the outside, around normal people. Their lives were going to get better. He was starting medical school. Their futures were bright. All they had to do was head east, to Charlotte. Out of Whaley's reach.

John glanced at his watch. It was 6:40 p.m. The two-lane wound down to US 74. He'd traveled it hundreds of times. Every second counted. He hit the gas.

"Slow down," Jessica said.

"I'm going the speed limit."

Jessica's phone rang. She looked at the screen. It was her mother. Her parents knew. Whaley knew. The police probably knew, too.

"Don't answer it," John said.

This was part of the escape plan. They'd agreed they wouldn't answer their phones.

Jessica looked ahead, staring at the white lines on the road. Only a few more miles and they'd jump on the highway and leave Rutherford County behind. But a car appeared in the rearview mirror, speeding in their direction. Could it be the security team?

They couldn't stop. Their future depended on it.

1

MOVING DAY, SEPTEMBER 19, 1993

Suzanne Cooper checked off the last item on her list. The boxes were labeled and loaded in the vehicles just outside the door. She'd make one last sweep of the house to be sure nothing was left. Someone tugged on her pant leg: Benjamin, grinning the gap-toothed grin of a seven-year-old. "Mom, when are we leaving?"

Suzanne sighed. "Real soon."

"Can we still play?"

"Yes. Keep an eye on your little brothers."

Benjamin bolted to the front yard to join his older siblings, Jeffrey and Lena. Five-year-old Peter was trying to keep up with them. Meanwhile, Suzanne's husband, Rick, had his hands full with the two toddlers, Chad and John David. Six Cooper kids, each born two years apart, running around the yard with their dad. Who almost qualified as another child, Suzanne thought.

She smiled at the sweet scene, pressing it into her memory. She wouldn't see it again.

She forgot for a moment the Ryder truck parked in the driveway, packed with all of their possessions. Their blue Chevrolet cargo van was parked just behind it, likewise stuffed with clothes, books, games, and flash cards to keep the children busy during the long trip.

They'd lived in Darien, Georgia, for four years, and Suzanne had loved the old rental house with its big yard, the neighboring couples with children, the friendly townspeople.

Darien had offered Suzanne stability, something she'd missed for the first twelve years of her marriage. Her husband was a sailor, an engineer on a US Navy nuclear submarine. Every time they got settled and made friends they'd up and move again, usually just after a baby arrived. They'd lived in Hawaii, Washington, Italy, and Florida. Darien, Georgia, was their latest stop, a community of cypress trees, cobblestone streets, a simple, very Southern place. Neighbors looked out for each other. Everyone went to church on Sunday morning.

After twenty years, Rick had retired from the Navy, and the family now would move to Spindale, North Carolina, where he'd study to become a pastor.

The screen door slammed. Rick had John David in his arms. "Are you ready?"

She nodded.

"OK, let's get everyone in the van," he said.

"I'll be out in a minute," she said.

Suzanne was apprehensive about this move. It didn't help that Rick made this life-changing decision without consulting her. It was typical Rick; he never thought things through, and it was up to Suzanne to make it work out. *Maybe that's how Christian marriages work*, she thought.

Rick "had a calling," and had started preaching on weekends at Christian Life, a nearby nondenominational church. The parishioners liked Rick. He wasn't the most dynamic pastor, but he was earnest, and a good family man. With close to one hundred members, congregants believed Rick was the kind of minister they could build a church around. They paid him $300 to preach each Sunday, and with Rick's growing family, every bit helped.

Just before he left the Navy, the church leaders made Rick an offer: How would he like to become their full-time pastor? When Rick told Suzanne, she was overjoyed. They could put down roots. Her two youngest children, Chad and John David, had been born in Darien. It was the perfect location. Her mother, Wanda Henderson, and her four sisters lived in Florida, an easy drive away. Everyone thought it was the perfect next step.

Everyone but Rick.

Rick's mother, Cora, lived in Forest City, North Carolina, and for ten years had attended Word of Faith Fellowship, another, newer kind of independent Protestant church. At Word of Faith the believers sang loud, talked loud, and prayed loud. They were led by Jane Whaley, a charismatic woman preacher. The congregation swore she'd turned around many troubled lives. Rick thought Jane Whaley could open up the Bible to him, enlighten his faith in Jesus, and help him launch his career.

For a decade, whenever the Coopers visited Cora, Rick and Suzanne attended services at Word of Faith with their growing brood. The congregation showered them with love. The Coopers went to their dinners and family gatherings. They praised the children. The Coopers were a picture-perfect young family. Everyone said so.

Word of Faith was founded by Sam Whaley and his wife, Jane, but she was clearly the feature attraction. Jane was a small woman, and with her big blond hair, power suits, and flashy gold necklaces, she looked more like a businesswoman than a pastor. But Jane Whaley was more than that. To many in her church she was chosen by God, larger-than-life, a prophet with a special gift.

In her thick Southern drawl, she told stories about her life before she was born again, before she found Jesus. She'd start slowly, talking in general terms about how Satan constantly worked to turn good people bad. Inevitably building to a crescendo, she'd narrow her message down to here and now, calling out the particular devils she saw hovering near one follower or another, threatening to inhabit their lives.

Her doctrine was clear and easy to understand: Satan employed an army of invisible demons on the earth, supernatural beings sent from hell to manipulate humans into addiction, illness, and wrongdoing. But believers were not helpless. They had the Bible, strong mutual ties, and frequent worship services to keep their minds trained on higher things. When the devil threatened, Jane Whaley used a dramatic high-decibel technique she called "blasting"—shouting and screaming—to drive the evil back to the pit of hell.

"You literally scare the demons away," one congregant gushed as he explained the technique to Rick.

Jane used Scripture to justify the church's practices, including blasting. One of her favorites was Mark 16:17–18, where Jesus lists the many spiritual powers given to his followers. Among them was "deliverance," driving away evil spirits. Whaley singled this one out as a commandment.

She cited Acts 10:38, too. "We are told that Jesus was anointed with the Holy Spirit and power to heal all who were oppressed by the devil," Jane said during one fiery sermon. "As believers, we are to take that same healing and deliverance to those who are oppressed. God has revealed to us that demonic oppression is present in those who have been born again, as well as those who have not.

"Many have been set free from the devil's torment and oppression as the result of believing prayer and submission to
God. Those who were once drug addicts and alcoholics are
now delivered by the power of God and are living normal
lives, serving God and doing His will," she shouted.

The dramatic prayer could "break the power of Satan" so
"the demons can come out," she said. It didn't matter that
nothing akin to blasting appears in Scripture. This was her
personal revelation, straight from God.

Once started, a "blasting" session could go on and on. People would get so worked up they'd wail, scream, convulse, or
vomit into buckets. Members left services hours later, hoarse
and spent, but cleansed.

Odd as this appeared to outsiders, Jane Whaley's congregation fawned over her. "Isn't she wonderful?" they said. "God
speaks to her."

Rick found it a bit much at first. Too much noise and commotion. But slowly, over time, he came to understand the end
justified the drama: church members were happy. They shared
a spiritual bond forged by helping each other get rid of their
oppressors. Heroic pastors held the keys.

Rick was so impressed by the Whaley technique he introduced blasting at Christian Life back in Georgia. But what
worked in Spindale didn't fly in Darien. Congregants complained about the bizarre ritual. Salvation is powerful and
dignified, they said, and a life dedicated to Christ does not
require ongoing exorcism. When church leaders offered Rick
the pastor job, they made one condition: no blasting.

Rick turned them down flat. If he couldn't share "the whole
gospel," if he couldn't practice blasting and preach about devils and deliverance, then to hell with all of them.

He made up his mind to leave Darien. Rick knew the
Whaleys ran a Bible school at their compound in Spindale.

He'd take classes there and open his own church when the time was right.

Rick told Suzanne he had turned down the pastor job.

"Rick, what did you do?" she cried, horrified.

They had no savings, no money. They lived from paycheck to paycheck. They barely had enough to get by.

Rick tried to articulate his vision. He truly believed that God would come through for them. But Suzanne knew better.

Shortly after they'd married in 1981, Rick wrote a check for a $5,000 living room set. They only had $10 in their account. Suzanne blew up. Rick said if he prayed long and hard enough, the Lord would provide the money.

Suzanne went to the store and begged the manager to cancel the transaction.

Years passed. Rick was always listening to "prosperity preachers" who promised every dollar donated would be multiplied by God and providentially returned someday.

The stress had taken its toll on Suzanne. She had just turned thirty-two but felt more like sixty. She was still pretty—tall and thin with long, shiny brown hair, green eyes, and high cheekbones. But now this: turning down an opportunity to pastor a growing church. What was he thinking? His Navy pension was only $1,200 a month. Suzanne couldn't work, not with six kids to care for.

If Suzanne had to leave Darien, she'd rather go home to Florida, to be nearer to her sisters and mother, Wanda— "Mama-Gail" to her grandchildren. She was outgoing and fun, the life of the party.

Suzanne, Wanda's eldest child, was the fruit of an unplanned high school pregnancy, a scandal back in 1961. Wanda married and had three more daughters in quick succession. She worked several jobs to make ends meet.

Wanda was not a model mother, but she cared about her

girls. She was a master at thrift-store shopping, so her daughters dressed like they were better-off than they really were.

When her husband abused her, Wanda got a divorce. She remarried, had another daughter, and divorced again. She worked hard. She vowed to never marry again. She didn't need a man, she said.

Wanda finally landed a legal secretary job and settled down. Suzanne, the responsible honor-roll student, kept the house and made sure her sisters' chores and homework were done. When graduation day came, there was no money for college.

"Get out of Florida and see the world!" Wanda told her daughter. So Suzanne enlisted in the Air Force.

Mother and daughter remained close. While serving a hitch in Hawaii, Suzanne met Rick Cooper, a decent, handsome Navy engineer, a strong Christian. They fell in love, more or less.

Suzanne knew from the moment she said "I do" that marrying Rick was a mistake. Now, twelve years and six babies later, it looked like she was about to make another.

Suzanne had told her mother everything and found her sympathetic. "Let Rick go on to his Bible school. You get those children in the van and come back to Ocala," Wanda told her daughter.

But Rick already had a plan. They would move in with his mother, Cora.

"It's only temporary," Rick promised. Soon as he got his degree from Word of Faith Fellowship Bible School, he'd find a church of his own, in the town of Suzanne's choice. He would be a pastor. God would provide for their needs.

Suzanne was skeptical. She'd grown up in the Bible Belt and had heard salvation messages from childhood, but she no longer believed in a loving God. The only God she'd seen was an angry, miserable taskmaster, always testing people's faith. Her children were the only beam of light in her life, her only joy. She invested all her time in them—homeschooling, playing games, planning excursions. They had become her whole life.

Out in the driveway a car horn beeped. Suzanne picked up her handbag, stuffed the paper and pencil inside, and walked out the front door. The children were loaded in the van. The back door of the Ryder truck was shut tight; the engines were running.

"Just follow me and we won't get lost," Rick said to Suzanne. He climbed into the driver's seat of the truck.

Suzanne buckled herself into the van. The children chattered with excitement, but she blocked out the noise. Down the driveway and out toward the highway, her mind raced. How would they ever fit all their furniture in Cora's little house? How long before Rick found a job, how long before they could have their own place again? How much would the Bible school cost? How could Rick support them all, and go to school, too?

As they approached the Interstate 95 on-ramp, Suzanne looked at the highway signs. She could take the southbound exit and head to Florida, to her mother's house. But she followed Rick, like she always did. It was the way God commanded, after all, and children need a father.

Rolling northward, Suzanne erased her negative thoughts and focused on the highway. She didn't know she was driving her family to hell.

2

SETTLING IN

Cora Cooper's white bungalow was tucked between an auto-repair shop and a Coca-Cola bottling plant. Suzanne pulled the van into the driveway and killed the engine. Her mother-in-law stood smiling on the front porch.

Suzanne took a deep breath. This wasn't her kind of place. Sure, the Blue Ridge Mountains were picturesque, but the narrow, winding roads into town were lined with derelict factories and stores. The clapboard houses had appliances rusting on the porch, and Fords rusting on the lawn.

Jeffrey, Lena, Benjamin, Peter, and Chad poured out of the van and into their grandmother's arms. Suzanne pulled John David from his car seat. Rick parked the truck in the space behind them.

The house was dark, smaller than Suzanne had remembered.

"You can stay as long as you like," Cora said, almost reading Suzanne's thoughts. "I'm happy you're here. Happy to have my grandbabies right here, where I can hold them."

Suzanne walked from room to room, trying not to feel horrified. Elvis figurines and other knickknacks covered the tabletops. Suzanne envisioned six little pairs of hands smashing it all to smithereens. The worst awaited on the enclosed back porch. Out there was the bathroom: one toilet, a claw-foot tub, no shower. No lock on the door. No privacy. No laundry facilities. She'd have to use the coin laundry down the street.

Rick called in the older children. Suzanne washed walls, floors, and baseboards, Cora watched the babies, and Rick and the bigger kids carried in boxes and tidied away the clutter.

It was close to midnight when they finished. Everyone collapsed into sleep.

Everyone but Rick. He sat up in the kitchen and looked forward to his bright future. The tight quarters didn't bother him. If he could live on a submarine, he could live anywhere. Life was about pleasing God. Hardship was part of the journey. If Jesus was leading them here, who was he to question it?

Word of Faith Fellowship pulled the Coopers into a whirl of worship services, parents' meetings, weddings, and noisy Friday night fellowship dinners.

The children enrolled in the church's Christian school and nursery programs, and a few weeks later Suzanne found she was pregnant again. She wondered how they could manage another child, but Rick was upbeat. Children are blessings, he said. Didn't Genesis command the faithful to "be fruitful and multiply"? But Suzanne knew the new baby had more to do with Rick's libido than God's will.

Meanwhile, Rick set aside his Bible school plan. He'd need to work to support his growing family, and two of the church leaders offered him a job at their construction company. But he saw that life at Word of Faith was an education in itself. He listened to every word Jane Whaley uttered during Sunday morning and Wednesday night services, and when weekday morning sessions were offered, he went to those, too.

The church numbered five hundred souls and was growing fast, and Rick felt he was on the ground floor of something big.

This wasn't just a church; it was a community. It stood on
thirty-five acres on the edge of Spindale. Sanctuary, fellowship hall, classrooms, and executive offices were clustered in
a main building, with smaller buildings scattered over the site
serving other needs.

The perimeter was secured by a line of tall, sturdy pine
trees. Old Flynn Road, a narrow two-lane, was the only way
in and out. Members of the security team manned the front
gate and monitored every car. Services were private, by invitation only.

The Whaleys had bought the property in the mid-1980s.
Everything was neat and clean—just the way Jane Whaley
liked it. Sam and Jane had preached all over the world, and
forged ties with similar churches overseas. Twice each year,
their weeklong Bible seminar sessions at the Spindale campus attracted thousands. When the week was up, followers
often stayed behind and joined the church. It was a multicul-
tural place, with members from England, Scotland, Switzerland, Germany, Brazil, and Ghana as well as Americans from
all over.

The diversity was a selling point. People of all races and
nations prayed together, with a leader who herself defied the
old white male preacher stereotype. It was a safe, clean, popular place, on its way up.

"This is what we've been looking for," Rick told Suzanne.
They joined the church. Suzanne was dismayed one Sunday
morning when church elders surrounded little John David,
laid their hands on him, and shouted for the demons to leave
the boy and flee back to hell. The ritual dragged on for a good
ten minutes, and Suzanne could see the fear in her son's face.

Yet many of the other members were smart, fun people, welcoming and exceedingly kind. And Jane Whaley's personal attention opened Suzanne's heart. When Suzanne cut her finger at a church function, Whaley lovingly bandaged her wound. She held Suzanne's hand and told her how much she loved her family. It was a sweet, motherly gesture by a woman revered by hundreds of followers.

When Blair, the Coopers' sixth son, was born on February 10, 1994, Whaley made sure the family had everything they needed, from a crib to diapers. Members visited the hospital and prayed with them, babysat, cooked, and cleaned. Suzanne was amazed.

Whaley took a personal interest in Suzanne's life. She phoned several times a week to see how she was doing. She gave clothes and other gifts to Suzanne and Lena, the only girls in a family of men.

Slowly, over time, Suzanne found herself agreeing more and more with Jane and her ministers. When Whaley praised her, it made Suzanne's day. She began to believe what Rick always said: God is good. Maybe the Lord didn't want Suzanne to suffer, after all. She found satisfaction in volunteering for nursery and kitchen duty at the church and school, babysitting, and carpooling, helping other mothers the same way she had been helped.

Even if she and Rick had nothing in common except their children and church activities, by early 1994 Suzanne felt hopeful and happy.

After Blair was born, Wanda Henderson came from Florida to meet her new grandson and give Suzanne a hand. She found her daughter had changed.

The Suzanne she knew loved to gossip about her sisters and updated her mom on her children's progress in math, their outgrown shoes, the funny things they said. She'd sometimes complain about Rick, but then they'd talk about politics or movies.

But now her daughter only wanted to talk about Jane Whaley and Word of Faith Fellowship.

Wanda worried. Suzanne was a caretaker, a natural follower; she had always been easily led.

She was sad when her daughter went to North Carolina, but she knew if she'd gone to Florida it would've meant the end of Suzanne's marriage. Suzanne had grown up without a father, and she didn't want her children to suffer that fate.

Wanda recalled the first time she heard Jane Whaley's name. A month or so after the Coopers settled in, Wanda sent nine-year-old Lena a pair of shiny white ankle boots. Soon after, during a church service, Jane criticized Suzanne for letting her daughter wear "go-go boots" to church.

"Parents, God cares what we wear and what we allow our children to wear," Whaley said. "We've got to mind how our children are dressed."

Embarrassed, Suzanne called her mother after the service and told her what had happened.

"The preacher stopped the church service to tell you that Lena wasn't dressed right?" Wanda asked.

"Yes. I don't know what to think," her daughter said. "They're just a fun pair of little-girl shoes."

"Goodness, I don't think I would want to go to a church where they tell you how you can dress your kids," Wanda said.

Suzanne was quiet for a moment. "Well, it's not that bad," she said softly. "I just didn't expect it. But maybe they are too grown-up a look for a little girl. Jane was probably right."

Wanda had come to North Carolina to cuddle the new baby, but while she was in town she decided to see Jane Whaley for herself.

The Sunday service was weirder than Wanda could have imagined. In the sanctuary there were no windows, no natural light. No pews. The wall-to-wall burgundy carpet was covered in rows of stackable chairs. Five steps led up to a stage with a big arrangement of artificial flowers. A lectern—Jane's pulpit—stood in the middle, surrounded by drab white walls. Ornate bronze chandeliers hung from the ceiling.

The congregation was striking. Everyone was dressed in suits, ties, dresses, and heels, like they were attending a wedding or a funeral. Back in Ocala, many churchgoers wore jeans. The preachers Wanda knew didn't care what people wore, as long as they showed up on Sunday morning.

Recorded music filled the room, and at the crescendo, Jane Whaley swept to the pulpit like a movie star at a premiere. Whaley looked the part, Wanda thought, with that white St. John Knits dress and a tailored jacket, a thick gold necklace, and bracelets on each wrist. Her fingers sparkled with diamonds.

She stepped to the pulpit, and the service took a surreal turn, a strange mix of Home Shopping Network and televangelist Tammy Faye Bakker. The glamorous preacher pulled a pair of ladies' shoes from behind the lectern and lifted them up to show the congregation.

"God is speaking to us today," she shouted. "Who has it in their heart that these belong to you?"

A woman raised her hand. "I feel led to have those shoes," she said.

What the hell? Wanda thought.

Whaley presented another pair of shoes, which were quickly claimed by another congregant. Then a belt, and a blouse. Wanda scratched her head. *Is this church, or an auction?*

Whaley and Brooke Covington, her most trusted confidante, loved shopping for bargains at discount clothing stores.

They often brought their booty to church services and "shared the blessings" with the community, Suzanne explained later.

When her shopping bag was empty, Whaley opened with a Bible verse and began to preach. But to Wanda, it was more of a public shaming than a sermon. One after the other, Whaley singled out her followers, using Scripture to describe the sin in their lives. When time came for the offering, the plate was sent around the church three times.

Wanda felt a chill creep down her spine. *There is evil in this room*, she thought.

When the service ended, Jane Whaley's followers fawned over her, but Whaley often didn't return their kindness. She was cruel, lashing out at some of them, scolding others. Wanda had seen enough.

That night she sat down with Suzanne.

"Do y'all know God or do you just know this woman?" Wanda asked. "I mean, what is going on in this church?"

"What do you mean, Mom?" Suzanne asked.

"Well, y'all treat Jane like she is some kind of star. Some kind of prophet. I mean, what is all that stuff about God telling people to buy a pair of shoes? It's crazy."

"Oh, Mom, Jane wants us to have nice things—maybe we'd never be able to afford a pair of shoes like that, or we'd never buy them for ourselves. This way, we can have nice things, and support the ministry, too. Try to understand."

"You're right, I don't. Help me to understand."

"If you stayed here longer, you would get it. It just hasn't been put on your heart yet what the church is trying to do The church is saving people's lives. We have a prison ministry. We visit nursing homes. We help drug addicts and alcoholics."

"That's fine, Suzanne, but I get a bad feeling about Jane. It's like she wants to control everybody."

"Well, look how great the kids are doing," Suzanne said.

"They're getting a great education. And most important, they are learning to be godly people."

Wanda pressed on. "Maybe, Suzanne, but there's just something about this place that isn't right. What do you really know about this woman? What do you really know about this place?"

"I don't know what else to tell you," she said. She stood up abruptly and went to her room.

Wanda had a hard time sleeping that night. She blamed Rick for getting her daughter and grandchildren into this mess. Back in 1982, Wanda had spent a month in Honolulu after Suzanne gave birth to Jeffrey, her first child. She remembered being jolted awake in the mornings by the sound of Rick casting the devil out of the house. Her new son-in-law had bought into a doctrine of devils and deliverance long before he joined Word of Faith Fellowship.

"I command you, Satan!" he'd shouted. "Get out of this house, in the name of Jesus!"

Religious drama was nothing new in Wanda's part of America, and it had never done her much harm. She believed in God, but she'd never been one to pound on a Bible.

When Wanda had her own family, she let her girls go to church when they wanted. At one point a church bus came and picked them up every week, but as they got older, they lost interest. It never bothered Wanda.

She had her own relationship with the Lord. She saw God all around her, in the kindness of strangers and the beauty of nature. She could look up to the sky and think, *That's God's ceiling right there. Thank You, Lord.* The created world was God's church. Staring at the ocean, she could feel God in her bones. A relationship with the Almighty was a gentle, personal thing, Wanda thought, and faith was not something that should be rammed down anyone's throat.

But Rick was another kind of believer. To him, God's love was not something to be cherished in the solitude of his own heart. It was his duty to evangelize others, whether they liked it or not.

She recalled a night in Honolulu. Rick and Suzanne had packed a basket of sandwiches and headed out to evangelize in the red-light district. Wanda swallowed her doubts and tagged along. They headed to Hotel Street, a seedy strip lined with bars and tattoo parlors.

For Christians like Rick, the street was target-rich, full of sinners in need of redemption. Wanda was afraid. Homeless men slumped against the walls of vacant buildings. Sex workers waved down passing cars.

Rick strode confidently through the dark streets, handing out sandwiches, shaking hands.

"Don't y'all think this might be a little dangerous?" Wanda asked.

"Oh, no," Rick said. "The Lord always watches over us, long as we're doing His work. Nothing bad is going to happen. God is good."

A shabby man came around the corner and nodded in their direction. Rick's attention was piqued.

"Did you see the devil in that man's face?" Rick whispered. "Poor man. I've got to get the devil out of that guy."

Rick ran after the man. "I want to talk to you!" he shouted. "I want to help you! I want to talk to you about Jesus Christ!"

The man bolted down the street, terrified. Rick followed, sprinting faster and faster until they disappeared around a corner.

Rick was a religious nut, Wanda concluded then. But now, with this wacko Jane Whaley woman, Rick had finally lost his mind.

She didn't know what to do. Suzanne was obviously being

brainwashed, but if Wanda kept criticizing Whaley, Suzanne might cut her off.

She decided not to say another word about the church. She'd try to gently steer her daughter in the right direction. It might take time for the light to come on, but Wanda wouldn't give up.

A few days later Wanda hit the long road back to Florida. A more terrifying thought occurred to her: What if the Fellowship was a doomsday cult, and Whaley was another Jim Jones or David Koresh? More than nine hundred of Jones's followers had swallowed cyanide-laced drinks in 1978 at his compound in South America. And Koresh and seventy-five of his followers were killed in April 1993 during an FBI raid on the cult compound in Waco, Texas.

Wanda suddenly felt sick.

Rick drove nails all afternoon, rehearsing what he would say as soon as he got home. Believers had to keep their families in order, or else be left behind when Jesus came to gather His saints to glory. How could the Coopers be found worthy if his mother continued in her worldly ways?

Cora was a member of Word of Faith, but every week she played sweepstakes. She dyed her gray hair black, listened to old Elvis Presley records, and sneaked off to Nashville to the Grand Ole Opry on Saturday nights. His mother was divorced, and Rick suspected she had a boyfriend who was not a congregant.

He mulled over her rebellion. He was the man in the house now, and it was his duty to confront her, for her own sake.

Rick had already proven that a troubled soul could turn around. He grew up nearby in Boiling Springs, a hardscrabble factory town. When Rick got older his dad taught him how to box, and Rick put those skills to work.

No matter who called him out, Rick wouldn't back down. He never lost a fight. In 1969, when everyone else was growing his hair, Rick got a crew cut. He was six foot two, all muscle, a badass with a chip on his shoulder.

Rick turned eighteen in 1972. His military draft number was twelve. Instead of chancing being drafted by the Army and ending up in Vietnam, Rick enlisted in the Navy. The world opened up for him. He was stationed in Hawaii, where he studied hapkido with a world-class sensei.

He excelled in his training classes and became a sonar technician on a nuclear submarine. Rick was always good at fixing things. He worked all over the ship—rebuilding a diesel engine, fixing hydraulic gears and heating systems. He became the go-to guy on his vessel, and later traveled to other bases to teach troubleshooting.

In his off-hours Rick drank and picked up "bar girls." He woke up hungover, his knuckles bloody from fighting.

Then, one afternoon in 1980, he had a dramatic conversion. Rick heard a voice in his apartment, then was struck senseless by a power outside himself. The next thing he remembered he was lying on the floor, with no idea how long he'd been there or what had happened. When he sat up, he felt a peace he had never felt before. This had to be Jesus, he thought. Rick bowed his head, closed his eyes, and prayed for Jesus to forgive him for all the people he'd hurt, and to turn his life around. Rick promised to devote the rest of his life to God, and never do violence again to another man.

When he opened his eyes, Rick was a new man. He began to purge all the sin from his life, starting with the beer, whiskey, and girlie magazines in the apartment.

Rick's family was delighted. The badass was now a decent, God-fearing man. He took up Bible studies and church services at First Southern Baptist of Honolulu. There he met an

Air Force sergeant named Suzanne, a good Christian woman, his miracle in blue.

All these years later, Rick still believed God had brought them together, and had sent them to North Carolina to be part of something great. Here at Word of Faith was the spiritual camaraderie he'd dreamed of for years, a community of people who were as serious about God as he was.

He listened intently when Jane Whaley and the other ministers spelled out the tactics for the "spiritual warfare" that Christians must wage each day. She cited 1 Peter 5:8: "Discipline yourselves, be alert! Like a roaring lion, that adversary of yours, the devil, prowls around, looking for someone to devour."

Whaley named the demons: ask too many questions and you had the "sneaky devil." Spend too much time following sports and you'd invite the "soccer devil." Effeminate mannerisms meant the "homosexual demon." Erotic or lustful thoughts meant you had succumbed to the worst demon of all, the "unclean devil," which could even take hold of children. Pubescent boys were tormented by erections, which Whaley called a "manifestation of their bodies," a shameful failing that required repentance.

Word of Faith used several Bible verses to justify the exorcism of demons, including Matthew 9:32–33: "Behold, a dumb man under the power of a demon was brought to Jesus. And when the demon was driven out, the dumb man spoke; and the crowds were stunned with bewildered wonder, saying, Never before has anything like this been seen in Israel."

A few months after they arrived, a minister pulled Rick aside and told him, "Rick, you're full of the unclean devil and need prayer."

Rick couldn't think of anything he had done that would

qualify as "unclean." But he listened to the minister. It was his turn to be blasted.

He sat in a chair and closed his eyes as a dozen people encircled him. They laid their hands on his head, shoulders, and arms, and called on the demon to go, shrieking, "Come out, devil, in the name of Jesus!" Some of them leaned in, their faces so close he could feel the heat of their breath and the spray of their saliva. Their hands squeezed down; they gibbered in nonsense syllables, speaking in tongues. Rick squeezed shut his eyes and held his breath, tamping down the fury that rose up in his gut. In the old days, nobody would have screamed in Rick's face like that—not without consequences. The old Rick Cooper would have knocked them all on their asses.

He used every technique he knew to keep the old Rick in check: the promise he'd made to Jesus to never fight again, thoughts of his children fitting in and earning good grades at the Word of Faith Christian School, thoughts of his job and all the friendly new people he'd met in Sunday school. If this was the price to pay for all those good things...he'd absorb it, like Jesus did as He carried His cross along the Via Dolorosa.

His first blasting session had a profound impact. Afterward, Rick accepted the church's doctrine without question. He began calling Jane Whaley "Mother" like her other followers did. Rick accepted whatever punishment the church meted out. He found it easy to help discipline other believers. He thought he might soon join the ranks of the ministers himself.

But first, he had to deal with his wayward mother, Cora. He knew she was playing the sweepstakes. In Rick's mind, it was gambling.

Rick drove home in a fury and stormed into the house. Cora sat at the kitchen table, reading a magazine.

"Ma, do you know what it's like to burn?" he said, a little too loud. "What do you think hell is going to be like if you don't repent of this?" He slammed his hand down on the table. "Is that what you want, Ma? To burn in hell?"

Cora sat in silence. Suzanne ran into the room. She knew the look on her husband's face. "Rick, please," she said. "We have children in the house."

Cora wasn't one to take abuse quietly. She was only a shade over five feet two inches tall and thin as a rail, but she was tough. "Who do you think you are?" she snapped. "What gives you the right to say these things to me in my own house?"

The drama was getting too much for Suzanne to handle, especially with the new baby added into the equation. She had learned many of the Cooper family's dark secrets in the past few months. Rick had painted his mother, father, sister, and relatives as devout Christians. But Suzanne had heard disturbing stories of violence, infidelity.

"You're my mother, but you're a harlot," Rick shouted, a common word in Whaley's lexicon. "Can't you see that I'm trying to save you?"

But Cora cut him off: "Jesus is my savior, not you. Go save your own damn self."

It seemed that the more Rick absorbed the teachings of the Word of Faith Fellowship, the more he fought with his mother. So in May 1994, Suzanne shared her burden with an assistant pastor, saying she would have to leave if the fighting didn't end soon. She had to protect her children, and her sanity.

And that was when Jane asked to speak with the couple in private.

Rick and Suzanne appeared at the appointed time. Whaley didn't give them a chance to speak. She praised their hard work and faithful attendance, saying she was proud of their progress. They'd proven their loyalty and trustworthiness. Now it was time to take the next step.

"I want you to attend our leadership meetings," Whaley said.

The Coopers were stunned. Only a handful of congregants attended leadership meetings, which were held in Whaley's office a half hour before each religious service. How many times had Rick walked by that closed door and wished he could be inside? Members got a heads-up about upcoming seminars, weddings, or other events. They also talked about who in the church was slipping, not living a godly life, and what kind of intervention it merited.

"What do you think?" Whaley asked them.

Rick and Suzanne said they would be honored.

But Jane Whaley had one qualification: the Coopers would have to undergo marriage counseling with a church minister and get their relationship back on track.

They didn't hesitate. They said yes.

Rick and Suzanne were filled with joy. Yes, they had problems, but maybe they could overcome them. They had to try! They were poised to become church royalty. They were now part of Jane's inner circle, and everyone would know. On Sundays and Wednesdays, they'd be the ones basking in Jane's light. They had joined the elite.

Brooke Covington and Karel Reynolds didn't have psychology credentials, but they were two of Jane's "daughters," confidantes she trusted enough to counsel married couples. In the Fellowship, that was all that mattered.

For Suzanne, it was one thing to talk about Rick without him in the room, but another to reveal her true feelings with him just a few feet away. She didn't like hurting people and hated confrontation, but today she had no choice. If they were going to achieve a breakthrough, she'd have to tell them everything.

Covington and Reynolds settled in with stern looks on their faces and several notebooks in their hands. This was going to take a while.

"We can sense that there's strife in your lives. Tell us what is going on," Reynolds said.

Rick had no chance to respond. Suzanne told the ministers their marriage had been on the rocks for a very long time. They fought over everything, she said. Money was tight, and Rick always made family decisions without her input.

"He wants sex constantly. All the time," Suzanne blurted out. In a church that punished followers for having erotic thoughts, Suzanne's confession was shockingly frank.

She had no idea if Rick's sex drive was normal, because she had little experience with men before she married. Although Suzanne was a pretty teenager, she didn't have boyfriends in high school, busy as she was caring for her younger sisters.

In the Air Force, she'd tried drinking and partying, but never really enjoyed it. She started attending a Baptist church on Sundays, and that was how she met Rick.

Back then, Suzanne thought Rick was boring and humorless. All he talked about was God, and he recounted every detail of his personal testimony every chance he got.

But Rick was determined. The night of their very first "date," a Sunday evening church service, he told her, "I'm going to marry you."

Suzanne laughed at him.

But over the next few weeks, it seemed that Rick was always around. He told her he wanted to be a pastor. He showed her department store catalogs. "I want you to pick out your ring and dress for the wedding," he'd say.

Suzanne got used to Rick being around. And one Sunday night at church, something odd happened.

Rick stood up before the congregation to "testify," to give a little speech on how God was working in his life. He talked about Suzanne. She was the most wonderful woman he had ever met, he said. He loved her deeply, and he'd do everything in his power to make her love him.

It came straight from Rick's heart, passionate and moving. And when he finished, Suzanne stood up and said, "I love you. I'll marry you."

The congregation erupted with joy.

Rick and Suzanne married a week later at a justice of the peace. Suzanne would later say she knew right away she'd made a mistake, but everything moved so fast... And even though she didn't love Rick, he seemed to really care for her. He seemed so sure, so righteous.

When her term expired, Suzanne didn't reenlist in the Air Force. She was pregnant within a few months, and Jeffrey was born on July 26, 1982. After that, it seemed that every time Suzanne called her mother or sisters it was to announce another pregnancy.

Mothering was the only thing that made Suzanne feel alive, but children were not enough to keep her marriage going or make her life meaningful.

By the time they moved to North Carolina, Suzanne was dead inside, she told the counselors. But now, under Jane Whaley's mentorship, she was coming alive again. Maybe that's why she felt so free to disclose so many details to these ladies.

She finished, and the room fell quiet. No one seemed to know how to respond.

"I think we all agree you two need a bit more counseling," Reynolds said, "especially now that you're in leadership."

The women closed their notebooks. The counseling session was over. They'd meet again in a week.

Rick and Suzanne left the office. Not a word was spoken, but the next move was clear. Rick knew that he'd have to change, or Suzanne was going to leave him.

He'd have to get them out of his mother's house. They didn't have money to buy their own place, but he would find something. God would provide, if he'd only believe.

3

A FOX IN THE FLOCK

Pete Evans peered into the rearview mirror.

Powell Holloway pulled off the road and killed the engine. He turned to Evans and smiled. "You ready?"

Evans nodded. He bounded from the station wagon, opened the tailgate, and pulled out a folded-up tent, knapsack, and a bicycle.

Holloway left him with some encouraging words: "You can handle this," he said. "Remember, you're doing the Lord's work. You're never alone. I'm praying for you, man."

Evans watched the taillights disappear. He felt very alone. This was his most important undercover assignment yet, and so far there wasn't anything glamorous about it. Evans and Holloway were Christians, garden-variety mainstream evangelicals. They worked for the Trinity Foundation, a Dallas, Texas, watchdog group that investigated allegations of religious abuse.

The Trinity Foundation was created in the early 1970s by Ole Anthony, a charismatic minister in the evangelical "Jesus Movement." It began as a small Bible study group and grew into a witty Christian humor magazine and a ministry to the city's homeless population. But by the late 1980s, Anthony was seething at public scandals involving wealthy televangelists like Jim and Tammy Faye Bakker, a North Carolina couple who created, then lost, a religious broadcasting empire.

The Bakkers were the darlings of the televangelist world from the late 1970s through the mid-1980s. Their "PTL Club" national cable network reached an audience of millions. Americans were attracted by Bakker's lively, apocalyptic preaching and his wife's cheerful, mascara-tinged tears.

As time went on, the Bakkers dipped into the offering plate to fuel an opulent lifestyle—their air-conditioned doghouse made national news. Heritage USA, their 2,300-acre Christian theme park outside of Charlotte, North Carolina, offered skyscraper lodgings, giant waterslides, a shopping mall, and Christian counseling, and at its peak drew six million visitors per year—all of it tax-free. But it all came crashing down in 1987, when word leaked of Bakker's affair with a church secretary, and the PTL Club money he used to pay her off. Bakker later served five years in federal prison for defrauding his followers.

Ole Anthony felt the Bakkers made a mockery of Christ and Christianity. He didn't have anything to do with their downfall, but he was determined to help root out similar religious charlatans. He and his companions began secretly working with news organizations to expose ministries they believed were corrupting God's Word and defrauding the credulous.

And that was what put the thirty-eight-year-old Evans on the Rutherford County roadside in late August 1994. The Whaleys were in the Trinity Foundation crosshairs.

Evans, a longtime Christian believer, had been a member of the Trinity Foundation since the mid-1970s, when he was a student at Austin College. After graduating in 1976, Evans drifted from job to job. In 1989, Anthony offered Evans full-time work in the ministry. Evans used his carpentry skills to build a guesthouse on the group's property in Dallas. He helped with a homeless housing program.

Evans had proven himself a capable undercover investigator with a small operation in San Antonio, and now he was after a bigger fish: televangelist Robert Tilton, whose *Success-N-Life* show had aired on more than two hundred US television markets. Tilton wrote inspirational bestsellers like *The Power to Create Wealth* and *How to Be Rich and Have Everything You Ever Wanted*.

But it was his TV show that brought him national fame. His shows were part revival and part infomercial, with a message built on money. Tilton told viewers that donating to his church was an investment that would pay off in answered prayers and financial success. Tens of thousands of followers mailed Tilton heartfelt prayer requests along with cash, checks, and gifts, certain that miracles would follow. Tilton's ministry flourished.

Anthony had long suspected that Tilton was fleecing his flock. In 1991, Trinity Foundation opened an investigation. They covertly attended services and combed through dumpsters at the mail depot in Tulsa, where Tilton's prayer requests were processed.

Investigators learned Tilton's staff had stripped valuables, checks, and cash from the envelopes, and dumped the prayer requests without opening them. Anthony shared his findings with ABC News's *Primetime Live*.

The broadcast triggered federal and state fraud investigations and Tilton's empire tottered. But the case wasn't over. Trinity learned that Tilton had ties to a secretive North Carolina church called Word of Faith Fellowship.

When Anthony asked Evans if he'd go undercover to investigate, Evans jumped at the chance.

Evans knew all about Tilton. One of the televangelist's former followers had filed a civil suit against the ministry, and Evans had been sitting in on the fraud trial. He was pretending to be a transient from Texas who was looking for better odds in North Carolina. Holloway, his contact and driver, was staying in Asheville, North Carolina, about an hour west of Spindale. Holloway was Evans's "emergency exit" if things went sideways.

During the thousand-mile drive from Dallas, they'd gone over every detail of how they'd infiltrate the church. Evans would introduce himself as John, his real name. (Pete was a childhood nickname that stuck. If anyone asked for his identification, it would prove he wasn't lying about his identity.) The main question they wanted answered: Was Tilton attending the church? If so, what was his role? And did other members of Tilton's congregation follow him to North Carolina?

Evans knew the investigation went beyond Tilton. He was going undercover to scrutinize Word of Faith Fellowship. The Trinity Foundation had received several reports that the church, led by a middle-aged cultlike leader named Jane Whaley, abused its congregants.

But right then, he needed a place to make camp. He'd been an Eagle Scout, so he knew exactly what to do. He found a flat spot, cleared away sticks and stones, and pitched his tent. He asked an old man at a nearby house if he'd be OK there and got the all clear.

The Word of Faith Fellowship compound was less than a half mile away. He'd studied maps of the property, and already knew the shortest route to the front gate.

Getting inside would be the next puzzle. Evans couldn't walk into a service unannounced or knock on the door of the pastor's study and ask for help. This was no ordinary American church. He'd have to be invited in.

Every morning Evans rode his bicycle to the local service station and washed up in the restroom. In town, he approached as many people as possible with his hard-luck story, and a mechanic offered him work and a place to stay on his property. After three weeks in Spindale, Evans finally met some Word of Faith Fellowship members, owners of a local diner. Evans told them how his faith kept him strong even through trying times. How he had been unemployed and had to leave behind his hometown and family to find work.

The couple was impressed. To them, Evans was a decent Christian guy trying to live through a bad patch—a perfect candidate for the church. They invited Evans to a Sunday service, and he quickly accepted. He called Holloway to tell him the news.

That Sunday, as Evans dressed for church, he once again rehearsed his cover story. No slipups. And when he was ready, he jumped on his bicycle and headed down Old Flynn Road. As he pedaled up the drive into Word of Faith's neatly manicured campus, he felt out of place. The men and women were dressed up like they were going to a White House dinner. Evans was wearing blue jeans, sneakers, an old pullover shirt, and a windbreaker. He had to remind himself that he wasn't there to join the church; this wasn't for real. Still, it was a bit unnerving. He could feel the stares.

It didn't take long. As soon as he got close to the church buildings, several men with sunglasses moved toward him. But the couple who owned the restaurant appeared, waved off the security team, and ushered Evans inside.

Not only did he attend that Sunday service, but he showed up again that evening, and again on Wednesday night. It didn't take long for Jane Whaley to notice him. His third time in the church she pointed to him and shouted, "You have a generational curse. We better get those demons out of you."

Evans had seen other congregants, including children, blasted into submission. It was an extreme practice of peer pressure, emotional manipulation, browbeating. Ushers kept buckets nearby because some congregants yelled and cried until they vomited. (The spiritually cleansed were expected to clean up after themselves.)

Now it was Evans's turn. While the bulk of the congregation sang choruses, he was taken to a chair near the front of the sanctuary. A bucket was placed by his feet, and more than a dozen people surrounded him. Nothing could have prepared him for the shrill, ear-piercing screams and guttural groans. The people swung their arms and punched at the air like they were fending off ghosts.

"Devils, come out!" they yelled. "We bind you, Satan. Get back. We rebuke you in the name of Jesus!" Others began babbling in strange languages. Although it sounded like gibberish, Evans knew they were "speaking in tongues," a common practice in the Pentecostal world. If that wasn't enough, a man began slapping Evans's back. Another grabbed his shoulders and shook him.

Keep it together, Evans told himself.

Easier said than done. His chest heaved as he struggled to control his breathing. His ears rang, his head pounded. He was getting dizzy. He just wanted it to end, but the believers were determined. Finally, after an hour, the shouting stopped. Evans was exhausted and nauseated. He bent over and spit phlegm in the bucket at his feet. Evidently that was what they'd been waiting for.

"Praise God!" the congregants shouted.

Evans was shocked, but he soon learned it could have been worse. That same evening, after an hours-long blasting, he saw a man vomit blood. He quickly discovered that nobody except Jane Whaley was immune to demons. She'd even call out her own husband from the pulpit.

"Sam, you've got those demons," she'd say. "You better go take a seat, and let's get 'em out of you. Take hold."

In the church's matriarchal world, Sam Whaley could offer no resistance. Like everyone else at Word of Faith Fellowship, he obeyed his wife. He took the chair near the stage, closed his eyes, and was blasted for a good forty-five minutes. Evans couldn't imagine what went through Sam's mind during his wife's deliverance session. When it was over, Sam looked like a beaten dog.

Evans fit in well at the auto-repair shop. His boss liked him, and eventually let him use one of their cars. He began volunteering at the church—cleaning, painting, whatever was needed. One evening after the service, Whaley pulled Evans aside and scolded him about his clothing.

"God's children should always wear priestly garments," Whaley said. "God demands that all of His followers wear the most royal of outfits when they come to worship."

"But these are the only clothes I have," Evans said. "You know I've been down on my luck lately. I'll buy some better clothes soon as I have enough money."

Whaley pulled a big shopping bag from behind her lectern and handed it to Evans. "These are for you," she said. Inside were expensive-looking clothes: slacks, dress shirts, and a stylish, knee-length black wool coat, nicer than any jacket Evans had ever owned.

"These are gifts from Joe English," Whaley said, motioning toward a clean-cut man with a slight paunch and short black hair. With his suit and tie, the forty-something English looked like a successful businessman.

Evans turned to English. "Thank you, sir. This means a lot to me."

English only nodded. He didn't say a word, but Whaley filled the silence.

"Well, I expect you'll be dressed more appropriately for the house of the Lord at the next service, right?" she said.

"I sure will, Jane. Thank you again," he said.

Evans had heard English sing at the church a few times. The guy had a powerful voice that filled the room, and his face lit up when he sang.

What Evans didn't know was that English was a world-class musician who had performed with rock royalty. English was a drummer and vocalist in Wings, a band founded by Paul McCartney in 1971, after the Beatles broke up.

A New York native, English played drums early on in a rock band called Jam Factory. The group signed with Epic records in 1969, recorded an album, and spent the next few years touring, opening for Jimi Hendrix, Janis Joplin, and the Grateful Dead.

English was also in demand as a studio musician. He played rock, blues, jazz, and fusion, and partied hard in his off-hours. He was staying at the Allman Brothers ranch in Macon, Georgia, in 1975 when he got a call from a friend working with McCartney on his new album.

Paul McCartney needed a drummer, the friend said—would English be interested? The following day English was in a New Orleans studio, recording what would become Wings' hit album *Venus and Mars*.

English was the only American in Wings, but he fit in well with the rest of the group, which was just beginning its most commercially successful period. English played dozens of live gigs during the band's Wings Over the World tour, which was filmed and turned into the 1980 feature film *Rockshow*.

English absorbed as much as he could from McCartney. He'd always been a freestyle drummer, but English learned to play "compact, tight little three-minute songs." In the studio, English and his bandmates worked the mixing board with McCartney, throwing around ideas.

He got along well with McCartney. Maybe it was because English was laid-back, or perhaps because he was a left-handed drummer playing a right-handed drum set. McCartney had had pretty good success with another left-handed drummer who played a right-handed set: Ringo Starr.

An after-concert interviewer asked Joe English what it was like playing with Wings.

"I think this is the greatest thing that ever happened to me since my first communion," he said. But on a personal level, Joe English was a mess. He was addicted to drugs, and his wife, Dayle, was pushing him to get clean or he'd soon be single again.

English knew he couldn't afford to lose Dayle. She had her own ties to rock-and-blues stardom: she played keyboards in a traveling band, and her first husband was Dickie Betts, a guitarist in the Allman Brothers Band. Their marriage didn't last, but Dayle continued working at the Allman Brothers farm in Georgia. That was where she met English, who had been hanging out, partying, and jamming with the band.

Rock and roll stars had easy access to drugs, but Joe's addiction came on just as his wife dedicated her life to Jesus Christ. She urged him to ask Jesus for help in kicking his habit, but English was too busy. In early 1978, Wings had just started recording its new album *London Town*. In the middle of a session English got an urgent call: his wife was in a serious car accident. The doctors didn't know if she'd live.

He flew back to the United States and stayed by his wife's side until her condition stabilized. He then had to make a difficult choice: return to Wings and England, or help Dayle through a long rehabilitation. The couple prayed together, and English decided to stay. He turned his life over to God.

Dayle and English attended a Bible study group with Christian music producer and promoter Ray Nenow, who convinced English to switch to Christian music. The couple moved to Nashville, where English reinvented himself as a Christian rocker.

"I'm doing it all for the glory of God," English told a Christian radio host during a 1981 interview. "I've had my glory. Being in the biggest band in the world with Paul didn't do it. So I give all the glory to God."

English put on a good front, but he was still using drugs. His wife wasn't fooled. He'd sometimes disappear for days and come home strung out and exhausted.

Nenow stepped in. And this time, English made the spiritual commitment that enabled him to kick his drug habit permanently.

Then, in 1990, Nenow brought the couple to the Word of Faith Fellowship. By the time Evans arrived to investigate Word of Faith, English was a loyal member, a willing volunteer who did janitorial jobs in the sanctuary.

The man who had jammed with Paul McCartney, Jimi Hendrix, and Jerry Garcia, who'd had all the cocaine, heroin, and women he could want, was now swabbing toilets in a church.

Within a month of arriving, Evans was being mentored by Sam Whaley and Douglas MacDonald, another minister. They asked him to open up his heart to them, and he did, confessing his loneliness and lack of spiritual direction. The bullshit worked. Evans was invited to more prayer meetings. He shared the details with Holloway.

Whaley was a micromanager, controlling everything in the church from the finances to the curriculum in the K–12 Christian school. Her followers were afraid to make a move without her approval, for if they did, they could be rebuked from the pulpit.

Evans hadn't seen Robert Tilton, but he'd heard a few people mention his name. Meanwhile, Jane took an interest in Evans. She'd invite him to her office to chat. She said God hadn't told her if he could join the church. Not yet. That'd take more time. But she was encouraged by his progress. He was "dressing more godly." If Evans became a congregant, the Lord would find him a "righteous woman for a bride."

He smiled and continued doing everything possible to fit in—attending every service, Bible study, and group meeting. The church's practices were stranger and darker than he'd anticipated. He planned to use his backpack to prove it.

He carried his backpack everywhere, even though he knew it made the church security guys suspicious. Evans left it unattended a few times during services, and when he retrieved it he could tell it had been inspected. He was careful. At first, he carried nothing but a Bible and notebook. Over time, people got used to seeing him with the bag.

Now he was ready to take the next step. He started carrying a video camera in his bag. He cut a small hole for the lens.

At church he casually put the bag on the floor in front of him during blasting sessions, moving it with his foot to scan the room. Sometimes he'd keep it in his lap, shifting his knees to move the lens. He shot footage of the sanctuary facilities.

The nursery was striking. There were no toys. Children were not allowed to play. Evans saw fussy children taken into a tiny bathroom to have their demons exorcised. Shouts and crying echoed down the corridor outside.

During one Sunday service, Evans watched as the entire

congregation blasted a six-month-old baby. The screaming was so loud and up close that Evans feared the terrified infant would suffer hearing loss.

One Sunday night in November 1994, as Evans was getting ready to film a service, a ripple of excitement passed over the sanctuary. When the grand entrance music blared, Robert Tilton strode into the sanctuary with Jane Whaley, followed by dozens of the televangelist's followers.

Evans rushed to a bathroom stall to make sure his video camera was ready. He popped in a fresh tape and jammed the camera into his backpack.

By the time he got back, the sanctuary was filled, and "the spirit had fallen" on the assembly. The congregation was whipped into a frenzy by Whaley's preaching. Tilton was there on the stage, but Whaley had the upper hand. Tilton had strayed, she shouted. He'd come to her for help, and everyone in the auditorium were going to expel the demons that had brought down this fine man of God.

Evans eased closer to the front of the room so he could get clear shots. Whaley and the leaders surrounded Tilton and began blasting. The audience of more than six hundred prayed along, screaming, shouting, and punching the air. Evans ran back and forth to the bathroom several times to change batteries and tapes.

When Evans got back to his tent that night, he realized his camera had malfunctioned. It hadn't recorded anything.

Evans opened his notebook and began writing details about the service. At the very least he'd been an eyewitness. He added to his list of "findings" about the church. Jane controlled every aspect of her followers' lives. They were told where to work, where to live. They were warned not to have contact with their families on the outside. Congregants were told they couldn't go on trips or vacations because, in the church, there is no "vacation time."

Evans wrote up a report about the Tilton service and the following morning Holloway picked up the documents and videotapes.

But it wasn't enough to film hysterical worship. They needed more. Late at night, they began rummaging through church dumpsters, looking for letters, receipts, or notes…anything that could help in their investigation.

Evans knew there was always a risk of getting caught, but he was careful. He made sure he wasn't being followed and always had an excuse ready in case he was questioned.

But as careful as he was, it was a chance encounter in a church hallway that ended Evans's undercover operation— and opened up a criminal inquiry that exposed the church to the world.

4

BUSTED

Evans knew he should've paid better attention. He was getting so comfortable inside the church he'd let his guard down. He joined in the hours-long, high-decibel deliverance at just about every service. It was like a mass primal-scream therapy session, and it was tearing up his voice. He'd phoned his mother one Sunday afternoon and she didn't believe it was him. His voice was all raspy from blasting.

One weekday in January 1995, scurrying down a hallway to a Bible study, Evans didn't notice a familiar figure headed his way until it was too late.

It was Robert Tilton. Evans stayed calm and managed to avoid making eye contact. He kept walking, but from the corner of his eye he saw the televangelist stop and stare. Evans ducked into the Bible study. But as the ministers taught the Word, Evans's mind was stuck on Tilton. If he'd recognized him, he'd go to Jane.

By then Evans had been filming for months. Trash bins had yielded information about the church and letters congregants had written to Jane. It gave them a clear picture of how the church operated and continued to manipulate members, even after they left.

One letter addressed a couple who had moved away. It said state law allowed the Word of Faith Christian School to withhold their children's transcripts until they paid off their tuition fees.

"We have heard from several people that since you left, you have made slanderous statements against the church, spread gossip and rumors, and sowed seeds of strife against your brothers and sisters in Christ. If what we've heard is true, God would not allow us to release the girls' records until all matters of contention are resolved."

The letter was signed Jane Whaley.

Other letters to Jane showed congregants were encouraged to expose their problems and sins in writing, with signed statements detailing "carnal desires" and financial and family troubles.

With all the information he already had, was it really worth risking his safety to try to get video of Tilton and Whaley together, praying, repenting for his sins like he did at the service in November?

Evans pondered the question. The church's practices were violent, but would they hurt him if they discovered what he was doing? Anything was possible. Still, Evans wanted to collect more information. The Trinity Foundation had been sharing their work with *Inside Edition*, a popular syndicated television show hosted by Bill O'Reilly.

Inside Edition planned to launch an investigation into Word of Faith Fellowship, and Evans knew they might need more video. He decided to stay.

Jane Whaley told everyone in the leadership meeting to have a seat and listen up.

"Remember that God sees and hears us, always. He cannot

be deceived. So, think hard about this," Whaley said. "Are there any Judases among us?"

Suzanne Cooper and the others looked at one another, shaking their heads.

"God has spoken to me," Whaley said.

She said John Evans was a "plant," but she didn't want anyone to speak a word about it. She wanted them to continue treating Evans like they would anyone else in the church.

"God told me John will come around. He's going to have a heart change," she predicted.

Whaley was convinced she could win over Evans, just like she did Rick and Suzanne Cooper, Joe and Dayle English, and so many others. She was confident in her ability to bring people into the fold.

When English first arrived at the church, he was impressed that Whaley didn't care he was a rock celebrity. She treated English as a lost soul, no different than anyone else in her flock. English needed answers, and she had them.

But with Evans, Whaley left nothing to chance. She assigned a trusted minister, Joe Franta, to dig into Evans's background and find out what he was up to.

It was an important time for Word of Faith Fellowship, and Whaley didn't need any distractions. Tilton needed Whaley's help. Not enough money was coming in, and he'd had to cancel his TV show. He continued to hemorrhage followers, too. He turned to Jane Whaley to help resurrect his image.

Tilton had met Whaley two years before, at the height of his fame. Newly divorced, he'd started dating Leigh Valentine, a former beauty queen and a member of Word of Faith Fellowship. Valentine was proud to bring her celebrity boyfriend to meet Jane.

Valentine was in her midthirties—tall and thin with long blond hair, high cheekbones, and teeth that were perfectly straight and pure white. She was well educated. She had found Christ after a near-fatal auto accident.

Leigh brought Tilton to the November 1993 Word of Faith Fellowship Bible Seminar, a weeklong event that attracted thousands to the church each spring and fall.

Before Tilton arrived, Whaley warned her congregation to avoid "loose lips" with Tilton, not to gawk, and to be wary of idolatry. She bragged that Tilton's "preachings" were inferior to hers, but she'd try to help him nevertheless.

When the moment arrived for Tilton's blasting, he was escorted onstage by the church's top leaders. Other followers were told to stay back for fear their demons might contaminate Tilton. Then the church leaders blasted Tilton for hours, shouting themselves hoarse, soaking their suits and dresses with sweat. When he returned to Dallas, Tilton incorporated some of Whaley's dramatic methods into his ministry.

Whaley was thrilled. Even though she knew Tilton's career was in free fall, she believed he could help put her on the map.

Respect and recognition from her fellow Charismatic ministers were things Jane had been craving for years, ever since her days back in Tulsa, Oklahoma, when the wives of the TV preachers had made fun of her. It would erase all the slights and indignities she'd faced growing up in rural North Carolina, and later on her journey into the male-dominated evangelical community.

Margaret Jane Brock was born October 22, 1939, near Morganton, North Carolina, a small town with furniture and textile factories. She was raised in nearby Forest City, a flyspeck in the Blue Ridge Mountains. Tough mountain folk lived in the area—men like William "Bill" Brock, Jane's father, who owned a plumbing supply store.

William and Blanche Mae Brock had three children: two boys and a girl. Jane was the middle child, the only girl, the quiet one. Painfully shy and awkward, she loved the outdoors, swimming in the river, and taking long walks in the woods. Her mother didn't have a lot of time for Jane. She was always cleaning, cooking, entertaining the couple's large group of family and friends, or helping at the store. Blanche would later say she regretted not spending more time with her daughter.

But it didn't matter. Jane was Daddy's girl. She'd spend after-school hours at the store, listening to customers' tales about everything from running moonshine to finding religion. She really loved being around her father. She wanted to make him proud. (Later, he'd attend her services, beaming as she preached the Gospel.)

When Jane started high school in 1955, she was barely five feet tall, thin with frizzy blond hair. By her own accounts, she was a homely girl. She didn't have boyfriends, but she excelled at school, especially in math.

Jane went on to attend Appalachian State Teacher's College in Boone, North Carolina. She threw herself into her studies and athletics. She joined a swim team called the Flying Fish, and played on the soccer team. After three years she graduated with degrees in math and physical education. She decided not to return to Forest City. She wanted more out of life. So she headed for the big city: Charlotte.

She took a job teaching math at Coulwood Junior High. In the summer of 1962, her brother Ray introduced Jane to Sam Graham Whaley, Jr., one of his employees in a consumer finance company. Sam was a serious young man from South Carolina who had just left the US Army, he said. They were perfect for one another.

On their first date, Sam discussed his religious beliefs. God had a plan for him, he said. He was going somewhere, maybe overseas, to preach the Gospel. Jane listened intently. Wherever Sam was headed, she wanted to go, too.

They married six months later. Time passed, and they had a daughter, Robin. In 1974, Sam quit his finance job and the family moved to Tulsa, Oklahoma. Kenneth Hagin, Sr., was a rising star in the Charismatic Movement, where enthusiastic followers, "baptized by the Holy Spirit," cast out demons, laid hands on the sick, and sent preachers, Bible teachers, and missionaries around the globe to spread the Word. Hagin had just opened a Bible school there. Sam would only have to spend a year at the Rhema Bible Training College and then he'd be ordained.

The Whaleys had enough savings to tide them through, but the career change was a leap of faith. In the mid-1970s, Tulsa was the epicenter of the televangelist movement. Oral Roberts had opened his Christian university there ten years before. His television ministry brought Pentecostalism—which promoted dramatic worship, faith healings, and "praying in tongues"—to the American mainstream. Like the Reverend Billy Graham, Roberts called his television specials and live events "crusades."

"Brother Hagin," as he was called by his followers, preached the "prosperity gospel." His philosophy: find a Bible verse that applies to your personal desire, and repeat it at high volume, over and over. Pray loud enough, and believe long enough, and God will give you what you want. Brother Hagin told his followers that faithful prayers—and generous tithes to church leaders—are paid back on this side of heaven with financial riches, health, and sobriety. It is a powerful, simple, and uniquely American blend of capitalism, fundamentalism, and magical thinking that continues to be preached by televangelists like Joel Osteen, Creflo Dollar, and Joyce Meyer.

Hagin's Bible school in Broken Arrow, Oklahoma, was the cutting edge of the fundamentalist Charismatic Movement. Sam studied hard, and Jane did, too. Rhema's program required students to listen to taped lectures of Hagin's philosophy and method. Jane listened. She learned about the different kinds of prayer, and how to use each one. She took notes. She began to form her own ideas about Jesus and the power of prayer, concepts that would later define her ministry.

Hagin's prosperity gospel was presented together with traditional Pentecostal practices like speaking in tongues, prophecy, and faith healing. Like any good fundamentalist, she combed the Bible to prove her points, just in case anyone questioned her beliefs. The Bible was God's Word to mankind, the ultimate truth. If the Bible says so, it cannot be questioned.

She didn't know it then, but Jane was preparing herself for a life in a Pentecostal pulpit, a place where the shy, plain girl from Forest City would find real power.

When Sam graduated from Rhema, he formed Sam Whaley Ministries, Inc., and joined a worldwide "revival circuit." The family crisscrossed the United States, England, Sweden, Germany, and Brazil. Sam preached to small groups in tiny churches, or large gatherings under tents pitched in the middle of fields.

At first Jane spoke only to introduce her husband, but in time her role expanded. Jane found that she enjoyed being in the pulpit, and the crowds were gratifyingly responsive. She loved telling people, especially disempowered women, how she had "received the call of God" in her life.

But she was torn. Sam was the pastor, not Jane. But more and more, she believed that of the two of them, she should be the one, the leader. She knew that time would eventually come.

In 1979, Sam and Jane Whaley formed Word of Faith Fellowship, and began holding services in a former steak house outside Rutherfordton, North Carolina. They chose "Word of Faith" because Sam felt God gave him that name. And "Fellowship"? Sam just liked the word.

Soon after opening, Sam was offered a job at Rhema as the dean of missions, a great opportunity. They were in on the ground floor of a worldwide movement. Rhema was growing more influential in Christian circles every day. They placed their new church in the hands of local pastors, including one of Jane's family members. They came back to preach from time to time, but their lives were centered in Tulsa.

They bought a house and Sam held an administrative post and taught at the Bible school, but his wife grew restless. She tried to fit in. She hobnobbed with Sam at Kenneth Hagin's house, but she felt the Hagins didn't like her. And there was something else bothering her: the wives of high-profile televangelists were creating their own ministries. They flew into Tulsa in private jets, dressed in fur coats, flashed big diamond rings, and held seminars. They were paid generous "honorariums" for their work.

Whaley wanted to be like them.

"They had entourages and got thousands [of dollars] in honoraria for speaking," said Sheri Nolan, who attended Rhema in the early 1980s. Jane went to the after-parties when the seminars wound up, but the glossy women shunned her.

"She didn't have the right clothes and didn't sound like them. She had this hick accent and bad teeth. She felt like they made fun of her," Nolan recalled.

Envious, and believing she had more to offer, Whaley began holding prayer meetings in her friends' homes. And they started spreading the word about this charismatic woman who had the "gift." So many began showing up, she rented a former car dealership that had been converted into a church. Most of her followers were associated with Rhema.

They were single women, some who attended the Bible school, alone on the weekends, women like Brooke McFadden. Some had experimented sexually with other women and were overwhelmed by guilt and shame. In their religious world there were few things worse than being gay or a lesbian. Jane Whaley could identify with the rejection they felt.

Jane had no formal religious training, but she had a natural gift. She was passionate, teaching "spiritual warfare," a belief that Christians share the world with supernatural beings, and the battle between good and evil is played out in each of their lives. Demons cling to humans, she preached, especially Christians, leading them to sin and sickness and blunting their spiritual effectiveness. It took special prayers to expel them, and Jane knew how. In an evangelical world dominated by men, her confident personality and message—strong prayer and dramatic deliverance to turn around troubled lives—resonated among women.

In her early forties, Whaley had become a mother figure to women struggling with their sexual identities, single mothers grappling with alcohol and drug abuse, and women whose marriages were falling apart. She had a way of making them feel they were God's beloved daughters, despite their rocky lives.

Jane had a complete makeover. She had her teeth fixed, began wearing expensive clothes, and practiced elocution and delivery for hours in front of a mirror. The impassioned shriek she used to cast out devils was part Jimmy Swaggart, part Billy Graham. She went from being "Sam's wife" to a minister with a faithful flock, followers who showered her with praise. And gifts. They looked after Robin after school. They put money in the collection basket. Soon the Whaleys moved into a big new house near an exclusive Tulsa country club.

Sam had an important job, but Jane was the rising star. When questioned, Jane said, "God spoke to Sam, and told him, 'Jane is the pastor.'"

"Jane was going to show everyone that she was important," Nolan recalled.

Jane's Friday night prayer services started at about 8:00 p.m. and often went on past midnight.

During the service, groups of Whaley's followers seated those who asked for special prayer in a "deliverance circle." They surrounded them, placed their hands on their heads or shoulders. Then they'd pray until they "had a breakthrough," confessing to sin and crying out to God for forgiveness.

The services were noisy and wild. By the end of the night the congregation was drained, their ears ringing like they had been to a rock concert.

As Jane's congregation grew, so did word of her practices. Rhema officials were worried that she was "corrupting" Hagin's teachings. Hagin's words and services were uplifting, with a focus on healing and salvation. Jane's message came from a "dark place." Her all-night services included shaming, exorcisms, and blasting, but the sessions weren't yet violent—just very loud.

It all reflected poorly on Rhema. During her sermons, Jane often invoked her husband's association with Rhema and "Brother Hagin."

The Bible school gave Sam an ultimatum: keep his wife under control, or they'd have to let him go. By this time, Sam knew the score. He resigned his post, and in 1985 the Whaleys moved back to North Carolina. They brought along twenty-two disciples, including Brooke, Jayne Caulder, and others who would become key ministers.

Jane liked to tell people she did not want to be the leader of a church, but she had no choice: it was God's will. "If we don't hate sin, we don't love God," she shouted out frequently. "If we don't point out sin in others, the same sin is in us."

The message resonated. Under her leadership, the Fellowship grew from a handful of people in an old steak house to hundreds of loyal followers and a manicured ministry complex.

Jane Whaley finally had the luxury cars, jewelry, and expensive clothing she craved to prove that she was chosen by God for success.

And now, with Tilton's help, she had a chance to take the next step, to become a household name. Even with all his troubles, Tilton was still one of the most famous preachers in America, and he was asking for Jane's help.

She had to win over Evans. She would use her "spiritual gift" to pull him inside, to stop him from doing anything that could hurt her church.

When the Wednesday night service ended, an usher asked Evans to wait in the sanctuary. After about an hour, a dour forty-something man with gray hair summoned him. It was MacDonald, his mentor, a longtime Whaley disciple.

"Come with me," MacDonald said sternly. "We need to go see Jane."

Whaley's office was packed. Her most trusted ministers were there, including Brooke Covington and Jayne Caulder, as well as Ray Farmer, the feared leader of Whaley's security team. Evans sat on the couch.

"John, do you know Ole Anthony?" Whaley asked, referring to the head of the Trinity Foundation.

Evans responded truthfully. "Yes, I do."

Whaley gasped, her eyes widening. Evans had never seen her look so surprised or worried. *Crap*, he thought. *I should have lied.*

"Well, John, we know you love everybody here. You've got a home here now. We've got a home for you, and a job for you, better than the one you have. We want you to work with Ray. We're going to give you a choice of staying here and being a part of the church family, or we can take you and drop you off somewhere. If you choose the second option, you are never allowed to come back."

Evans was terrified. *Drop me off somewhere? What does she mean?* He immediately regretted blowing his own cover. But for a moment, the truth felt good. He just wanted to go home. He was tired and afraid. All the screaming and long hours at the church had taken a toll.

"I think I would just like to go home now," Evans responded.

He wasn't sure what would happen next. Would they search his bag? Would they hurt him? But to his surprise, they let him walk right out the door.

Evans called Ole Anthony and Holloway to let them know he'd been busted. Evans wanted to get out of town, but he decided to stay with Holloway and help the *Inside Edition* reporters. He put the reporters in contact with former church members, briefed them on the church's practices, and gave them all his tapes.

One day Evans was driving through town with Holloway when a church member spotted them. Before long, several members of the church were tailing them in their cars.

"Is that Jane Whaley in that car?" Evans shouted. "We have to get out of here."

"What do you think they will do?" Holloway asked.

"I don't want to sit around and find out," he said.

Holloway sped down winding mountain roads to a crowded restaurant in a nearby town. Evans ran inside and took a seat at a table in the middle.

He never saw Jane Whaley in person again.

As for Whaley, she knew all about the Trinity Foundation, and the job it had done on Tilton. She braced herself and her congregation for the coming storm.

5

THE ATTACK

Word of Faith Fellowship was braced for the worst demonic attack in all its history. Satan was out to topple their church, Jane Whaley warned, and it was time for all believers to hunker down, pray louder than ever, and, most important of all, turn off their televisions.

Jane Whaley didn't disclose details. She didn't have to. Her followers believed that Jane was a prophet, and asking questions meant disloyalty, or a lack of faith.

Truth was, Jane was terrified: *Inside Edition* had asked to interview her about allegations of physical and emotional abuse inside the church. They had videos of children being blasted. The show's producers said several former members had claimed, on camera, that adults and children at Word of Faith were subjected to "extreme discipline."

Whaley had seen what became of Robert Tilton's empire after the *Primetime Live* piece aired. She had counted on his support, but as soon as *Inside Edition* contacted her, Tilton scurried back to Dallas. He didn't want any part of another scandal.

Now Jane was really seething. The investigation not only

ended her ambitious affiliation with the TV-star evangelist, it might also bring down the ministry she had worked so hard to build. She couldn't let that happen.

"Expect the worst," she intoned from the pulpit. "Tie up your loose ends and get ready for a satanic attack."

For Rick Cooper, that meant getting plans for his new home in order. A few weeks before, ministers at Word of Faith had approved his plan to buy thirty-three acres on Old Stonecutter Road, about a mile from the church. The approval was a reward for his family's steadfast devotion to the church.

By February 1995, Rick and Suzanne Cooper had become true believers. Any doubts they had about the church's practices had long faded, and they enthusiastically told friends and family members about Word of Faith Fellowship. The couple gushed about Jane Whaley's healing powers to anyone who would listen. They were evangelists, recruiters. A few of Rick's Navy buddies had moved their families to Spindale, and Suzanne was on the verge of the biggest coup yet: bringing her sister Cynthia Cordes into the fold.

If everything went to plan, Cindy, as everyone called her, her husband, Stephen, and their three children would be the Coopers' new neighbors—as soon as Rick closed on the Old Stonecutter Road property.

Once the papers were signed, Rick planned to sell half the land to his brother-in-law. The Cooper and Cordes families would then build homes for their growing broods. Rick also planned to build a small house on his side of the property for his mother, Cora. He wanted her close enough to keep an eye on, but not inside the same house. He and his mother were still at odds.

The same was true for Rick and Suzanne. The marriage counseling seemed to make things even worse. Sex was dirty and evil, they were told, and Rick needed to control his lust, or lose his soul. Their primary loyalty should be to the church, which should come before even spouse and family.

As Suzanne became more and more indoctrinated, she grew colder toward Rick. The church and the children were her priorities. She attended every school function and every service. Suzanne was strict with her children, believing that firm discipline had a godly effect on their lives. Television viewing was limited to chipper family-friendly programs or nature documentaries. The Cooper children did their home-work the moment they walked through the door after school. Suzanne's children loved to read, but now, aside from their textbooks, they could only read Bible stories, or the Bible it-self. Nothing else.

The children occupied themselves by memorizing Scripture passages. But at 8:30 p.m., no matter what they were doing, the children had to stop everything and go to bed. Even Jef-frey and Lena, who were practically teenagers.

Rick and Suzanne believed that Word of Faith Fellowship was the panacea their family needed. Their children were happy and healthy, they'd tell everyone. That was the sales pitch Suzanne used on her sister. For years, she had invited and accompanied Cindy and Stephen to church seminars and other events, and they'd grown in their Christian faith. Mov-ing to Spindale was their next step on the road to salvation, Suzanne told them.

Much like the Coopers, the Cordeses were the prototypi-cal Word of Faith Fellowship couple: decent, hardworking, and flawed.

Cindy was ten months younger than Suzanne, and they looked like twins with their slender figures and long brunette hair. When she was a teenager, Cindy was a party girl, pop-ping quaaludes and smoking weed.

By the time she graduated high school, Cindy's addictions

were taking over. Instead of continuing her education, she took a job sweeping the floors in a water-filter factory. And that was where she met Stephen.

Stephen's father was an engineer at the factory, and Stephen had been studying engineering himself when his family moved from New York down to Ocala. In 1982, when he took a draftsman job at an aerospace company in Orlando, he asked Cindy to move in with him.

Despite the change of scenery, Cindy continued to struggle with drugs. Wanda pushed Cindy to get out of Florida, to move to Hawaii and live with Rick and Suzanne. She even bought Cindy an airline ticket.

Cordes knew if Cindy went to Hawaii he'd never see her again. The night before she was to leave, he asked her to marry him. Cindy said yes.

The Cordes family was chasing the American dream. Stephen advanced in the company. They bought a house in 1986, and had a son, Brent. A boat, nice cars, and clothes didn't bring happiness. When their second baby died soon after birth, their grief brought them to their knees. They found answers in the Bible, and comfort at a local church.

A job opened in Thomasville, Georgia, and Stephen decided to transfer. There they attended an Assemblies of God church, where lively music, healing, speaking in tongues, and other "gifts of the spirit" were common practice. Cindy gave birth to Heather in 1991. And as Cindy became more involved in church, she looked for a deeper relationship with her sister Suzanne, a fellow Christian.

Suzanne invited Cindy to a weeklong Bible seminar at Word of Faith Fellowship. Stephen volunteered to stay at home with the kids so Cindy could go with her sister. Cindy didn't know what to expect at the North Carolina church, but as soon as she opened the sanctuary door and heard the loud prayers, she "felt the love of God," she said.

On her return, Cindy praised everything about Word of Faith Fellowship. "This church is loving. They take care of one another. They're real people," she told her husband.

Stephen was glad she liked it, but they were staying put for now. They were making a life in Thomasville. But Cindy continued making trips to Spindale.

Soon after the death of Stephen's mother, Cindy persuaded her grieving husband to go with her to the next Bible seminar. During a noisy public prayer session, a visitor from Sweden approached Stephen. He had a "word of knowledge," a message for Stephen straight from the Lord.

"You are very bitter at God for your mother passing away, and you haven't forgiven," the man said. "It's like you have your fist raised at God and you are angry with him."

It was uncanny. Stephen broke down and wept. And when his tears dried, he felt cleansed, refreshed. God was doing something in his heart.

The Cordeses decided to move to Spindale, after all, for the sake of their spiritual growth. They waited until late 1993, for their daughter Danielle to be born.

Meanwhile, Suzanne continued sending glowing reports from Word of Faith Fellowship. When Rick offered them a plot of land next door to his, it seemed like a sign from above.

And then another of Cindy's sisters walked through the door.

Like Cindy, Shana Muse had made her share of bad choices. Although she was a licensed practical nurse, Shana was a drug addict.

In November 1994, Shana was living in Northern California with her sister Sonya and wanted to get away from an abusive boyfriend. She had just given birth to her fourth child. She told Cindy she wanted to get out of California.

Cindy didn't hesitate. She sent Shana enough money to get to Thomasville, and three days later, Shana and her children were at Cindy's house. Shana had to give up drugs, alcohol, and cigarettes, her sister told her. She needed a complete spiritual makeover, for the sake of her children, and for the survival of her own soul. Only Jesus could do that, and Cindy knew the perfect place for her to meet the Savior and get her life straightened out: Word of Faith Fellowship.

Shana wasn't interested in a religious conversion, but she needed a safe place to stay. It had been a long trip. "Later," she said.

Cindy broached the subject several times over the next few weeks. She told Shana about the plan to buy property in North Carolina and build a home near Suzanne. They were moving in the summer, Cindy said.

"It's empty land. Where will you live while the house is built?" Shana asked. "Why not wait?"

True, their home wouldn't be ready, but they'd worked that out, too. They would rent a house, maybe live with other church members, Cindy said.

Shana sighed. She knew from Suzanne that many church members lived in shared houses. Word of Faith Fellowship had promoted communal living, like hippies in a California commune. There were clusters of homes near the church where several families lived under the same roof. They shared expenses and helped raise each other's children.

But there was another reason the church endorsed communal living: members were accountable to one another. If someone veered off course and gave in to the "unclean" or "evil ways," the others were there to help rein them in. At least, that was the theory. In reality, members were encouraged to tell on one another, even if there was no evidence of sin. Shana would discover that in time. But for now, she was just happy to have a clean place to stay. She was taking it one day at a time.

It was different in Spindale, where Rick was juggling his work and home life. He had started a new job with an electronics company. He earned more money, but it was a forty-five-minute commute to and from work each day, and church services afterward. When he had time, he drew floor plans for the new house. Rick believed the new house would save his marriage.

Rick planned to build the house himself. He had spent a good part of his life working on building sites and home maintenance, helping his father through his school years. He'd learned electrical wiring in the Navy, and could subcontract the foundation work, plumbing, and finish carpentry. If everything went right, his children could learn how to frame and wire a house, put up cabinets and drywall. It would be a real family affair.

There was still some paperwork to track down, but he had a little time to pull everything together before the closing in the spring. But then Sunday came, and Sam Whaley took him aside for a private word.

"Rick, I know you're buying that property. But I wanted to let you know something. There are going to be some lies coming out in the news. If you want to buy that land, you'd better hurry. I don't know how the seller will react to the lies."

Rick grimaced. "We're supposed to close the deal soon."

"That's good. God's decided you should have that land. I just don't want the lies to mess things up for you," Sam said.

Rick had never seen Sam so distraught. He knew what he had to do. He called Cordes, the landowner, and his attorney, and on February 27, 1995, Rick borrowed $61,875 from

Centura Bank to help buy thirty-three acres. Then Rick sold half the property to Cordes.

That evening Rick stood in the middle of a farm field. He gazed at his land: the towering pines, the winding creek, the Blue Ridge Mountains in the distance. The Lord had heard his prayers. He was truly blessed.

But twenty-four hours later, everything changed.

The *Inside Edition* piece was worse than Jane Whaley had expected. Evans's secret videos made their worship services appear hysterical and violent. Former members exposed the church's secretive practices and aired old grievances.

The host, Bill O'Reilly, spoke in an outraged voice-over: "They say they are following God's will, but are they really abusing children?"

With footage of members going into the church building, O'Reilly revealed stunning details.

"Until now, many of the members may have been kept in the dark about allegations of child abuse, sexual molestation, and unlawful imprisonment and cultlike mind-control techniques," he said, noting that the church's leader, Jane Whaley, was a fifty-five-year-old "former schoolteacher with no formal theological training."

One former member said he had been hit so hard that he flew over a desk. Another said children were routinely spanked with wooden paddles, leaving deep bruises as well as emotional scars.

Local law enforcement had turned a blind eye, the segment suggested. In a small county, a church with hundreds of congregants could sway an election. County sheriff Dan Good and his deputies cozied up to Jane Whaley, they said. When police had a chance to take action, they did nothing.

The *Inside Edition* piece was an eye-opener for the people of

Spindale. Until then, the church's practices were largely hidden from the public, save for whispered rumors around town.

Most local residents only knew that church members and their children were polite, respectful, educated, and successful. Church leaders owned more than two dozen businesses. Their big new houses stood out in the poverty-stricken district.

The rest of the sect lived in clusters of family homes in middle-class neighborhoods. Members rarely mingled with the locals. Most of them held jobs at the businesses run by church leaders.

The images and audio descriptions were gripping. One showed a small group of people sitting in a circle with a man at the center, praying for him and "regularly screaming to split the ears of devils, delivering this man and others from demons inside them so they can walk with God." In another, children barely out of diapers were shouting to heaven to expel demons, aping the adults around them.

The people of Spindale saw the show, but the people of Word of Faith Fellowship did not. Jane Whaley had forbidden them to watch television.

Whaley knew she had to take action fast. She convened a group of her closest ministers and told them the *Inside Edition* broadcast was "all lies." She charged them all to call and write to law enforcement and local and state political leaders, to complain loud and long that Word of Faith Fellowship was being persecuted for their religious beliefs. Christianity was under attack by the legions of secularism. The congregation was called together for a videotaped rebroadcast of the *Inside Edition* report.

Whaley explained that a television show had broadcast a negative story about the church—and she wanted them to hear it from her.

Rick and Suzanne Cooper sat and watched while Whaley

controlled the start and stop of the videotape. She derided the segment as "nothing but media lies and persecution of God's children."

Like many congregants that day, the Coopers were outraged. Not at the church or Whaley, but at Pete Evans and *Inside Edition*.

After the service the Coopers drove to a nearby lake. While the children fed the ducks, Rick and Suzanne talked about what they'd seen. The church encouraged corporal punishment. They'd seen children tied to the chairs in the nursery. But was that really abuse? Were things at the church as bad as *Inside Edition* said?

No, Rick said. They weren't. People just didn't understand their practices. Yes, to outsiders they might seem strange. But so what? The outside world was godless. Outsiders didn't know Jane. The outsiders were wrong. The church was right.

So that day in the park the Coopers decided to stay. They'd build their house. They'd continue living Christian lives. Jane would continue to be their spiritual leader.

Sheriff Dan Good was feeling the heat. In 1990 he'd been elected by only a few dozen votes. Support from Word of Faith Fellowship had put him over the line.

Church leaders routinely examined candidates running for public office in Rutherford County. The person they chose could count on the votes of hundreds of congregants. Just before the 1990 election, a former sheriff's deputy, Wayne Hall, had stood up at a Word of Faith church service and told them Dan Good was their man.

Nothing had changed in the years since then. If problems cropped up at the church, security chief Ray Farmer called Good with a heads-up. Nothing major. Usually disgruntled former members upset with being asked to leave. If they tried to file a criminal report, Farmer did what he could to discredit the person.

Good tried to stay out of the church's business. They were nothing but trouble, but with the sudden national attention, he couldn't ignore the allegations. He sat down with the Rutherford County district attorney, and together they decided to punt the case to the State Bureau of Investigation.

The SBI was the law enforcement agency that handled high-profile criminal investigations in North Carolina. At the end of a probe, the agency presented a report to local officials, who ultimately decided whether to prosecute. If Word of Faith Fellowship members were charged with abuse, Good could blame the SBI. It would give him cover.

Jane Whaley was not happy with the decision. She went on the offensive and, on March 2, 1995, called a news conference at the church. Flanked by her husband and several well-dressed followers, she called the allegations a lie.

"These accusations were created to enhance a sensational and a very emotional story," she said.

Inside Edition then ran another damning episode, alleging that a member died after the church turned to blasting to cure the man's severe heart condition.

Darren Lloyd, who had never been a congregant, said that Word of Faith leaders withheld his father's heart medication in the summer of 1994, insisting that God would heal him.

Harold Lloyd died during a family dinner on July 2, 1994, two weeks after stopping his medicine.

Inside Edition asked a haunting question: Did Harold Lloyd die for his devotion to the Word of Faith Fellowship?

Darren Lloyd was certain that was what happened. "Sickness and death is of the devil, according to the church," he said. "Medical help is the last resort."

Whaley could only wonder what else *Inside Edition* was

planning. News stations still had satellite trucks stationed in Rutherford County. One was parked at the end of the road near the church. She'd heard reports of reporters knocking on doors, looking for people familiar with the church, hoping they'd talk.

Crystal Taylor stared out the window of the backseat, wondering where they were taking her. She'd been in the car a long time. They'd left the pine trees and mountains behind, the scenery was changing to sand and palms. She'd been doing her homework when the church men came in, saying they had to get her out of Spindale right away, before the reporters got to her.

She was only fifteen years old, a black girl, a motherless child. Just when she thought her life couldn't get any worse, it always did. She'd seen a lifetime's worth of abuse in her fifteen years and had finally shut down emotionally. She didn't speak often, and when she did it was in monotone. She didn't smile. She kept a blank, lifeless look on her face.

She was happy when she was little, even though she'd never met her father. Then her mother was killed in a car accident in 1989, and her world went black. The sexual abuse started soon after that. A family friend, then a relative, in the dark. Crystal and her sister and brother were sent to their step-grandmother, Janet Taylor, a member of Word of Faith Fellowship.

The children lived in a series of ministers' homes, or with other congregants' families. The Fellowship ministers were the worst, Crystal thought. The first one waited until his wife was off babysitting to take her to a room alone. There he touched every part of her body. If she told anyone, he said, something terrible would happen.

William Keith Grindstaff, another minister, said the same thing to her when she lived with his family. Grindstaff waited and watched the girl until he saw her go into a room alone. He'd then close the door and corner her. The assaults went on with other family members so near Crystal could hear them talking. She prayed they'd walk in on him and make him stop.

At night he'd sometimes come into her room. She stopped sleeping. She wanted to tell someone, but who? No one would take her word over his.

When the sexual abuse became too painful, Crystal told her aunt. The Rutherford County Sheriff's Office and Department of Social Services were called in. Deputies and social workers told her the first molestation was "too old" and "couldn't be proven," but they launched an investigation into Grindstaff. Crystal was removed from the minister's house.

Jane Whaley summoned Crystal to a meeting and asked the girl to tell her everything. She was scared, but Crystal disclosed how she had been sexually abused in the past, and how the two church ministers had molested her, too.

Whaley lost control. She stood up, jabbed her finger at Crystal, and screamed. "This is your fault," she told Crystal— the child had been carrying "sexual devils" and had released them on Grindstaff and all the men who had ever abused her. Whaley summoned other church leaders into the room and they blasted Crystal for hours. They called her a harlot, and said she was full of the "unclean," a catchall term used for a wide variety of sins. Finally, Crystal was told she must atone for her wrongs by telling the prosecutor she had seduced Grindstaff, that the abuse was her fault. Crystal agreed. She'd do anything to stop the screaming.

Whaley called the prosecutor and said Crystal had something important to confess. In an office at the county courthouse, with Jane Whaley standing by, the prosecutor listened in silence as Crystal asked him to go easy with the minister.

"It was my fault," she told him. She said she came on to him, that he didn't do anything wrong. The prosecutor asked no questions. When Crystal left the room, Whaley stayed behind.

Years later, Whaley would recount that meeting in a three-hour conversation with a former congregant that was recorded without her knowledge. (On the recording, Whaley acknowledged that she was aware of several instances of sexual abuse at Word of Faith Fellowship, but said she didn't have to report them because of "ministerial confidentiality." In fact, there is no such waiver for clergy in North Carolina.)

Whaley said she told the district attorney that Crystal was partially responsible for the abuse because she had previously been sexually assaulted by relatives. She said she told the prosecutor that Crystal was "thirteen, but she looked twenty."

Instead of facing sexual assault charges that could put him away for life, Grindstaff pleaded guilty to two felony counts of taking indecent liberties with a child. He was given a six-year sentence, suspended to five years' probation with two hundred hours of community service.

Grindstaff was barred from "going on or about the child's school, residence, or place of employment" during his probation.

Despite the order, Grindstaff continued attending Word of Faith Fellowship. He made a point of sitting right behind Crystal at Sunday services.

Crystal panicked when she saw Grindstaff, but she fought desperately to hide her fear. Any kind of outburst would bring on a blasting, or even a beating.

That was what she'd tell reporters if they ever found her. She'd tell them how she was sexually abused by church leaders, but no one cared. She'd tell them how she and her siblings were beaten for years by ministers and church members.

The car pulled into a hotel parking lot at the beach. Crystal knew that now she'd probably never get the chance.

6

THE INVESTIGATION

If anyone thought Jane Whaley might wilt under the hot lights of an SBI investigation, they were mistaken. Whaley held dozens of meetings with congregants, telling them they were under siege from satanic forces. School hours were changed from one day to the next, and a corps of drivers was recruited to deliver students directly to their homes when classes ended. The fearfulness eventually reached thriller-novel levels. Suzanne Cooper answered her phone one afternoon, and a strange voice said only "I'm about to deliver your apples." Evidently, the children were being brought home from school.

Whaley told her congregants to lie to authorities, and not to talk to anyone outside the church. During hours-long services she reminded the faithful of the miracles she had performed—how she'd healed the terminally ill and set the addicted free from their demons.

The paddles were gathered up and hidden away. Children who needed discipline were taken off church grounds for spankings, even if it was just across the property line. An abundance of new toys appeared in the nursery and schoolrooms.

Hundreds of followers signed "waiver and release agree-ments," a curious mix of Charismatic terminology and legal language that Whaley believed would protect the church if a follower was hurt during a ritual, or a demon did not leave as instructed.

The agreement said that Word of Faith Fellowship "believes in the Holy Bible as the true living Word of God; that it be-lieves in speaking in tongues, casting out devils, and divine healing, as taught by the Word of God as part of its worship services," much like many Charismatic evangelical groups. But it warned that "no guarantee or warranty of any kind is made" that "demons or devils will be cast out; that their bodies will be healed; that their souls will be saved or that their mental health and/or emotional condition will be cured."

By signing the form, congregants released the church "from any and all liability of any nature or kind, for whatever injury or harm or complication of any kind that may result whether directly or indirectly by reason of my subjecting myself to prayer and ministry during any services of the parties of the second part."

"I am fully aware of the danger that arises out of any men-tal or spiritual exorcism," the signers affirmed. They not only signed away their own legal protections. The church was also not held responsible if leaders harmed their children.

The legal papers were seen as loyalty vows, public declara-tions of unity and solidarity. Hundreds signed them.

Whaley's sermons painted a bleak picture. If members talked, the Rutherford County Department of Social Ser-vices would shut down the school and take away their chil-dren. The church would close, the flock would be scattered, evil would triumph.

It was the Word of Faith Fellowship against the world. Con-gregants were forbidden to read newspapers, listen to radios, or watch television. Instead of seeking outside information, her congregation listened to their spiritual leader.

Not long after the *Inside Edition* report aired, a county social worker knocked on the Coopers' door. One of the most explosive allegations in the program was that children at the church were tied to nursery chairs. Suzanne had seen it herself—her youngest child, Blair, spent hours each week in the church nursery. Suzanne downplayed the allegations, repeating what Jane had told her to say.

"The children aren't tied down like that TV show made it out to be. The thing is, there aren't enough high chairs for all the children," Suzanne said. "They were strapped in during meals for their own protection. You know, so they wouldn't fall out of the chairs and get hurt. It's not like the media is making it out to be."

"Well, what about television? Is your family allowed to watch TV?" the worker asked.

"We have a TV right there," Suzanne said, pointing to one in the living room.

"What about vacations? Do you have to ask for permission to take vacations?" she asked.

"I have a relationship with Jane. I tell her when we are going on vacation," Suzanne responded.

"But do you have to ask her?" the social worked snapped back.

"We let her know, but I wouldn't say we have to ask permission," Suzanne said.

The social worker thanked Suzanne for her time and left.

For John Huddle, it was a strange request from a powerful figure: Don't watch television. Don't talk to reporters. Don't let anyone know your business.

But Jane Whaley was a prophet, and Gerald Southerland, the man who carried her message to Huddle, was likewise anointed of the Lord. Huddle wasn't one to question authority. Besides, he never watched TV, anyway. He'd found the spiritual enlightenment he'd yearned for and, by March 1995, was spending his spare time buried in Bible study, listening to sermons on tape, making himself a worthy follower.

Huddle and Southerland lived in Greenville, South Carolina, a good fifty miles southwest of Spindale. But Word of Faith had a long reach, and Jane Whaley's teachings had taken hold at Grace and Truth Fellowship, the church where Southerland was pastor.

The men had known one another for several years, with the Southerlands acting as caring parent figures to Huddle and his wife, Martha.

John Huddle was an ordinary guy, born in small-town Virginia. His was a paperboy and Boy Scout childhood, attending Vacation Bible School each summer and church on Sundays. He grew into a practical man. He dropped out of the College of William & Mary after a couple of years when he realized his literature and world affairs classes weren't going to help him get a job.

He ended up working for a consumer finance company in South Carolina, repossessing cars through the 1980s. He met Martha on the first day of 1987 at a dinner party. They sat on the sofa and chatted for hours. She was unabashedly Christian, a former student at Oral Roberts University in Tulsa. She worked for an attorney, but she hoped someday to be a minister. John was overwhelmed. He'd heard the same call himself.

John and Martha fell in love, John proposed, and Martha's parents sent them for premarital counsel to pastors Gerald and Linda Southerland at Grace and Truth Fellowship in Greenville, South Carolina.

They married in 1988 and, in 1992, moved to Greenville to join the church that had treated them with great kindness. They attended early-morning teaching sessions at the church's "Training Center," and Martha took a job at the church school. Money was tight, but they looked at it all as an adventure. They enjoyed their new life.

Huddle threw himself into church. At first, he didn't know what to make of some of the church's strange worship practices: the shouting and loud prayer, the angry faces, fists punching, and fingers pointing up to the ceiling. Many of the words they spoke were not words at all, but "speaking in tongues." It was loud and radical but enticing. He wanted to learn more. He wanted to belong.

He asked Southerland questions: Where is blasting in the Bible? What does it do for you? How do you do it? He was told the answers could be found in Scripture, so Huddle studied harder.

Southerland taught the Huddles about the "move of God," and submitting their decisions and plans to spiritual authority. He focused on devils and deliverance, saying Christians can be plagued by invisible devils that require dramatic deliverance techniques to be expelled. If a believer was suffering or having trouble, a devil was probably "after him, in him, around him, or upon him," Southerland said. And evil is contagious. People nearby can "carry those devils and release them at you with their thoughts, their actions, their music, or their touch or their looks or their words about you."

Southerland's doctrine and practice originated with Jane Whaley. Southerland's church was a Word of Faith Fellowship affiliate. Whaley built up her church in part by forming affiliations with small, nondenominational churches like Grace and Truth. Once Whaley got a foot in the door, she placed her followers in critical positions. And when she had enough control—or when God told her, as she liked to say—she'd close the church and tell the members to move to Spindale.

Southerland's church was on that trajectory. Southerland first met Whaley twenty years before, when Sam Whaley was working for Kenneth Hagin, Sr., in Oklahoma. They reconnected in the late 1980s, and Southerland soon adopted Word of Faith practices at his thriving church.

It didn't go over well. Almost overnight his four-hundred-strong congregation dropped to one hundred. Southerland liked to say the ones who left wanted to "keep their devils, keep their sin."

Huddle got the chance to meet Jane Whaley in May 1992, when he attended the Bible seminar at the Spindale compound. Seminar Week was a big deal for the church. It attracted thousands of people in the United States, South America, Europe, and Africa.

The meeting opened a new world to Huddle. And it closed the world around him.

Huddle heard Jane Whaley preach several times, and each message was better than the last. Her followers were the chosen ones, she said. Jesus was coming back soon to gather them all into heaven. All others were doomed to an eternity of fire and brimstone. Meantime, believers were called to a lifetime of "spiritual warfare" here on earth.

He believed that Jane heard God at a level no one else could. The audience hung on to her every word. Huddle had never witnessed a minister with this level of charisma. She gave him a sense of purpose, a sense of urgency and power.

Huddle was embarking on a step-by-step journey of manipulation that would lead him to slowly relinquish his will. Whaley demanded that followers conform totally to her message from God, and that message encompassed every aspect of their lives. Family, career, and financial matters were all subject to her review, as well as individual spiritual concerns.

Clinical social worker Lorna Goldberg studied the phenomenon and said, "All cult leaders have a special vehicle to hook all of their followers into submission to their ideology. With Whaley, that hook was loud prayer, which had elements of both positive and negative reinforcement."

When John Huddle heard Whaley's "no television" edict, he didn't pay much attention. He was setting up a crib for his second baby, due any day. His family members saw the *Inside Edition* segment and called him to ensure he was OK. As instructed, he told them it was all lies.

Michael Huddle was born on March 13, 1995. That evening, Martha's hospital room was full of well-wishers, including Gerald and Linda Southerland. Church members took turns at the bedside, admiring the healthy newborn.

Then Southerland's mobile phone rang. He answered, frowned, then grabbed the remote control for the television on the hospital wall. The room fell silent as the local news channel appeared.

The fallout from *Inside Edition* had reached Greenville.

There, on the screen, was Southerland's church, with a live-shot truck from WYFF Channel 4 parked in front. Their affiliation with Word of Faith was mentioned, and then there was b-roll of Gerald Southerland, standing at the edge of the church property, talking to a congregant, looking bewildered. The Huddles watched Southerland watching himself on TV.

The Huddles spent one of the happiest days of their lives, the birth of their son, calming and comforting their pastor. Huddle promised his pastor he'd stay loyal, no matter what. Nothing was going to shake his faith.

Agent R. C. "Toby" Hayes leaned back in his chair and surveyed the documents stacked on his desktop. Hayes had been involved in dozens of SBI investigations, but he had never seen anything quite like this.

Hayes was the lead agent in the Word of Faith Fellowship investigation. His people had fanned out across North Carolina, tracking down and interviewing dozens of former congregants.

They said they were cut off from loved ones outside the church. Some said their small Pentecostal churches were taken over by Jane Whaley and her followers, their longtime pastors pushed out by new leadership. Word of Faith took control of church finances, and no one knew where the money went.

They said church membership included sheriff's deputies, corrections officers, and employees in the Rutherford County Courthouse. They gave Jane Whaley an inside track, from identifying the license plates of cars parked outside the church, to stepping in if anyone filed a complaint about the church or its members.

They said congregants were forced to work at businesses owned by church leaders. If it all was true, the church was one big criminal enterprise. But most of the members had no clue what was going on, or refused to accept the facts. They were "brainwashed," the escapees said—Word of Faith Fellowship was no church at all. It was a cult.

Leslie Martinez told investigators that she was restrained, choked, and held in a basement when she tried to leave. She said church leaders in 1988 had tied up another woman for nearly two weeks in an ill-fated attempt to exorcise her demons.

Martinez described what happened to Carol Pullen. Pullen's husband brought her to the church, saying she was acting crazy and needed help. The church summoned one of its members to examine her. Pat Pagter, a Duke-educated doctor and Navy veteran, said Carol Pullen was possessed by a demon.

Pullen was taken to the home of Sallie and Ollie Carlson, where she was tied to a chair and blasted through the day and bound into a bed and blasted at night. It went on for thirteen days.

Martinez said Pullen's husband, John, was skeptical at first, but Jane Whaley convinced him that radical action was necessary. After nearly two weeks of blasting, church leaders finally brought Carol Pullen to a hospital. There she was diagnosed as having an allergic reaction to cold medicine.

Hayes pulled the Pullen file. The Pullens had written letters to the church, and copied them to Kenneth Hagin, Sr., about the Word of Faith Fellowship treatment.

"My decision to bring [Carol] there and submit her to your ministrations was the greatest mistake I have ever made," John Pullen wrote. "It almost destroyed our marriage and could have caused permanent damage to her physical and mental health.

"According to four highly reputable doctors, Carol's problem was a psychotic reaction to the drugs that were administered to her while she was ill with flu; but we—you and I and others who helped me get her to Rutherfordton and keep her there against her will—assumed that she was possessed by demons. Then we proceeded to subject her to thirteen days of so-called deliverance, which, in reality, was nothing but torture.

"Carol was temporarily out of her mind because of the drugs that were poisoning her system, but you were in grave error when you called her responses 'the devils acting up,' and I was even more wrong to heed your advice to me, which was to 'torment the demons in her' in order to make them come out. Because demons were not the problem. Carol got better when the effects of the drugs wore off, not from any 'deliverance' she received from us."

Carol also wrote a letter just as damning.

"I have by the grace of God survived the horror of being tied to a bed and a chair under constant surveillance (even in the bathroom) with scores of people screaming at me and making me feel that you thought I was evil, when I was already frightened and confused because of foreign substances in my system," Carol Pullen said.

"It was very confusing to me that people in a church would behave the way you did," she said.

Parents told investigators that their children were spanked by ministers—and not just a few light taps on their butts. No, their children were beaten with paddles or belts until they bled. Some were left with deep bruises on their bodies. Agents were told about one child whose eardrum was ruptured from the intense screaming prayer. Others reported a child being thrown to the floor and an adult lying on top of her for an hour while she was blasted.

And then there was the case of Harold Lloyd—the man who was featured on *Inside Edition*. Lloyd and his wife sold their house in Lumberton, North Carolina, and moved two hundred miles west to Spindale in 1994 to join the church.

When his adult son, Darren, returned from an overseas assignment with the US Air Force, he visited his father, who was living with other members in a communal home.

On July 1, 1994, Lloyd's family, including Darren, his sister, and her boyfriend, Duane Drew, a church minister, cut short an outing when Lloyd, who had a history of heart problems, said he wasn't feeling well.

"Take hold," his daughter's boyfriend told him. "It's in God's hands."

Lloyd said he felt weak. Once home, he sat at the table and finally slumped over in his chair. "I'm having a heart attack," he said.

Harold's wife and daughter and Duane Drew immediately laid their hands on him and began screaming, "Get out, you evil spirits."

Darren was startled. "Get him his medicine!"

The three turned on Darren, telling him to leave.

Darren ran to get his wife, who had been napping. She knew CPR. "Get up!" he said. When they returned to the kitchen, his father was still seated in the chair. He was "purple," the report said, and "sweating profusely."

Darren watched as his father's eyes rolled back in his head "and he went into convulsions and slid out of the chair."

"Call 911," Darren screamed as his wife began administering CPR.

Instead, his mother and sister tied up the telephone "hysterically going down the church list, calling other members to blast for his father."

Finally, someone ran next door and called for an ambulance. It arrived too late. Harold Lloyd was dead.

Only later did Darren learn that his father had stopped taking vital heart medicine two weeks before, as part of a "spiritled" healing treatment the church leaders had prescribed for his condition.

Jane Whaley went with the family to a funeral home to help make arrangements. His service, a few days later, was called a "memorial celebration." Jane Whaley preached for an hour. Darren was furious. He'd later confront his mother about being in a "cult," but that only drove a deeper wedge between them.

Hayes thought this could constitute manslaughter, but in the Lloyd file was a letter from Whaley's attorney. It said that Darren had recanted some of his allegations. But what the lawyer called a "retraction" was Darren and his wife complaining about merciless harassment that followed his father's death.

"Because of some accusations brought against my parents' church in Spindale, my wife and I began to receive numerous telephone calls (at one point in time they were coming

daily all day long) concerning the events surrounding my father's death. These became almost unbearable harassment to
my wife and I," he wrote. "I was sorry I had ever made any
kind of statement to reporters."

Beginning in late March, agents began interviewing key
ministers, including Brooke Covington and Jayne Caulder.
Covington told them about graduating from Rhema Bible
College in 1982, following Sam and Jane Whaley to Spindale in 1985, and eventually working for them at the church,
mostly as a teacher at the school. But she didn't disclose the
critical role she played in the church.

Whaley treated Covington like family. She'd always introduce Brooke as her daughter. (Most people outside the church
didn't know they weren't related.) But Brooke was really the
daughter of wealthy Kansas farmers. She had always been devout and after high school in Goodland, Kansas, she traveled
with the Continental Singers, a Christian musical ministry.
At Rhema, she attended one of Jane Whaley's services. And
Jane quickly took Brooke under her wings. After her mother
died in 1987, Brooke used some of her inheritance to help the
Whaleys buy their home. (Her father had died in 1982.) Jane
later arranged Brooke's marriage to Kent Covington. Over
the years, she had become Whaley's trusted enforcer—the
one who made sure congregants were following the church's
practices.

Brooke admitted to an agent that she paddled students, but
only as a last resort. She said she used a thin ruler with kin-
dergartners and a paddle for older ones.

When asked about Carol Pullen, she admitted knowing
her. At first, Covington was reluctant to disclose details, but
she later said that Pullen was "masturbating incessantly and
would not stop and was acting irrational."

She denied that Pullen was restrained the entire time they

tried to expel her demons. Pullen's husband gave his permission for the exorcism, and she insisted that no congregant was ever harmed at the church.

Then it was Jane Whaley's turn.

The meeting took place in the office of her lawyer, James H. Atkins, in Gastonia, North Carolina, a city an hour's drive east of Spindale.

Whaley strolled into the office like she was heading into a Sunday service. She sat down and switched on her Southern charm. She told investigators she was glad to finally tell her side of the story and said so many "godless lies" had been spread about her church. She said the devil was working against them.

Hayes advised Whaley that she wasn't under arrest. She didn't have to speak to him. But she interrupted, saying she wanted to tell the truth.

Hayes pitched right in: Was Leslie Martinez ever restrained? Was she choked by another member? That never happened, Whaley insisted. No one at the church was ever abused. She stuck to the script: Word of Faith Fellowship was a loving community. They'd helped a lot of troubled people over the years.

"Do you tell members of your congregation where they have to work?" Hayes asked.

They didn't do that, Whaley snapped. But if someone came to them looking for work, they'd do their best to help them find a job.

Hayes pushed on. "Mrs. Whaley, do you separate families?"

No, but some families lived with others. It helped them keep up with rent.

"Does the church restrain congregants?" Hayes asked.

Whaley's attorney advised her not to answer. But again, she ignored him. It depended, she said. If demons were trying to get the person to leave, church leaders would talk to the member, to determine if they wanted to continue with the exorcism, she said. If the individual chose not to continue, they were free to leave.

But there was a caveat. Walking out halfway through a demonic deliverance could be dangerous for the possessed soul, she said. These individuals would be restrained because "people in deliverance are in a psychotic state."

Whaley had a snappy answer to every query. There was no hesitation. She loved to talk, and the interview went on.

Two hours in, Hayes asked about the nursery. "Are children ever tied up?"

At snack time, they used a soft baby blanket to tie around the children's waists so they'd not fall out of their chairs. She called it a "seat belt" for their protection.

After nearly three hours, Hayes ran out of questions. Whaley stood up, still as confident as when the interrogation began.

In August 1995, Hayes put the finishing touches on the agency's investigation report. It was 315 pages long, comprehensive, and very disturbing. It was clear that something ungodly was going on inside the church, but was that criminal? That was for others to decide.

Hayes's brief summary of the investigation said that most of the information described the church's unorthodox practices, which included individuals "being physically restrained and assaulted" during deliverance, and children tied to chairs in the nursery, and other children being "whipped with paddles and rods."

Nearly a dozen people said they were willing to testify against the church, but Hayes wrote, "Most victims were reluctant to come forward, and many indicated they did not wish to pursue any criminal prosecution."

That line cast a pall over the entire investigation. It was

one of the reasons District Attorney Jeff Hunt cited when he decided against prosecuting Whaley and other Word of Faith Fellowship leaders. Hunt had asked the State Bureau of Investigation to look into the allegations. And even though the investigators compiled a damning, 315-page report, Hunt declined to prosecute. At a news conference, Hunt said too many congregants had refused to cooperate. It would be too hard to get a conviction.

Case closed.

The SBI report was never released to the public. It was buried for more than twenty years. The triumphant church marched on and flourished, while its practices grew more violent and dark.

Years later, Pete Evans learned that his name was mentioned in the 1995 report. An SBI agent had written that Evans phoned him and said he did not witness abusive practices during his time inside the church.

Evans says he never called an SBI agent, and he was never contacted by one, either. If he had talked to an agent, Evans said he would've told him that abuse was widespread.

The church won, Jane Whaley bragged to her congregation. That was the first of many victories against what she labeled "the attackers."

7

LITTLE HOUSE IN THE COUNTRY

It was a happy season at Word of Faith Fellowship. The satellite trucks and reporters were gone, and the church compound slipped back into its normal rhythm.

Jane Whaley turned her attention to more important matters: her daughter's wedding. Robin Whaley was outgoing, slender, and petite with a warm, infectious smile. Her big curly blond hair was permed and lacquered to 1980s perfection.

Robin had been educated in upscale schools, like Victory Christian in Tulsa. When her mother gained an entourage, her followers doted on Robin, chaperoning her to school and social events. She stayed in their homes when the Whaleys traveled the world on evangelism tours.

Robin had a boyfriend back in Tulsa, early on, a "bad boy" from down the street named Jay Plummer. Jay's mother and sisters would later join the Fellowship, but Jane Whaley didn't want her daughter associating with a beer-drinking motorcycle-riding rebel like Jay. She had put a quick end to their flirtation.

Then Frank Allen Webster showed up at one of Whaley's

services with his parents. He was a nice, clean-cut kid, a business major at Oklahoma State University. He saw Robin, and that was it. His parents didn't move to Spindale, but Frank Webster did. And after years of courtship under Jane's strict supervision, they would tie the knot at the end of September 1995.

Weddings were elaborate affairs at Word of Faith Fellowship. Several congregants were seamstresses, and their custom wedding gowns and bridesmaid dresses were a cottage industry. The fabric came from a business owned by a church elder. The sanctuary was decked in white and beige silk flowers. Gifts were required.

And because this was Robin's wedding, expectations were extra high. Robin's bridal shower was coming up soon, and Suzanne Cooper was feeling the pressure.

Money was tight in the Cooper household. Rick earned a decent living at the electronics plant, but they still had seven children to support, and a big house-building project to finance.

Rick had stockpiled materials and drawn up plans for a nine-bedroom, five-bathroom house with an office over the garage. All told, the house would be 4,800 square feet. Work would start in the spring of 1996, and he intended to do most of it himself, keeping an eagle eye on expenses. It would take a year or more to finish, but Rick was determined to take his time and do the job right.

In the meantime, the Cooper family had just moved from Cora's place into another three-bedroom rental house. It was a temporary solution, a way station to their new home. Their new place was much like the old one: cramped and cluttered. The sooner they could move to their new home, the better.

Suzanne had another worry. She'd been feeling a little nauseated lately, but she wasn't running a temperature. That could only mean one thing: she was pregnant. She was scared. Rick would welcome the news, of course. But she knew Jane wouldn't.

The Coopers were still going to marriage counseling, and their relationship was still unhappy. They had sex, obviously. But Jane had filled the emotional void in Suzanne's life. The pastor had been nurturing, always asking if she needed help. In church, Jane praised the Coopers from the pulpit. They were role models for others with their bright, obedient children. Jane's father, Bill Brock, took a liking to the family. Before services, he'd often come over and chat with them.

But Suzanne knew the rules: couples needed permission to have children. Suzanne had been told time and again that she had too many children already. As far as the church was concerned, her childbearing days were over.

So if she was pregnant, Jane would be upset. As she headed to Robin's bridal shower, Suzanne blocked that from her mind.

The party was being held in Brooke Covington's new three-story brick home on Brooke Breeze Lane. Her old one had burned down a year earlier, and she'd used the insurance money to build a new home on a secluded two-acre tract less than a mile from the Whaley home.

Suzanne knew congregants had been shuttling in and out of Brooke's house all day. She hoped to go in, drop off her present, and leave. She didn't want Robin to open the gift in front of everybody. She couldn't afford to buy Robin something fancy from a department store. She'd put together a "practical gift": a pair of tweezers, a makeup pencil sharpener, nail-polish remover and cotton balls, and other personal-care items that women use every day. She didn't have money for a gift bag, so she put the items in a shoebox and wrapped it up in brightly colored paper.

When she drove up the long entryway, her heart fell. Cars

were parked bumper to bumper. Ladies carrying elaborate packages bustled to the big front doors. Suzanne felt like she was back in high school, wearing an out-of-style dress to the formal dance, facing the scorn of the better-off kids.

Robin sat on a couch in the big living room, flanked by Jane and Brooke. Others perched on chairs and couches, chattering and sipping punch. On a table nearby were stacks of presents. Robin would open a present, put it on coffee table in front of her, then move on to the next one.

Suzanne felt her heart racing. She wished she could go back in time and scrape together money to buy Robin the most expensive gift in the room. She wanted Jane to praise her thoughtfulness. Her thoughts were interrupted by Jane's shrill voice.

"YOU BACK UP, TERRI!" Jane screamed.

A congregant, Terri Franta, had leaned in to look at a present, and had moved a little too close to Robin for Jane's liking. Jane didn't let up. She ripped into the woman for at least ten minutes, telling Terri she had all kinds of devils hovering around her, and she needed to leave the house right away.

An uncomfortable silence fell over the room. What did Terri do that was so wrong? Terri was celebrating, Suzanne thought. She was happy for Robin, and what was her reward? She was humiliated in front of dozens of people.

Terri and her devils left the party, and the focus moved on to the next present like nothing had happened. While Robin opened the gifts, Suzanne placed hers in the pile and slipped out of the house.

Rick couldn't contain his joy. He loved children, and was going to tell everyone the news: Suzanne was pregnant! Yes, they already had seven children. But so what? His faith had carried him this far.

Suzanne called her mother for emotional support. Wanda took the news quietly. She walked a tightrope every time she talked to her daughter. Suzanne could talk about the slights and conflicts among church members, but if Wanda criticized them, Suzanne might stop calling.

Wanda was deeply disturbed by Word of Faith Fellowship, and it didn't help that Cindy and her family had just moved to Spindale. They were living in a small rental while their new house went up on the land they'd bought from Rick. They'd almost had their mitts on Shana, too.

When Cindy moved to Spindale, Shana and her four children tagged along. But after a few months of strict rules and bizarre worship, Shana gave up and escaped back to Florida, to be nearer to her mother. Neither could understand how Suzanne and Cindy couldn't see through Jane.

Experts who study cults say families have difficulty getting through to victims. They often feel like their loved one has become a stranger. The victims live in an alternate universe where they are relieved of daily decision-making by a leader who tells them how to think and how to live. The victim believes her family has changed, not her.

That was the case with Suzanne. Her reality was turned upside down. Even though she was the mother of seven children, church leaders could make her feel like she was a child herself.

Suzanne broke the news first to Brooke Covington. There were no smiles or congratulations, no questions about how far along she was with the baby, or how she was feeling. Brooke would have to immediately report it to Jane, she said.

A few hours later, Brooke told her that Jane was unhappy with her, and she was to write a note to "explain what had happened." Suzanne's hands shook as she wrote the letter. She said they didn't plan to have another child. It had just happened, but she was very happy about it.

Jane's response crushed her. Suzanne's baby "was not in the spirit of God."

She explained that "when you hear from God and do things in the spirit of God, then your child will be provided for"—clothing, food, everything they need in life. But when you "just go out and get pregnant," it's a sin.

On Sunday, Jane preached that message from the pulpit. Everyone in church knew who she was talking about. Jane was relentless. "You were only having babies to have babies," she preached directly at Suzanne.

The snide comments weren't confined to her pregnancy. Jane and other ministers began criticizing other things, too. Once, when Jane picked up little Blair in the nursery, he started crying. Jane handed the toddler to Suzanne and scolded her. "He did not take hold of Jesus. He did not do the will of God," she said. The other ministers followed, saying there was something wrong with Blair. He wasn't peaceful, they said, so they blasted him.

Suzanne, who lived for Jane's approval, was demoralized. She felt hurt and ashamed, and all the more determined to get back into Jane's good graces.

Suzanne was determined to follow Jane's advice on how to raise her new baby. She went to an obstetrician who treated other Word of Faith Fellowship women. She let a church member escort her to her appointments. She was told to breastfeed her infant by the clock, every three hours. "And if they don't want your milk, give them formula," the instructor told her. That way Suzanne wouldn't develop any "perversions" for the child.

She had nursed her other seven children on demand, and everyone was healthy and happy. But maybe she had been doing it all wrong. Maybe she really was a bad mother. She needed to learn about God's way.

★ ★ ★

Jeffrey Cooper was clean-cut, arrow straight, and tormented. Much was expected of the oldest Cooper child, and he didn't disappoint. Jeffrey followed all the rules, worked hard, and did what he was told. And like most young congregants, he referred to Jane as "Grandmother."

At a time when most teenage boys were watching television, playing sports, or hanging out with their friends, Jeffrey was studying math, reading his Bible, or "volunteering" to work at businesses owned by church leaders.

In the fall of 1996, Jeffrey was fourteen years old but acted like he was forty. As a responsible son, he welcomed his new little brother, Adam. Now there were eight Cooper kids— seven boys and a girl.

The family's new rental house was as crowded as the last. Without his grandmother Cora under the same roof, there was a little more peace. Still, it was hard for Jeffrey to find space to do his homework—or anything else. The problem was exacerbated when Word of Faith sent another family to live with them.

Melissa Hudson and her two children were new to the church. Jennifer, the pretty thirteen-year-old daughter, presented Jeffrey with his first distraction from schoolbooks.

Jeffrey had a crush, his first one, and like most teenage boys, he didn't know how to handle it. The church and its rules made it even more confusing.

It was exciting, terrifying, and embarrassing, finding out how to relate to someone of the opposite sex. Jeffrey knew "those" feelings were prohibited by the church. They meant he had "lust devils," or was giving in to the unclean.

But the feeling he had for Jennifer felt so right. They'd make eye contact and Jeffrey would feel giddy, but he knew he couldn't show his feelings. Time and again, he had heard Jane preach about the unclean, the impure thoughts that threatened to send her flock to hell. Boys were taught that an erection was "a manifestation of their bodies," something that should never happen.

But now it was happening to Jeffrey. He needed to confess his sin and clear his conscience. Only one person could show him the way: Grandmother. He was determined to tell her, but his nerve failed.

He was terrified, but it didn't matter anymore. His guilt was too much to bear. After the Sunday evening service, he waited for the sanctuary to clear, then slowly walked to Jane.

"What is it, Jeffrey?" Whaley asked.

He hesitated for a moment, then blurted it out: "I have sin in my heart."

Months of soul-twisting guilt spilled out. He told Whaley everything, how he couldn't stop thinking about Jennifer. Worse, he was having sexual thoughts. He tried to stop, but he couldn't. When he was finished, he stood there trembling, bracing for the worst. He fully expected to be blasted. But something strange happened. Jane wasn't mad at all. Instead, she smiled at him sweetly.

"You did the right thing, coming to me, Jeffrey. I already knew you were giving in to the unclean. But God told me that if I gave you time, you would do the right thing," Whaley said. "Now, I need to hear from God on what we should do. You are not the only one giving in to the unclean."

As Whaley talked to Jeffrey in the sanctuary, Ray Farmer was lurking. He found Suzanne waiting in the hallway.

"Jeffrey was very, very honest tonight. He opened his heart to Jane," Farmer said.

"About what?" she asked.

"He told her about the unclean, about the feelings he has

been having for the young woman living with your family," he said. Suzanne was shocked. She had no idea.

Over the next few days, Whaley showered Jeffrey with attention, praising him at Bible studies and holding him up as an example to others.

"How blessed you are to have such an honest boy," Whaley told Suzanne. "God is working on his heart."

Now it was time for the others to come clean. At the next Wednesday service, Whaley scanned the room, studying her congregation.

"I've had a young man come to me and open his heart to God. God didn't have to come to him and expose him," Whaley said, her voice rising with each word, building to a fever pitch.

"BUT HE'S NOT THE ONLY ONE WITH THE UNCLEAN."

She said she knew others in the congregation had similar thoughts. God would have mercy on them if they came forward, now. If not, they'd face God's wrath.

"We're not here to disobey God," she warned.

Some children and teenagers stepped up quickly. Others took longer. But soon a line had formed from the pulpit deep into the sanctuary. Suzanne went stiff. She didn't know what would happen to her own children, and whispered a quick prayer: "God, don't let them get blasted."

Then she turned to her children. "Benjamin, Lena, Peter, do you need to come clean about anything?"

They all nodded.

"OK, go get in line and tell Jane," she said.

For hours, little boys in suits and ties, and little girls in lace-collar dresses, lined up, weeping, to confess their dirty secrets. One boy had gotten an erection and he didn't know why. Another spent too long in the bathroom and had touched his penis. Some of the children told on their brothers and sisters. It went on well past midnight, but it didn't matter that children were up so late. Whaley said classes at the Word of Faith Christian School could start later the next day.

Jeffrey Cooper had started a "move of God." Even after the congregation went home, parents pressed their children to admit their wrongs. They called Whaley on the phone to confess.

Church leaders made a list of all the children who confessed to the unclean. More important, they made a list of those who had not. Elders spent the next week calling their parents to ask why their children were denying the move of God.

Whaley used Jeffrey Cooper's confession to hammer home to her followers that God's grace could not cover them if they carried their sins in silence. It morphed into a new strategy. If one church member was caught violating a commandment or rule, all members were expected to "take hold," to search their own souls for similar shortcomings and come clean to Jane. Since the church had escaped "the attack" without serious consequences, Whaley felt more powerful than ever. She had predicted that God would protect them. The fact that no criminal charges were brought against them only solidified her standing as a prophet.

Jeffrey soon blocked Jennifer out of his mind.

Crystal Taylor didn't have as much control. Throughout her teens, images of past attacks returned to her at night: men sneaking into her bedroom, slipping into her bed. Jane Whaley screeching into her face, blaming her for "allowing" herself to be assaulted. Policemen who took notes, asked odd questions, and then did nothing to help her.

But now it was 1998 and she was eighteen. Now she had hope.

Her uncle was on his way to pick her up. Her step-grandmother's parental custody rights could no longer stop her from leaving Word of Faith Fellowship. Just like that, she was free to go.

She had a path to follow, blazed by her brother, Eddie Taylor, who had left a few years earlier. He'd told reporters from *Inside Edition* about abuse inside the church, and he told the same to SBI investigators.

He had tried to run away several times, but was always caught and physically restrained. His hands were bound; he was slapped and punched. Another time, a "three-hundred-pound church member...held him down in his chair and would not let him leave."

He gave detailed descriptions of church leaders beating young children, but nothing changed. Eddie knew how closely law enforcement was aligned with the church. Several Rutherford County sheriff's deputies were church members. In fact, the church had set up a hotline of sorts with the sheriff's office.

If a campus resident like Eddie Taylor ran away, Ray Farmer would take over. He was the conduit between the church and civil authorities, Jane Whaley's fixer. If police saw a "Word of Faith kid" walking down the road, they detained him until church security came to collect him.

Crystal knew not to trust anyone at Word of Faith. Her "trip to the beach" back when the *Inside Edition* piece ran had made it clear that she knew things they wanted to keep in the dark.

During that long stay, elders blasted her off and on for more than a week.

They'd brought her back. The men did not bother her again, but the demons did. At night, mostly, she heard them shrieking at her again. She smelled their breath. She saw their angry faces.

She tried not to think about that. She didn't want another

panic attack. She took her things to the door and peeked out the window. Her little sister, Danielle, lived in a house down the street. Danielle was growing up, too. Crystal wondered if someone was slipping into her room at night.

"Please, Lord, protect my sister. Help me get through this," she whispered.

A car horn beeped. Her uncle was here!

Crystal didn't say goodbye. She grabbed her bag and ran outside. She was free. She'd never have to come back to this place.

But the abuse was seared into her memory. She carried that with her through life.

At sundown Rick Cooper stood in the front yard and marveled at the work of his hands. It had taken years, but he'd finally finished his dream house. His family and friends from the church were inside, setting up the furniture.

It was a dream come true in several respects. Rick had seen the project as a great way to bond with his children, and his three eldest—Jeffrey, Lena, and Benjamin—rose to the occasion. They spent after-school and weekend hours hauling lumber, handing off tools, and finally showing off real skills they'd learned on the job. The other boys—Peter, Chad, John David, Blair, and Adam—were still too young.

Rick had taken out a construction loan to pay for materials. He was finally making good money—$25 an hour—and picking up as much overtime where he could. He filled in whenever a coworker called in sick or went on vacation. Every extra penny went into the house.

Rick cut and shaped all the lumber. His older children helped measure and handle the boards and timbers—they'd framed the house, put up beams and joists, and nailed it all together.

He was a patient teacher, explaining the intricacies of construction and the importance of precision just as his father had done with him so many years before. When the time came for Rick to cut headers for the doors and windows, the children carried in the pieces and nailed them in place without his guidance.

They had fun together, and that was the point. Weekends at the property had become family outings. Suzanne and the younger kids played or laid out picnic lunches while Rick and the older children worked. On breaks, Rick played hide-and-seek with them, chasing the kids through the woods and across the creek, whooping and giggling like a kid himself. Those weekends were everything Rick had ever wanted.

As the project neared completion, church members pitched in. After a service, Jane announced that Rick needed volunteers to help him put up and paint baseboards and crown molding. That was no small task in a 4,800-square-foot home, but about fifty people showed up. They did it all over one long weekend, and they did it for free.

Now here he was, grinning, still amazed at how it had all come together. Stars emerged onto the fresh night sky. Rick looked up at bright Orion stretching up from the horizon.

He thanked God. This was the nicest house he'd ever lived in, a special place to raise his family. The future was out of his hands, but he did know one thing for sure: right here and now, he was truly blessed.

PART TWO

CHILDREN OF
THE DAMNED

8

DOUBTING THE WORD

July 14, 1999, was a big day for Sam Whaley, a moment when he stepped out of his wife's shadow. It was the payoff for years of faithful glad-handing, campaigning, and buffet lunches for the Republican Party of North Carolina. That day, Sam offered the opening prayer for the US House of Representatives.

The invitation came from Rep. Charles Taylor, a staunchly conservative Republican congressman from Brevard, North Carolina. For years, Word of Faith Fellowship had hosted lavish candidate forums and luncheons to support local, state, and federal politicians, including Taylor.

The Whaleys were longtime supporters of Taylor, a wealthy farmer banker who was elected in 1990 by only 2,700 votes. Taylor presided over weekly prayer breakfasts in Asheville, and Word of Faith parishioners frequently took part. They didn't give much money, but they cheerfully campaigned.

Taylor, a Baptist, offered his own support for the Whaleys' church. A year earlier, he'd donated several used computers from his congressional offices to Word of Faith Fellowship.

Now, four years after the SBI investigation, Sam Whaley

was ready to stand before one of the most important legislative bodies in the world. Word of Faith Fellowship had come a long way toward rehabilitating its reputation. And behind the scenes, its global power was slowly growing.

By the summer of 1999, Word of Faith Fellowship's affiliation with two Brazilian churches had strengthened significantly. They numbered more than a thousand members, and they were growing every day. The Brazilian groups routinely sent member contingents to Spindale for biannual weeklong Bible seminars, with some staying on through tourist or student visas.

Likewise, Word of Faith Fellowship formed ties to a congregation in Ghana run by a Whaley-trained pastor. His church near Accra, the nation's capital, had hundreds of members.

The Whaleys had speaking engagements in evangelical hot spots all over Europe, mainly Sweden, Switzerland, and Germany. People in those nations were encouraged to move to North Carolina.

Not only was Word of Faith Fellowship extending its reach overseas, it was solidifying its power at home. Member Laura Bridges was hired at the Rutherford County court clerk's office in 1997, joining Ramona Hall, another congregant who had worked there for a decade.

Leading the US Congress in prayer was another step toward respectability. Sam stood in the big room where just six months earlier, lawmakers—including Taylor—voted to impeach President Bill Clinton for trying to thwart a federal probe into his fling with White House intern Monica Lewinsky. The buzz was still in the air, the rush of righteousness.

Sam felt good, standing shoulder-to-shoulder with powerful, right-thinking men. At home his wife never missed a chance to belittle him. Once, when he took a second helping of spaghetti, Jane snapped, "Sam, you're giving in to the gluttony devil." But today the platform was his.

As the lawmakers began to take their seats for the start of the session, Sam headed to the dais. The portly pastor spread his papers on the podium, the same podium where US presidents had given their annual State of the Union addresses.

Sam bowed his head. "Let us pray," he said. The room went quiet. Sam took a breath. He could feel the C-Span television camera focusing on him.

"Father God, we count it an honor to come before You on behalf of our Congress and leaders. We need You to be in control of our nation," Sam said. "We are in desperate need of Your wisdom, Your will, and Your divine protection.

"We cry out for Your wisdom and courage to come to the hearts of our leaders so they will have strength to take a stand for righteousness. Cause them to be aware of how important it is to inquire of You before any decision is made, since You and You alone place them in the authority to execute Your righteous judgments.

"Have mercy on us. Put a heart of prayer in Your people. Thank You, Dear Lord. Amen."

The former used car salesman beamed quietly. The church's political connections now extended far beyond the foothills of North Carolina. Church leaders hoped those connections would serve them well in case things ever went sideways again.

Shana Muse paced her cell at the Marion County jail in Ocala, craving a cigarette. How could things have gotten so out of control? She'd always been a free spirit, but now she was thirty-six years old, with four children. She couldn't keep going on benders. Her children's fathers weren't around, and never had been. Those babies needed her more than ever.

But here she was, busted, in March 2000 for writing bad

checks to support her drug habit. Social workers had placed her children with her mother, Wanda. She had no friends. No money. No drugs or alcohol to help her forget for a while. *So, this is rock bottom*, she thought. She plopped down on the concrete bench and buried her head in her hands.

Shana started on this path in middle school, drinking vodka-and-orange-juice "screwdrivers." By eleventh grade she was using drugs. Cocaine was her favorite.

Like she'd done with Cindy, Wanda wanted to get Shana out of Florida and into the world. "You are going to live with Rick and Suzanne. You need to get out of here, get yourself straightened out, try something new," she told her.

A week before Shana's eighteenth birthday, Wanda put her on a flight to Hawaii. Shana settled in for a long-term party. Six months after she arrived in Hawaii, Rick was deployed to Florida. Suzanne urged Shana to return with them to the mainland, but Shana said no. She was having a great time.

Three years later, at age twenty-one, Shana made the move, this time to Orlando, to live with Cindy and Stephen Cordes. She met a handsome college student named Khalid, the son of a wealthy Saudi family.

Khalid made it clear he would go home after graduation, but Shana was living in the moment. Their daughter Sarah was born in January 1987. Khalid left five months later. Shana was crushed. Two weeks later, Shana got the shock of her life: she was pregnant again. Rachel was born the following January.

Shana headed west to live with her sister Sonya in Fontana, California. She took classes to become an LPN, or "low-paid nurse," as she liked to say. She met a man named Vincent, who gave her two sons in two years: Patrick in 1993, and Justin in 1994. Shana's relationship was turbulent, so she hit the road again when Justin was just ten days old. She loaded her kids up in the middle of the night and drove across the country to live with the Cordeses. She went along when they moved in July 1995 to Spindale to join the Word of Faith Fellowship.

From the start, Shana and the church were a match made in hell. The church expected total submission, and they weren't going to get that from her.

Church leaders—as well as Cindy and Suzanne—constantly criticized Shana and her children. Suzanne was especially hard on her, calling her sister to "repent" at the slightest provocation.

Shana moved back to Florida, where she again developed a cocaine habit. She moved on to crack cocaine, a highly addictive smokable form of the drug. Within three months she lost her job and her house. Her children were sent to live with Wanda. And now she was facing a felony charge for bouncing checks.

Shana was desperate. She couldn't turn to her mother. But her sisters came to her rescue.

"You have visitors," a corrections officer said. On the other side of the bulletproof glass were Suzanne and Cindy. Tough as she was, Shana burst into sobs.

"We're going to get you out of here," Suzanne promised. "But we want you to come back with us to North Carolina. Get yourself together and then we'll help you get custody of the kids. But first, right now, you have to get right with the Lord."

Those were not the words Shana wanted to hear, but she didn't have a choice: it was either Word of Faith Fellowship or jail. In her mind, they were almost synonymous. But she took the offer.

Suzanne, Cindy, and Wanda joined together to hire an attorney, who asked a judge to give Shana a chance. The judge sentenced Shana to five years' probation. He gave her permission to move to North Carolina, and in a separate hearing, Suzanne was given temporary custody of Shana's children.

When everything was over, Shana apologized to her sisters and mother for all the grief she'd caused them. She thanked them for not abandoning her. She'd messed up, but this time—with their help—she really was going to turn around her life.

All three sisters climbed into the car for the long drive back to Rutherford County.

Rick Cooper glimpsed out the window into the darkness. Benjamin had school the next day, and it was getting late. He didn't know exactly where Benjamin was, if he was working at the Whaleys' or on a church "work project," which meant he was helping remodel someone's home.

Rick only knew his fourteen-year-old son was coming home later and later every night, and he didn't like it. It had been going on for a long time.

He thought he'd created a perfect Christian world for his family. But shortly after they moved in 1998, other families were sent by the church to share the house with the Coopers. The families helped with expenses, but the house was starting to feel a lot like a commune. People and their things were all over the place, and it was clear the Coopers were not in charge. Every time Rick or Suzanne did something the housemates didn't like, they'd go to leadership, saying the Coopers had "given in to the devil."

Punishment could include "discipleship," which meant one of them could be taken out of the house and sent to live with another family, sometimes for months. And it wasn't confined to adults. It was happening to more and more teenagers, too. In fact, some kids whose parents were found wanting were being raised instead by ministers.

Rick felt that was wrong, that families should live together in their own homes. His own children were turning into teenagers, and he didn't see them more than an hour or two each day. Cooper had to stop himself from thinking too long about it.

For Rick and Suzanne, the children's education was one of the reasons they bought into Word of Faith Fellowship. All of the students at the school seemed to get excellent grades.

But now it seemed like the church leaders' businesses had a first claim on the youngsters. Children were spending more time than ever toiling at businesses and doing housework, babysitting, and maintenance jobs in the ministers' homes.

It was cutting into their study time and music practice. Rick's children not only excelled academically but had started playing instruments. Benjamin was getting good on the cello. Jeffrey and Peter played the trumpet and trombone. Lena, Chad, and John all dabbled on piano.

But now, they hardly had time for music. Jeffrey, Lena, and Benjamin wore themselves out working after school and on weekends. Children as young as ten and eleven years old were starting to "help out" in the businesses.

Not only that, Jane had said she wasn't sure she could allow the students who graduated from the high school to go on to college. There were just too many temptations in the outside world.

What, then, was the payoff for working so hard in high school? Rick thought.

Jane permitted a few teenagers to go to college, but only under pressure, and only if they met her conditions. They had to start at nearby Isothermal Community College. Word of Faith students had to commute to school together, so they could keep one another in line. And if they did well enough after two years to transfer to a four-year college, the same rules applied. They'd have to go in clusters, and they couldn't live on campus.

But students in the ministers' families were allowed to continue their education. Ray Farmer's son, Josh, was about to go to law school, as was Jane Whaley's son-in-law, Frank Webster. Somehow, the leaders thought the followers wouldn't notice the inequity.

Rick was too scared to discuss his doubts with Jane, ministers, or even Suzanne. Beyond that fear were more hard facts: the electronics factory was about to close. Rick didn't know where he'd find work that paid enough to meet his mortgage payments. Jane kept asking members to tithe more, and the kids kept growing out of their clothes and shoes.

"God never gives you more than you can handle," Jane liked to say. Just pray loud and faithfully, and the Lord will provide.

He peeked out the window again. Still no Benjamin. He didn't mind the boy mowing the Whaleys' lawn or cleaning their house on the weekends. It was the "work projects" that got his goat.

The Farmers owned several apartment complexes, and the church owned other rental homes. The ministers had put together work crews to remodel and maintain the properties. Teenagers helped paint, put up cabinets, do all sorts of construction work. They sometimes came home after midnight. Some of the jobs were paid a minimum wage. Others were not.

Rick knew their education was suffering. If they worked late, church leaders sometimes canceled or delayed the start of classes the following morning. Parents just couldn't say, "No, not my kid. Not tonight."

A car door slammed. Rick stepped to the door and waved to the driver. Benjamin slipped safely into the house. Rick didn't bother asking him about homework.

Shower. Bed. All his children would sleep under the same roof tonight. Everything looked fine on the surface, but Rick knew he had to do something. He'd just wait until the Lord gave him the answer. Just what that might be, he didn't know.

9

NO ESCAPE

After six years away, Shana was shocked at the changes at Word of Faith Fellowship. Dozens of new rules had been added, and old ones tightened. Members were kept from the world outside, and deeply dependent on the church. The edicts had nothing to do with the Bible, but what Jane Whaley justified as "God's will" was as good as gospel to her hundreds of followers.

Many of the rules focused on "the unclean," Whaley's catchall term for intimacy or sex. Congregants required permission to marry. Afterward they weren't to "come together"—have sex—until the elders decided the time was right. Sex outside marriage was the ultimate sin.

Followers knew that at some point, no matter what their age or gender, they'd be accused of masturbation, or having erotic thoughts. From the pulpit one Sunday Jane Whaley described something diabolical she'd seen during a drive into town: a man standing with his hands in his pockets. This clearly meant the man was masturbating, she said, and from that day forward, Word of Faith followers were not allowed to put their hands in their pockets.

Sexual demons were supposedly attracted to youngsters, so boys and girls were forbidden to speak to each other without a "guard" present. Swimming was an occasion for sin, so children could swim only in same-sex groups. Men and boys had to keep their shirts on in the pool.

It wasn't just sex. Shana saw that Whaley was stepping up restrictions on followers' contacts with "outsiders"—family and friends who weren't Word of Faith Fellowship members—a common cult tactic.

Experts say cult leaders consistently isolate members from people who question their beliefs. They hate others influencing their flock, so they manipulate followers' lives to maximize contact with fellow members and minimize their contact with people outside the group, especially trusted family or friends who might oppose their involvement.

At one time, Whaley allowed members to watch "family-friendly" television shows and movies. Then she banned Disney movies because they depicted "wicked fantasies." And nowadays, Shana thought, just about every medium was off-limits. No radio, no television, no magazines, or newspapers. Forget about movies or videos. Whaley issued her edicts from the pulpit. Nobody dared object.

Birthday celebrations came from a pagan tradition, she said, and should thus no longer be honored. Christmas was a birthday, so it was banned, too. Thanksgiving, Easter, and every holiday on the calendar eventually were "normalized."

Shana hated rules, but she wasn't going to buck the system. Not now. She had to stay focused if she was going to get her children back.

She had to change her ways, and fast. She quit using drugs and faithfully attended church services. She made herself participate in a blasting. She still didn't embrace it, but at least she tried.

She accepted a machine operator job at a plumbing parts factory owned by church leader Kent Covington. She earned $8 an hour and was surrounded by fellow church members throughout the day.

Meanwhile, Suzanne and others in the church did everything they could to prove to social workers in Florida that the children were safe. Justin and Patrick were sleeping on twin beds in the hallway of Suzanne's house, but Suzanne sent pictures of another child's furnished room, making believe Shana's kids were living there. They sent them the Word of Faith Christian School curriculum, along with glowing reports of the children's educational progress.

The social workers were impressed. Shana's children were living in a big house and attending a private school. Shana was sober, showing up for regular drug tests. She had a job. She was attending church. So after a few months, social workers closed their investigation and Shana was given legal custody again. She was thrilled. She tried to abide by the church's rules. She stayed clean and sober. Still, by the summer of 2001, Shana was sure Word of Faith Fellowship was not the right fit for her family.

Ministers routinely belittled her and her kids, calling them wicked. Her older children were forced to work after school and on weekends, sometimes without pay. Church leaders struck children, and sometimes took them from their families "on discipleship."

But what could Shana do? She was stuck. She wasn't financially or emotionally stable enough to make it on her own outside, but not indoctrinated enough to turn a blind eye to the abuse and hypocrisy.

Rick and Suzanne were having doubts, too.

Jeffrey was a sticking point. He was a brilliant student who'd graduated from high school with honors. His college placement tests would get him into just about any school he wanted to attend, but Jane Whaley had said no, Jeffrey wasn't allowed to go to college. Jeffrey was devoted to Jane. He seemed to be happy spending his days doing odd jobs at her towering white-columned house. That was not what Rick and Suzanne had envisioned for him.

More were being taken from their families. It was only a matter of time before it happened to them.

The Coopers kept their concerns to themselves because they didn't trust one another. Each was afraid that if he or she expressed their fears, the other would run to Jane. A lack of trust was only one of the fatal flaws in their marriage. Rick still hoped the relationship could be salvaged. Suzanne knew it was beyond repair.

But it rolled on, powered by the momentum of everyday circumstance. Their daughter, Lena, was about to graduate from high school, they had money troubles, Rick had no employment security. In 2001 he ruptured a disk in his neck, an injury that required surgery.

With Suzanne sitting alone at his hospital bedside, Rick seized the moment. Maybe because they were so rarely alone together, or maybe the pain medicine lowered his defenses, but he opened up and told Suzanne he was worried their children were being exploited by the church. He was disillusioned with Whaley's teachings. He had been studying other Christian teachings and traditions, and believed Whaley was corrupting the Bible's meaning.

Suzanne sat silently for a few moments.

"You're right," she said. "We have to get out."

Rick sighed with relief.

"But for me it's not the teachings," she said. "It's the kids."

The work projects, the late nights. Church leaders constantly telling her how she should raise her children—it had started with all that shaming before Adam was born, and hadn't let up.

But how could they get out? Ministers had been assigned to each family to keep them in line, to make sure they didn't attempt such a move. The Coopers would have to figure out a way to plan their escape without tipping them off. It would cost Rick his job. Since the electronics plant had closed, Rick had worked for one of the ministers. He made only half what he used to, and the hours were growing longer.

The Word of Faith Fellowship had been the center of their lives for years. Some of their children didn't know anything else. What if the kids didn't want to leave? Rick and Suzanne had seen what happened in similar cases. The church forced children to turn on their parents, and sometimes even went to family court to seize custody.

Since his confession to a schoolboy crush at age fourteen, Jeffrey had become the one Cooper Jane found acceptable. He often stepped proudly alongside Jane when she walked into church for services. He was nineteen, old enough to make his own decisions. Rick and Suzanne knew he would want to stay. They weren't sure where their other children stood. The last thing they needed was a protracted custody battle.

And there were other issues: Should they stay in Rutherford County or move away? Florida seemed the obvious place to go. Wanda was there. And what about Cindy? Should they broach the subject with her?

The Coopers decided to wait until Lena graduated to make their move. It was only two months away. At some point, they'd approach Cindy. It was risky, but if she and her husband were on board it would make their departure easier. At least, that was what they thought.

Time passed quickly. Two weeks before Lena's graduation, in the van on the way from the grocery store, Suzanne stunned her sister with the sudden revelation. She waited for Cindy's reaction, her heart racing.

Cindy sighed. "Yes," she said. "I've been thinking that, too. We're not being treated right."

Cindy didn't know if she could get Stephen to agree, but she'd try. They agreed to keep it from Shana, at least for the time being—she never was much good at keeping secrets.

It was a long time to keep silent.

Shana tried to conform. She tried to convince herself that she was Word of Faith Fellowship material, but after nearly a year in Spindale, she knew she was living a lie. She couldn't bury her head in the Bible while her children were being abused.

She had a meltdown one afternoon at work. She had to get out, right then and there. The kids were safe at Suzanne's house, so she checked into a cheap hotel in Spindale and spent the night eating pizza, drinking Coke, smoking cigarettes, and watching MTV. She needed a plan.

The following morning she called Suzanne to pick her up. The van pulled into the parking lot. Shana rehearsed her apology and braced for a lecture.

But Suzanne didn't launch into a sermon. She said she could only dream of a night of pizza and TV. She understood her sister's pain.

"We're not happy, either," she said. "Rick and I have been planning to leave for months."

Shana shook her head in disbelief. Did she just hear that right? "Are you serious?"

Suzanne nodded.

"Why didn't you tell me?" Shana said.

"We didn't know if we could trust you."

She told Shana about the plan, then swore her to secrecy. "We don't know what Jane would do if she found out," Suzanne said.

The sisters sat in the van, hugged, and cried.

When they returned, Jane appeared with Shana's punishment: Suzanne was told to call her sister's probation officer and demand a drug test. Shana was forbidden to attend Lena's graduation celebration.

That night they huddled in Suzanne's bedroom with the ceiling fan turned on High to drown out their whispered conversation. How far would they need to go? How clean did the break need to be?

"If we have to start over from nothing, that's OK," Shana said. "What price do you put on freedom?"

Whatever happened, they'd face it together, as a family, Shana said. They just had to make it through graduation.

The timing was perfect. Wanda was coming up from Florida for Lena's graduation. If anyone could make it happen, Wanda could. It would be a clean break.

Lena graduated, but the big day dawned the following morning. The Coopers hadn't told their kids what they were planning. First, they had to talk to Stephen Cordes.

Rick and Suzanne had led him into the Word of Faith Fellowship. Now they hoped they could get him out.

Stephen was the key to their next move. They still didn't know if they'd stay in Rutherford County, or go to Florida. If the Cordes family stood with them, Jane Whaley would never boss them around again.

Wanda sat at the Coopers' big kitchen table with her daughters, smiling and hopeful. She had been waiting for this moment for almost a decade. She told them all, right out in the open, to stop calling Word of Faith Fellowship a church.

"It's a cult," she said. "Call it by its name. It's almost destroyed my family. It's broken my heart. Where's the love of Jesus in that?"

No one could argue with her. For the most part, church leaders had forbidden Suzanne, Cindy, and Shana and their children from calling or visiting Wanda. Now there was a chance to undo the damage.

Cindy phoned Stephen and asked him to come over. It was important, she said. When he got there, Cindy, Suzanne, and Wanda took him for a drive in the van.

Shana and Rick stayed behind. They took the kids outside to play in the yard.

Rick's mobile phone rang. It was a former Word of Faith member, an escapee, congratulating him on his decision. How did the man know?

Rick hung up, spooked. As the kids played, Rick paced the driveway in a daze.

"Are you OK?" Shana asked.

"I feel like I have a black cloak over me, like death," Rick muttered.

Despite all their planning and secrecy, the Coopers had made critical mistakes. They'd disclosed their plans to the wrong people. Suzanne had called a friend who had been considering moving to Spindale, to warn her away. She told her the Coopers were leaving.

More loyal to the church than the Coopers, Suzanne's friend took the juicy gossip straight to Jane Whaley. The phone lines around Spindale lit up as word spread from house to house.

The van pulled into the driveway at the Cooper house. Stephen Cordes leaped out, ran to his car, and sped away.

Rick walked up, looking like he'd seen a ghost. Suzanne could see that he was losing his nerve.

"I'm getting calls from the wicked already," he said, shaking his head. "I've changed my mind. I don't want to leave."

Suzanne was floored. "What? Rick, we have discussed this! We took a long time to come to this decision. Why are you doing this?"

"The presence of God will leave me. I'm making a huge mistake," he said.

For a moment, Suzanne just stood there in stunned silence. She was overwhelmed by both grief—and fear. She wanted to grab her kids, throw them in a car, and peel out like a bank robber fleeing from a heist. She wanted to get as far away from this damn place as possible. But she was stuck, in a bad dream. The more she tried to move her feet, the more they felt like they were encased in cement. Everything was unraveling in front of her, in slow motion. And she knew it was only going to get worse.

Jane Whaley had dispatched her troops to deal with the revolt, and carload after carload was wheeling into the driveway.

"Don't listen to them, Suzanne. Just tell them to get off your property!" Shana pleaded. "You've made up your mind. Please don't let them do this to you!"

It was too late. Dozens of people barged up the drive and into the Coopers' house, screaming and praying, pulling the children inside, splitting up the family for intense, individual blasting sessions.

Minister Mark Doyle pulled Jeffrey aside.

"Do you know what your parents are planning?" he asked. Jeffrey said no, he had no idea.

"They are planning to leave the church. They want to leave the will of God," he shouted at Jeffrey.

It was like a scene from a horror movie, with people rushing around the house, shouting in tongues, calling out demons and devils. Suzanne looked at her mother. Wanda's eyes were wide, terrified and confused.

"Let's go next door to Cindy's," Suzanne said.

Things were even worse there. Screams rang through the house. Ministers isolated the older Cooper children, putting them under intense pressure. Did they want to die suddenly, and to go to hell? That was certain to happen if they left the church, the ministers said.

Suzanne prayed her family would stick together. But when Jeffrey confronted her, she could see that he'd made up his mind.

"Mom, you don't want to do this," he warned. "We can't leave the church."

She knew it was over. Suzanne knew she couldn't force Jeffrey to leave, but if she escaped without him, Whaley would cut off all contact. She couldn't abandon her child.

Back at the Coopers' house, Wanda slammed her bedroom door on the chaos in the hallway and packed her bag. She returned to Cindy's on her way out. The screaming from the house traveled down the driveway. Rick opened the door, sweating and crying. "I can't leave, Wanda. I just can't. I love my kids too much," he said.

"That's bullshit and you know it," she told him. "If you love those kids you'll get them out of this madhouse. If you loved them you would have never come to this godforsaken place."

Wanda's worst fears were confirmed. She drove away in tears. Her family was in too deep.

Over the next two days, ministers streamed in and out of the Cooper and Cordes homes, blasting for hours on end. Shana stayed in her room as much as possible. Late one night she crept downstairs for a glass of water.

She peeked into the darkened den, where worn-out "spiritual warriors" were draped over the couches and floors.

"Y'all are weirdos," Shana said, shaking her head in disbelief.

She turned the corner into the kitchen and was startled by god-awful shrieks coming from the bathroom. She opened the door, thinking one of the children was hurt. Her sister Cindy was standing inside, watching impassively while Lynn Millwood, one of Jane's lieutenants, held four-year-old Stephen Cordes on her lap atop the toilet seat. Millwood, her face contorted, was screeching in the child's ear, maniacal rants about demons and devils. The boy wailed and struggled.

"Cindy, look what you're doing to your child!" Shana screamed.

"She's helping him," Cindy said.

"She's terrorizing him, Cindy! This is so wrong!"

Millwood told Shana to leave.

"You're a bitch," Shana shouted, slamming the door behind her.

Shana looked up and saw Rick and minister Mark Doyle walking toward her.

"Shana, we can't have that talk in our house," Rick said.

Shana was stunned. Jane's followers were occupying the house like the Manson family. There was a madwoman in the bathroom terrifying an innocent boy. And Rick was worried about Shana saying *bitch*.

"You know what, Rick? You need to stand up and be a man," she snapped.

She scurried to her room, grabbed a few things, and took off. Rick, Suzanne, and a couple of ministers chased after her. Shana made it as far as Cora's little house next door. She sat down at an outdoor table. That was when it hit her: she had no car, no house, and no money. She worked for a church minister. Her mother had left her behind. She lit up a cigarette.

Suzanne leaned in, whispering in her ear, "I love you, Shana. We can work this out."

"No, get away," Shana said, taking a long drag off the cigarette. "You promised me. You've got no backbone. You let me down, Suzanne."

Shana resisted for an hour. But in the end, she knew she was fighting a losing battle. Rick and Suzanne had changed their minds about leaving. For now, she was stuck. The worst was yet to come.

10

THE FIVE BOYS

The Cooper house was quiet again. After days of chaos and shouting, the devils had finally been expelled. By early 2002, the family had settled back into its routine. Suzanne tended to children, her own as well as other members'. She had slipped back into Jane's orbit, a true believer once again. Rick continued working at Kent Covington's business. Most of the Cooper children attended school during the day and worked for church leaders afterward.

Things seemed to be getting back to normal. But something was brewing. Jane Whaley had been seething for months. Children in the church were too independent, breaking the rules.

Jennifer Creason was in the middle of a lesson when a minister barged into the classroom, whispered something to her, and left. Creason turned to her students.

"Jane is really upset. Everybody up," Creason said, clapping her hands. "Walk quietly, single file, to the sanctuary."

Jamey Anderson felt a lump in his throat. Something was terribly wrong. Jane was mad all the time, but Jamey knew something was different this late February day. He glanced at his friend Peter Cooper. Peter shrugged.

Jamey had spent most of his thirteen years in the church and couldn't recall Jane ever calling a church-wide meeting during a school day. She wanted everyone there—students, teachers, parents, and ministers.

He and his little brother, Nick, were toddlers when they came to Word of Faith. His mother, Patti, was sent to Spindale from Greenville in 1989 by Gerald and Linda Southerland. She and her boys settled into a communal house with other congregants.

Jamey couldn't remember a time when he wasn't blasted or beaten. It became apparent early on that he was one of the children who couldn't do anything right.

As a child, Jamey cut his left eyebrow while speeding down a hill in a red wagon. His mother had warned him not to go, and when the wagon crashed and a scar bisected his eyebrow, she told him God had placed a permanent record of his disobedience where all could see.

He was labeled "anathema, accursed." And he couldn't recall how many times he had been pinned to the ground while a group of congregants, including his mother and stepfather, beat him with a paddle. The attacks wouldn't let up until he had confessed to something and cried out to Jesus.

Sometimes even that wasn't enough. If he "really needed a breakthrough," they locked Jamey in a damp, windowless storage room he called "the green room," for the color of the outdoor carpeting. Long hours in the dark, the constant hum of a dehumidifier, and the smell of mildew drove him to the edge. He'd bite his arms and bang his head against the cement-block wall, hoping to die.

He worked, too, sometimes during school hours, on construction and real estate projects. He was diagnosed with

asthma in middle school, a condition aggravated by the outdoor work. If he stopped to catch his breath, he was rebuked
for "laziness and foolishness."

He developed a sarcastic sense of humor. He became the
leader of "the Rebels" or "the Underground," an informal
scattering of misfits. None of them used four-letter words or
drugs, or carried knives, or painted their names on the wall.
Their "wild side" was making funny faces, or cracking jokes
in the hallways. Jamey was careful not to reveal that side to
too many people. Someone might turn him in.

Jamey's mind raced as the kids marched to the sanctuary.
He replayed the last few days in his head. Had he done anything out of the ordinary? Somebody probably ratted them
out for something, but what could it be?

In the sanctuary Jamey caught a glimpse of Jay Plummer II,
one of his friends. Jay hated the place as much as Jamey did,
and Jamey had spent a lot of time over at Jay's house lately. He
felt safe with Jay's parents. But today, Jay looked scared, too.

Jamey slid into the seat next to his mother. Jamey was a
handsome teenager, bright and talented, but in Patti's eyes he
was the bad son, always in trouble. Nick was the chosen one
in their house. Jamey didn't care. He was counting the years
until he turned eighteen and could leave.

Jane stormed into the sanctuary, screaming.

"YOU ARE ALL WITH THE DEVIL!"

She pointed out five boys, one by one. Peter Cooper. John
Blanton. Liam Guy. Micah Gwartney. And Jamey Anderson.

She called them "the Five Boys." They were a locus of evil,
she said, possessed by devils. Over and over, she used the name
"Five Boys" to describe their transgressions. They kept secrets.
They "gave in to the unclean." They made jokes. They talked
trash about ministers. The list went on and on. The Five Boys

personified everything she hated. They were independent. They didn't submit to authority. They were "satanist rebels."

They had to be broken.

Jamey froze. He was confused and humiliated. It felt like the eyes of the congregation were boring into him. Jamey didn't know why they were singled out. Sure, they were all friends. But what did they do that was ungodly?

They were friends, and in the end, that was what bothered Whaley. She knew they wouldn't turn each other in. They trusted each other.

Jamey knew what was required to end the theatrics. Jane expected them all to fall to the floor and cry out to Jesus for forgiveness. That was what the others did. But for some reason, Jamey was too scared to move. Jane turned on him, screeching that his "heart was hard"; he was unreachable. She moved inches from him and stuck a finger in his face. "You are a devil!" she shouted. She was so close he could smell her hot breath. Spittle flew from her mouth with every terrifying shriek.

She yelled and screamed, and the congregation yelled and screamed, surrounding the boys and blasting in unison. Patti prodded Jamey to cry out to Jesus. Jamey wanted to, but he couldn't move. And that was when minister Mark Doyle appeared and ordered Jamey to follow him into the hallway.

"Sit down," Doyle said, pointing to a chair. Then he handed Jamey a legal pad and a pen.

"You are going to write everything you have done wrong on a piece of paper. We already know what you have done. Your other friends have exposed it to us. You're not going home until you write it all down," Doyle said. Jamey had no idea what they were looking for. Doyle saw that Jamey wasn't writing.

"I told you I want to know everything. I want to know

your sexual thoughts. I want to know if you like boys or girls. I want to know if you masturbated. Your friends have already told us everything. You will not leave here until you confess your sins," he said.

So, Jamey started writing. He wrote that he liked girls, not boys. He scribbled that he masturbated, even though he didn't know what the word meant. He confessed to having unclean thoughts about girls in his class. He wrote whatever he thought that they wanted to hear. He could handle the beatings, but his mind kept returning to that green room, his worst fear. He filled so many pages so fast that his hand began to hurt. When he finished, he was told to go home with his mother. He'd find out his punishment later.

In a room nearby, Peter Cooper was going through the same torture. Peter was smart, like his brothers, and was probably the most athletic of the Cooper boys, tall and thin with a runner's build. He and Jamey did everything together. They were supercompetitive. If they played basketball, Peter made sure he guarded Jamey. They pushed each other to be the best.

Now here he was on the floor, crying out to Jesus, but that wasn't enough for the ministers. Peter had to write his confessions, too. Yes, he thought of girls. Yes, he masturbated. He knew they were trying to break him. There was no escaping, so he did everything they asked. By the time it was over, he wanted to die, right there.

It was the worst day of their young lives. But they had no idea how bad it would get.

Over the next year, Jamey, Peter, and the others weren't allowed to attend classes. They sat in a room during school hours and watched countless videos of Jane Whaley sermons. They couldn't move, because at any moment Jane or a minister could barge into the room.

After school and on weekends they were confined to their

homes. Family members weren't allowed to speak to them. The boys were moved back a grade, and were rarely allowed to do schoolwork. When they did, they were under intense scrutiny.

Jay's mother, Susie Plummer, taught at the school. One day, Susie was assigned to the room where the Five Boys were being held. She was teaching them about the North Star, the guiding light for centuries of travelers. She wrote on the blackboard: "Another name for the North Star is Polaris." In his notes, Jamey scribbled, "Polaris is another name for the North Star."

When a teacher saw it, she berated Jamey in front of the entire class, calling him "full of pride and haughtiness," and summoned Mark Doyle. The reason: rebellion. He didn't copy the phrase exactly as the teacher had written it.

Doyle's verbal bashing was even worse, screaming about Lucifer and evil. He wanted Jamey's fear of God to be "tangible," to see Jamey "tremble before God."

"Every time the devil rears his head, we're going to drive him out," Doyle said.

He took Jamey to the principal's office and pulled out a wooden paddle. By then, Jamey was broken. He felt worthless, "like the gum on the bottom of someone's shoe." He knew what was coming. He bent over the desk. Doyle hit him hard, several times. Jamey didn't resist like he had in the past, when people had to physically restrain him so he would keep still. He just didn't have it in him. Not now. Doyle stopped when he was satisfied that Jamey had submitted.

When it was time to eat for Jamey and some of the others, someone would open the door and slide food in on a tray, like in a prison. They were told they were full of "witchcraft and warfare," and constantly grilled with sexual questions. Who did they fantasize about? Did they act on it? The ministers were relentless. If the boys didn't answer the "right way," they were blasted and beaten.

John David Cooper saw the way his brother was being treated. He knew it was wrong, but what could he do? If he was spotted talking to him, he could be punished. He loved his brother, yet the church wanted John to hate him. His sense of justice wouldn't allow that. He was torn. How could "God-fearing people" treat Peter like this? And why weren't their parents saying anything? They had to know this wasn't right.

Over time, John saw his brother change. Peter used to tousle John's hair when he saw him, a little mark of affection in a household devoid of positive emotion. In a normal school, Peter could have been the star of a sports team. The girls would have been all over him. Even at Word of Faith Fellowship, Peter had a confident air about him.

But now Peter's shoulders slumped when he walked. He stared straight ahead, avoiding all eye contact. He didn't smile or say a word. When Peter walked into the house after spending the day watching Whaley tapes, he went straight to his room. His eyes were blank, like a zombie's.

Peter and the other boys were prisoners without a sentence. They didn't know how long their punishment would last.

Six months in, Peter heard a rumor that maybe he'd be allowed to go outside for a physical education class. That night he decided to do stomach crunches and push-ups in his room, just to make sure he could keep up.

Someone outside his window saw him. They told Suzanne, who immediately called church leaders. The next day, instead of physical education, Peter was ordered to stay in his room. Doyle came to visit. He brought a wooden paddle, and after a thorough beating, Peter confessed. Yes, he had been exercising. Doyle wanted to know why.

Peter didn't know what to say. Doyle warned that if Peter ever wanted to end his punishment, he had to tell him why.

"It was pride that made me do the push-ups," he said.

But Doyle didn't buy it. "No. God told me it wasn't pride. It was something else."

Peter racked his brain, annoyed with this guessing game. He had to figure something out before Doyle picked up the paddle again. Then he hit on the answer. Peter was trying to build up his body to compete with his brothers. "It was the bodybuilding devil," he said.

And to his surprise, Doyle bought it. "That's what God told me, too!" Doyle said.

Like Peter, Jamey felt dead inside. Years later, he was still haunted by that day in the sanctuary. "Of all of my memories, those were some of my darkest times," Jamey recalled. "It was extreme, even for there."

He paused for a moment, brushed back tears.

"It's disgusting and revolting what they made us tell them, what they made us do. We were forced to tell things about our personal lives, and volunteer information. It's always the accusation. They will hammer you until you admit to giving in to the unclean—and they want details.

"If there was ever a time I was broken, that was it."

John Huddle felt like Abraham, called by the Lord out of one country to take possession of a new land. The word had come from above. It was time to move his family to Spindale.

He knew this day would come. Gerald and Linda Southerland had predicted that Jane Whaley would eventually hear God's voice and close their church. And just a few months earlier, in January 2002, Whaley said God wanted everyone in Greenville "home" to the Spindale headquarters. Jane herself had come to Grace and Truth and told them the time had come.

The news had caught Huddle off guard. Jane had singled him out, and he'd chosen the right response. Everyone in the room applauded the Huddles, hugged them, and offered their congratulations.

Huddle had just bought a house in Greenville, and had to put it back on the market—not a great financial move. But John knew exactly what to say to family and friends who questioned the wisdom of this move: they were going to live in the "spiritual Mecca, among the Chosen."

Huddle worked for a credit union in Spartanburg, which was only thirty-five miles from Spindale. His seven-year-old son and eleven-year-old daughter were thrilled. They attended the church's private school in Greenville, and many of their friends would be making the move, too. The school in Spindale was bigger and better. Huddle loved to see his kids so happy.

Not every family decided to move to Spindale. Those who stayed behind were, evidently, not spiritual enough to hear God's voice, too worldly to step out in faith. But Huddle and those who followed Jane believed they were moving into the "will and the move of God."

On moving day, his excitement was "so thick he could taste it." As the moving truck backed up to his door, he couldn't stop smiling. They were on their way to the promised land.

11

"HAPPY ARE THE CHILDREN"

John David Cooper didn't look like a troublemaker. Like his brothers, he was well-behaved and squeaky clean, with a square jaw, round brown eyes, black hair, and a big smile.

But trouble dogged him, especially at school. He asked questions in every subject, especially science—difficult, insightful, outside-the-box questions that in other schools would have earned him praise and respect. But at the Word of Faith Christian School, he was punished for having "inquisitive devils." The rules were simple: Teachers taught. Students listened. They didn't ask questions.

Even in the sixth grade, John was extremely analytical. The sixth of the Cooper children, he questioned everything, and formed his own opinion, and was one hundred percent convinced he was correct. This led to problems in a place where only one person's opinion counted. At Word of Faith, the members followed the leader. They did not question authority.

John disliked school and the part it played in the general monotony of his daily life. Wake up. Say prayers. Get dressed. Crowd around a big table for breakfast with his siblings and whoever else was living in the house—the Hudsons, the Smiths, or Shana and her kids. Pack a lunch, grab the backpack, pile into the van for the drive to school. A monitor posted at the door watched his every move, in case he dared to touch anyone, especially a girl. Lower grades were co-ed, but John now spent his days in the company of other boys. Girls, from here on out, were segregated, off-limits.

It wasn't all darkness, because John had friends. His best buddy was Josh Valentine, and this morning they were actually looking forward to school. They had something to show off to their friends.

Class began with Bible study, prayers, and singing. John sang along with the familiar choruses. He played along, trying to stay out of trouble. Any infraction could mean blasting, or a beating, or worst of all: discipleship. John hated that the most. He couldn't stand the isolation and boredom.

John and Josh had been close since Josh moved to the church with his mother, Leigh Valentine, one of Jane's confidantes. She returned to Spindale after her contentious divorce from televangelist Robert Tilton in 1997. Josh's father, Robert Valentine, was a preacher in New York City. He pastored churches in Manhattan and later in Connecticut, but Robert Valentine refused to join Word of Faith Fellowship. Periodically, Josh got to experience the outside world.

And during walks in the woods, Josh filled John's eager ears with descriptions of television, music, video games, and movies. Life was different outside the church walls, he said. John wanted to know every detail.

The boys climbed trees, laughed at stupid jokes, and acted like normal kids. John knew Jane would hate it. He could hear Jane's voice in his head: kids were supposed to be serious. There was no time for foolishness. Laugh with your friends and you risk possession by the "buddy-buddy devil." The boys joked about how fun that devil was.

John trusted Josh. He knew his friend would never turn on him. The previous day, Josh's mom had taken them to see Chimney Rock, a tourist attraction in western North Carolina. Most church members didn't get to do things like that, but Leigh enjoyed more freedom than other members. After her divorce from Tilton, she'd founded a cosmetics company that became a fixture on the QVC shopping network. She was a blonde beauty from an important family, and church leaders coveted her money and connections.

At the outing the boys climbed to the top of Chimney Rock, a towering granite slab rising more than three hundred feet on the edge of the Blue Ridge Mountains. They soaked in the views, climbed trees, and skipped down trails. The highlight for John was the gift shop, a wonderland of books, toys, and games.

"Look at this," said Josh, holding up a glittery plastic ring, flashing a mischievous smile. "I'm going to buy this for Jeanna."

John laughed. "I'll buy her one, too." He had a little bit of money on him—just enough.

Both boys had a crush on Jeanna Powell, a Whaley cousin who was born into the church. The boys would have to figure out how to give the garish jewels to her without getting into trouble.

Sifting through the toys, Josh picked up a toy sword and turned to John. "Wow! Look at this," Josh said. When he pushed a button, it lit up like a strobe.

"Wow, I want one of those!" said John.

Leigh bought one for each boy. John and Josh couldn't wait to get back and try them out. Leigh's backyard became a ninja warrior training gym, and the boys leaped and slashed theatrically at one another until one of the swords broke off at the handle.

"Oh, man, I wanted to take those to school to show everybody," Josh said, disappointed.

John shrugged. "Too bad it's broken."

But Josh wasn't about to let that stop them. He was on a mission to show everyone they were the cool kids. "Listen," he said to John. "I'll take the sword to school. You still have your penlight, right?"

John said he did. Leigh Valentine's new boyfriend had given it to him. The penlight was one of his favorite possessions. For a kid with next to nothing, it was everything.

"We might get in trouble," he warned.

Josh wasn't going to take no for answer. "It's just a light. What's the big deal?"

So when John got dressed for school, he slipped the penlight into his back pocket. There was a church event coming up, which meant the students had to clean up their classrooms after Bible study. And that meant more free time, if you could call it that. Boys moved furniture while the girls swept and mopped. That was what they were doing when Josh pulled out the sword.

"Look at this," he said. The sword lit up. Curious kids gathered around and admired the toy. Josh reached into John's pocket and pulled out the penlight.

"And look at this," he said, flashing the light.

That was all it took. An older student saw the toys, and went to tell a teacher, who grabbed them away from the children. John braced for the worst, but to his surprise, that was it. No blasting. No spanking. Nothing. He was angry that his penlight was taken away, but he knew it could have been worse.

"I'm glad we didn't get kicked out," John whispered.

Josh nodded. "Me, too."

To John, there was nothing worse than getting kicked out of school. That would mean discipleship. John preferred beatings. School beatings lasted for a few minutes and left welts and bruises, but at least he knew what to expect. It was anybody's guess how long the isolation of discipleship could go on for—weeks, or even months. Children in isolation weren't even allowed inside the sanctuary during church. They were sent instead to an adjacent room to watch Whaley on a monitor. Education was limited to Bible lectures and preaching videos.

The child was publicly shamed, and his family shared in the punishment.

The boys thought they'd escaped the worst. But the next day they were sent to Whaley's office.

John couldn't recall ever being called there. Spankings and isolation were handled in the school.

The boys stood in the hallway for hours, until every muscle in their bodies was stiff. John's palms were sweaty, his knees shook with nerves. *Just get this over with*, he thought. *Give me a spanking and let me go.*

When the boys were finally summoned inside, Rick and Suzanne were already there, seated on a sofa. Leigh Valentine sat in an upholstered chair. Whaley stood in the middle, holding the sword and penlight. She scowled at the boys, then turned to Valentine.

"Leigh, you ought to know better than to take children to a place like that, out of authority," Whaley said. "Just look at this," Whaley shouted, shaking the toys. "It's wicked. You boys have the foolish devil."

Whaley broke the toy sword into pieces and tossed it in the trash along with the penlight.

"You boys have the buddy-buddy devil," she said, jabbing her finger at them. "You've been sneaking around, giving in to foolishness. I know it. And God sure knows it. But we are fixing to put a stop to it. I have heard from God. You boys have been spending too much time together. So from now on, y'all are not allowed to speak to each other. I mean not at all. Not until I hear from God. I will make arrangements to have you separated at school."

The boys looked at one another. John was crushed. Josh was his best friend. Whaley pulled out her big wooden paddle. The boys knew the routine. They bent over. Jane swung the paddle, whacking their buttocks and the backs of their legs.

"Take hold," she said. "Let's get those demons out."

WHACK. WHACK. WHACK. John was too mad to care about the pain. As Jane continued to hit him, John kept thinking how everything about the church was unfair. Everything good would eventually die. Everyone he cared about would be taken away.

His mother and father would just take Jane's side.

John's mind reached back to a time when all the kids, twenty or thirty of them, gathered in their yard to play tag and hide-and-seek. Then one day, that was gone. The church decided that children should not touch one another, so tag was banned. They came up with a new game and called it dodge-ball tag. The rules were the same, but instead of touching, they threw a ball. Soon that was outlawed, too. They played hide-and-seek until the church decided that children should never be out of sight. Even board games were banned for making the kids too competitive.

No TV, no trips, no toys, no friends. John wanted to be like the kids he saw at Chimney Rock—free to explore the world around them, to be inquisitive, to have fun.

As Jane swung the paddle, he thought about a church song. If one of the teachers said the words *happy, happy, happy*, it was a cue, an order. Put on a smile. Put on a happy face and start singing a church chorus over and over, no matter how you were really feeling—or else. So, at that moment, he closed his eyes while the melody played in his head and the rhythm was pounded on his backside.

"Happy, happy, happy
"Happy are the children
"Whose God is the Lord."

12

SURROGATE PARENTS

Benjamin Cooper stretched out on his bed and stared at the ceiling. It was May 21, 2002, and today things were going to change. Soon as everyone was asleep, he'd slip out the door and down the road. He was going to catch a bus to Wanda's house in Florida.

He knew his grandmother "Mama-Gail" would help him. It was just a matter of getting there. Benjamin's mind drifted back to Darien, Georgia, to vivid memories of Saturday morning cartoons and backyard football games.

The Coopers had joined the church when Benjamin was seven, plenty old enough for him to remember the way life could be. For so many years, he wanted to play sports, to hunt and fish, to go camping with his dad.

Now, at sixteen years old, Benjamin was angry. The Word of Faith Fellowship had stolen his childhood, and there wasn't a damn thing he could do about that. His parents had done this to him. Benjamin never had a close relationship with Rick, who was always working, or always at the church. And lately, his mother was always so angry. It was obvious she still resented Rick for backing out on their chance to break free in 2001. She wasn't a consistent mom. Sometimes she was so friendly and kind to Benjamin, then suddenly she was a stickler for the rules, phoning Jane Whaley and reporting her kids' bad behavior.

Benjamin was old enough to recognize hypocrisy.

He had been raised on Bible stories and verses. He had studied the book from cover to cover. Whaley's teachings did not match what he read there. He was tired of being shamed, called unclean, accused of erotic thoughts. He was deeply offended at what was happening to his older brother Peter and the rest of the Five Boys.

The beatings, violence, and shaming at school seemed to be getting worse. Benjamin was through. If his parents wouldn't leave this place, screw them. He'd go by himself. He had $60, and he knew which way the town was.

But somehow his mom seemed to know something was up. She kept popping into his room.

"Why are you still up?" she asked.

"Oh, it's nothing. I just can't sleep."

An hour later, she was back. "Why are your socks on?"

"My feet are cold."

After midnight, when the house was silent, Benjamin put on his shoes and slipped out the door. He didn't know where the bus station was. But guided by the stars and a bright moon, he headed east, walking more than a mile down Old Stonecutter Road, past two homes occupied by church families on the rural road leading into Spindale.

When he reached Oakdale Road, he stopped in a convenience store for directions. The cashier said the transit station was on the other side of town.

It would be a long walk. He'd have to head north, right by Old Flynn Road, which led to the church. Then he'd have to cross the interstate and head through an industrial part of town. Even then he'd only be at the county's public transportation terminal. He'd still have to find his way to a Greyhound station.

Benjamin walked, his heart racing, his eyes scanning the dark road ahead. He wasn't sure if he understood the directions he was given. And he could not escape his fear. Every time a car passed, his heart fluttered. What if someone from the church saw him? Even worse, what if Jane was right? God could make their brakes fail, and the car would go off the road and strike him down.

The fear escalated with every step. His chest was tight with anxiety. He'd only made it a mile or two, but hard as he tried, he just couldn't force himself to go any farther. Deflated, he headed home and slipped back inside. He needed to talk to someone. Someone who was wise, and knew him well, and wouldn't mind if he called at 1:30 a.m. There was only one person like that in his life. He picked up the phone and called Jane.

"I'm running away," Benjamin told her, explaining what he'd done. "I hate this place. I don't want to be here."

"Do your parents know you ran away?"

"No, ma'am. I didn't tell them anything. Because I know they're going to do whatever you want them to do. So, how do I get out of here?"

"Are they awake?"

"No, I don't think so."

"We need to meet and talk about this. Are you comfortable spending the night at Mark Doyle's house? We can talk about all this tomorrow."

"OK."

"I'll send Mark over now."

Minutes later, Suzanne and Rick were jarred awake by the telephone.

"Suzanne, it's me," said Jane.

"Is something wrong?" Suzanne said.

"Benjamin left."

Suzanne wasn't surprised. "I suspected he was going to," she said. "I had been checking his room. I must have fallen asleep. Is he OK?"

"Don't worry. He called me. He said he wanted to leave, but I talked to him. He said he'll stay with Mark Doyle until we figure this out, so I sent Mark over to pick him up."

"Thank God he's OK."

Suzanne swallowed the lump in her throat. She hung up the phone and began to sob.

"What was that about?" Rick asked.

"That was Jane. It's Benjamin. He told her he's been planning on leaving the church, but she talked him into staying. She gave him the option of staying with Mark Doyle, and he said that's what he wants to do."

Rick grimaced. "I don't understand, Suzanne. Why is God doing this?"

"I don't know," she said. "The only thing I've ever wanted to do in my life is to be a good mother. Now my son doesn't want to live in the same house with me."

"Don't say that, Suzanne. It's part of God's plan."

But Suzanne wasn't buying that. Her sons, one by one, were being taken from her. And now another one was gone.

Jane Whaley knew she was losing her grip on Benjamin. Mark Doyle was the man to change his mind.

Doyle was one of her most reliable ministers. Just recently he'd taken in some brothers from Chicago, newcomers to Spindale. They were "worldly," full of bad habits and lazy attitudes, but Doyle straightened them out in no time, like a drill sergeant shaping his soldiers.

Before going to bed every night, they had to set the table for breakfast. The place mat had to be a half inch from the edge of the counter, no excuses. If it wasn't right, those boys were spanked. If he said to be ready to leave for school at 7:15 a.m. sharp, and the boys weren't ready, he'd make them walk.

Doyle was in his late thirties, somewhat effeminate and moody, a survivor of a dysfunctional family in upstate New York. He'd first heard God's voice over the noise at an AC/DC rock concert, and while the stoned-out crowd chanted along to "Highway to Hell," Doyle heard a voice asking him, "What are you doing here?"

He came to Jesus in New York City, on the 700 Club TV evangelism hotline. The person on the phone referred Doyle to a small, nondenominational church that met in the Empire State Building. It was Leigh Valentine's church. They welcomed him like a lost son.

Doyle dedicated himself to the church. He met Sam Whaley during a mission trip and moved to North Carolina in 1994. He became a Realtor, married, and devoted himself to Jane.

At Word of Faith Fellowship, Doyle had a reputation for discipline. In 2001, Doyle allegedly punished Benjamin Talley, a sixteen-year-old boy, for not raising his hands during a song rehearsal. Talley said Doyle beat him mercilessly for hours with a wooden paddle until he was bruised and bloodied. Doyle was tried for assault in 2003 and acquitted.

Benjamin Cooper didn't want to leave his house, but now he didn't have a choice. He knew he'd miss his siblings. Jeffrey was the firstborn, but Benjamin played the role of the protective older brother. He was easygoing, accepting, and supportive, and he'd step in if he saw his siblings being bullied. When blasting started up, he stood in the back of the crowd. He only took part if one of the church leaders scowled at him.

It didn't take long for Benjamin to figure out the dynamics

in the Doyle home. Doyle was the unquestioned leader, but he asked deep questions, and really listened when Benjamin spoke. Doyle seemed to take a genuine interest in him, something he'd never really experienced before. Sure, Doyle was strict, but Doyle, unlike his parents, seemed to care about him.

Benjamin had always been skeptical of church doctrine, but Doyle "got inside his head" and met his doubts with stories of his own experience "on the outside." To hear him tell it, Doyle had seen and done it all. He had money. He had moved around the country and seen firsthand how ugly the world could be. He'd discovered the truth: the only path to peace, happiness, and salvation was through the Word of Faith Fellowship.

It was working, just as Jane Whaley had planned. Jane knew it was imperative to keep the children of the church inside the fold.

She recognized that Benjamin was a natural leader. His brothers and friends looked up to him. He could prove useful in the future, so Whaley and Doyle were determined to whip Benjamin into shape. That meant breaking Benjamin down and changing everything about him, right down to his hairdo.

Benjamin brushed his hair into place while it was wet, then sprayed it with hair spray. Whaley detested the "wet look" and shamed Benjamin in front of everyone. It was "harlotry," she said. It looked "homosexual."

This had started even before Benjamin moved in with Doyle, but now Jane seemed obsessed with his hair. No matter what Benjamin did with his hair, it was wrong. Whaley wanted all the men to wear the same style as Sam Whaley: parted far to the side and combed over. One day when the high school kids were singing in the sanctuary, Whaley called Benjamin down to have a word.

"I have told you about this hair," she said. "You need to go with Mark."

Doyle told Benjamin to follow him into a bathroom. The door shut behind them, Doyle ordered the teenager to get on his knees so he could fix his hair.

It was weird, but Benjamin did as he was told. Doyle took out a comb and started parting Benjamin's hair to one side. A few minutes later, he finished.

"Do your hair like this from now on," said Doyle, pleased with his work.

Benjamin stood up and looked in the mirror. He was horrified. He lashed out at Doyle. "Why do y'all care about my hair? What's the big deal? It looks stupid, what you're doing. I look like Ronald Reagan!"

"You need to open your heart about the unclean," Doyle snapped. "You need a heart change."

Benjamin knew he had to stop. If he said another word, he'd get blasted. He heaved a great frustrated sigh.

"Let's go see Jane," Doyle said.

Benjamin was embarrassed. He hung his head, hoping his friends didn't see his ridiculous old-man hair. When they entered Whaley's office, a few of the elders were already there on her white couches. Benjamin sat in a burgundy armchair while Jane inspected Doyle's work.

"That looks good, Mark," Jane said.

Benjamin was humiliated. He was a teenager, dealing with the usual insecurities, and now he couldn't even brush his own hair his way.

"I look like Ronald Reagan," he cried.

"No, it's just different than what you had," Whaley said, laughing. "This is how it should be."

And for years, that was how it stayed.

13

MONEY AND INFLUENCE

Shana Muse couldn't take it anymore. She had fought so hard to get legal custody of her children, only to have them labeled as misfits and blasted in the name of God. It seemed like they were constantly in trouble, especially the boys.

The summer of 2002 brought a pivotal moment for the church. Jane Whaley's father, Bill Brock, died at the age of eighty-six. It seemed that Brock was the only person who could talk sense into Jane. Brock challenged Whaley when he believed she had crossed a line. After he died, there was nobody left to put brakes on her behavior.

Once again, Shana's family was on Whaley's radar. One of her children was being punished and was barred from attending Brock's memorial service. Shana didn't much care about the old man's funeral, but this was another slap in the face.

Yes, Shana was fed up. So on a Friday in September 2002, she picked up the phone and called Wanda.

"Mom, I can't take it anymore. I'm sick of it all. The way they treat the kids. I'm leaving."

Wanda didn't hesitate. "I'll be there next Friday to pick you all up. Everything will be OK."

The following Monday, Shana was excited as she got dressed for her job at Kent Covington's plastic molding plant, where she worked for $8 an hour. *Just a few more days*, she thought.

When she got to work, Kent Covington pulled her aside.

"I thought I'd let you know your kids are in discipleship. They sinned. They have to repent."

"Well, nobody talked to me about this," Shana snapped.

"Calm down, Shana. This is God's will."

"You people have no right to discipline my children. This is just wrong. I don't know who you people think you are. They are my kids. It's my decision when and how they are punished."

"Shana, it's for their own good."

But Shana refused to back down. "Y'all think you can do whatever you want. That's why I'm getting out of here."

"Wait. What did you just say?"

"My mom is coming Friday to get us. I'm done. I'm leaving. I can't stay here anymore."

"Shana, you need to think about what the church has done for you. Sam and Jane lay down their lives for the people. They saved my life."

Kent had a checkered past, too. The son of an alcoholic father, Covington spent eight months in a North Carolina prison in 1974 for breaking and entering and larceny.

He was introduced to the Word of Faith Fellowship by one of his sisters in the late 1980s and credited the church with saving his life. Kent married Brooke McFadden in 1991, elevating his status in the church. He managed successful businesses, and hired Word of Faith members "so he could be their spiritual guardian while they were away from the church."

He was one of Whaley's top ministers, and he was going to bring Shana into line.

"Shana, you can't make it out there in the world," Kent said. "And what about your kids? Those two girls of yours. I hate to think what is going to happen to pretty girls like them. The men are going to chew them up and spit them out. And there's no telling what will happen to those sons of yours. You know they are going to end up being drug addicts. They'll end up dead, or in jail. You're being selfish. Think about your family. It's just the devil working on you. You need prayer."

Shana had no car, and only $80 in her pocket. She was appalled by the conversation but attempted to steady herself as she got ready for the day's work.

But Kent wasn't finished. The next thing she knew, the machines in the factory were shut down, and all twenty employees, all members of the church, surrounded her in Kent's office. They blasted her, but Shana shut them out. Nothing they could do was going to change her mind, and she wasn't going to roll around on the floor to make them happy.

At the end of the workday, a coworker dropped off Shana at Suzanne's house. The house, usually bustling with activity, was dead quiet. She called out to her children.

"Kids, y'all come here. We need to talk," Shana said.

There was silence. Shana searched the house. No one was home. Kent appeared.

"Shana, let's just talk about this," he said.

"I've said all I have to say. Where are my children?" Shana answered.

"The kids are fine. Let's just talk about what you're doing. You are going against God's will for your family. Are you sure you want to turn your back on God? And even if you are willing to walk away from God, do you really want to lead your kids back into the lifestyle you had before coming here?"

Shana was frantic. She picked up the phone and called her mother. "Mom, the kids are gone. They took them somewhere and won't bring them back. I'm trying to get out of here, but they're not telling me anything. I don't want a confrontation, but I don't know what to do. Kent is standing here, but he won't tell me where they are."

"Let me talk to him," Wanda said.

Shana handed him the phone. Wanda asked Kent about the children. He assured her they were fine, but he refused to say anything else.

When Shana got back on the phone, she knew what her daughter had to do. "Shana, if they won't let you have your kids, you need to call the police."

Shana immediately called the sheriff's office. When two deputies arrived, she explained the situation. The deputies drove Shana to the church. They stopped when they saw Ray Farmer. Shana jumped out of the car. "Ray, I want my children," she said.

"I'm not sure what's going on here, and I don't know where your children are," Farmer said.

"Yes, you do, Ray. You know everything that happens in this place. I just want my children and I want to leave."

Farmer said the children were with Kent and Brooke and they'd bring them to the church. Instead, Rick and Suzanne showed up in the sanctuary. At first, Shana was happy to see her sister. Suzanne told the deputy she could straighten out the matter. But as she spoke, Shana's world turned black.

"My sister has been abusive to her children. I have custody of the kids, so I cannot let her take them," she said.

"What? That's not true," Shana cried. "I got custody back a long time ago."

Shana picked up a phone and called Cindy. She asked her sister to bring her file with the custody paperwork to the church. Cindy had no idea what was going on, so she did what her sister asked. But when Cindy arrived at the church, Shana snatched the file from her hand.

"I'm sorry, Cindy, but Suzanne is trying to steal my kids," Shana said.

The sheriff's deputy reviewed the paperwork, but said he was required by law to call social services because there had been an allegation of abuse. When social worker Robert Boykin arrived, he interviewed Shana and the children.

Shana swore that she didn't abuse her children. Boykin listened, then called a supervisor. After he got off the phone, he avoided making eye contact with Shana.

"Ms. Muse, I'm sorry. My supervisor said we can't make any decisions until we investigate further. Because they say you abused the children, I can't let you take them tonight," he said.

Shana was beside herself. But what she didn't know was that church leaders had coerced Suzanne into lying by threatening her own family. Shana was out of options. She turned to Kent.

"Kent, do you mind if the kids stay with you tonight? I'll get this all worked out tomorrow."

"Of course they can. You know we love those children."

So that night, Shana checked into a hotel. She cried herself to sleep. By then, James Lewis, a reporter for the *Daily Courier* newspaper got wind of Shana's situation. He knocked on the door of her hotel room the following day. Shana explained what happened and told Lewis she was going to get her kids back. After the interview, Shana rented a car and drove to the Rutherford County Department of Social Services. A social worker handed Shana a paper saying the agency had found no evidence of abuse. He also gave her some advice: "If I were you, I would go get those children right now and get out of town."

Shana called the sheriff's office. She wanted an escort. It

took hours of reviewing paperwork, but after authorities were satisfied that Shana had legal custody of the children, she went to pick them up. Lewis, who had written about the church in the past, met Shana there and decided to follow her to the Covingtons' house.

When she got to Kent's, the children, ages eight to fifteen, did not want to leave. Shana's children believed they would go to hell if they left the church and had grown close to the Covingtons. They yelled and screamed, but somehow Shana managed to coax them into the car. But as Shana started driving away, Rachel opened her door and jumped out.

"I don't want to go with her!" Rachel screamed. "I want to stay here and do what God wants!"

The kids were hysterical, screaming at the tops of their lungs. Shana should have driven away, jumped on the highway, and headed south to Florida. Instead, she went back to the hotel and called her mother.

"Mom, they won't stop screaming. They say they want to go back to the church. I don't know what to do," she said.

"Let me talk to them."

Shana handed the phone to Sarah. "Sarah, what is going on?" Wanda asked. "Why is everyone screaming?"

"We don't want to be with her. We want to be with God."

"But, Sarah, your mother loves you."

"No, she doesn't. She's trying to take us straight to hell."

"OK, Sarah, let me talk to your mother."

Wanda was stunned. "Oh, my God, Shana."

"I don't know what to do, Mom. I don't want my children to hate me. I'm taking them from their school, their security. My nursing license is expired. I'm broke I have no place to stay. I don't know what to do!"

And like Benjamin Cooper did on his way to freedom, Shana reached for the only steady hand she knew was near.

"Sorry, Mom," she sobbed. "I'm going to call Kent and see if we can work something out."

Wanda knew that was the wrong move, but nothing was going to change Shana's mind. Shana called the Covingtons. She said she hoped they could keep her kids until she rented an apartment and got back on her feet. They could still go to the church school. Shana said it was a compromise she hoped would please everyone.

Kent offered to help Shana find an apartment, but first, she'd need to sign a document that would allow him to get the children medical care if needed.

That's fine, Shana thought. *It's only temporary.*

The children left with the Covingtons. Shana paced and chain-smoked, wept, and finally fell asleep.

The next morning, Brooke arrived with a notary public and several other church leaders, including Ray Farmer, who had a pistol tucked into his waistband. The document gave the Covingtons full custody of the children. Shana, "under pressure and in a fog," signed it without reading it first.

For the next few weeks, Shana was allowed to meet with her children in Kent's office and help them with homework. She could see they were changing. She noticed that Patrick signed his last name as Covington. Soon Brooke began pressuring her to change all the children's names.

"The girls have Arab names, Shana. Don't you think it would be better to change them after 9/11? You can change your name to Covington, too, so then your whole family will have the same name," Brooke said.

The children called Brooke "Mom." Shana became "Mama Shana." Shana got another job in a plastics factory and moved into a small apartment, but she saw less and less of her children. When she called the Covingtons, they didn't pick up.

Shana knew something bad was going on. She couldn't

sleep. She was feeling numbness on the right side of her body. She was in a mess, and she knew it.

Brooke phoned one day to say that Jane Whaley was on her way over to visit. Shana cleaned up the apartment, opening the doors and windows to air out the cigarette smoke. Jane came prepared with her own can of disinfectant. She sprayed inside each room before she walked in to inspect the pictures on the walls. She picked up a family photo that Shana kept on her nightstand.

"Jane, I miss my kids so bad. I kiss that picture before I go to bed every night," Shana said.

"Well, that's good. Whatever it takes to get you through this," Jane said, taking a seat on the couch. But this wasn't a social visit. Jane was there for a reason.

"I want you to know something, Shana. You are never to step foot on church property. And don't let me find out you have gone to Brooke's house or anyone else's in the church until you write a rebuttal in the newspaper," Jane said.

"A what?"

"A rebuttal. To take back the lies."

"Why?"

"Because you lied. You told the newspaper that Kent was a kidnapper, didn't you?"

Oh, shit, Shana thought. Lewis had written a front-page article and Whaley was fuming about the negative story in her local newspaper.

"I didn't use that word. That's the way they wrote it. I just told the reporter that when I got home the kids were gone and I had to go find them with the help of the sheriff's department. That's it. I don't see why I should take it back. That's what happened," Shana said.

"If you want to make things right, Shana, this is something you have to do."

"But I wouldn't know how to write a rebuttal."

"That's all right. We'll help you write it. So just let me know what you want to do."

Shana watched Jane walk out the door. That was when everything became clear to her: they had taken her children away from her.

Shana's family outside the church could see she was teetering on the edge. Her sister Sonya had been researching a cult deprogramming facility in Albany, Ohio, named Wellspring Retreat and Resource Center. Sonya called and broached the subject with Shana. She needed help. It didn't take much prodding. Shana agreed to go.

Wellspring was in the foothills of the Appalachian Mountains, a place that looked a lot like Rutherford County.

Shana's fellow patients were a lot like her, people who had escaped cults like Scientology, and several more she'd never heard of. She was pleased to meet Holly Hamrick, another Word of Faith survivor. Together they came to terms with what had happened to them: their abuse, manipulation, and shame.

Their stories were eerily similar. Although the cults' messages were different, their practices were more or less the same. Cults controlled how members dressed, who they married, their contacts with the outside world. They made it difficult for them to leave.

Counselors showed how cult leaders use disasters as a way to convince followers that God is angry with them, to frighten them into submission. Shana recalled what happened on September 11, 2001, when terrorists flew passenger planes into the World Trade Center and the Pentagon. Since they weren't allowed to watch television or read newspapers, Jane rolled a television into the sanctuary and people huddled around the screen. Jane told everyone it was a sign of the imminent second coming of Jesus. Everyone had to be on their best behavior if they wanted to get to heaven. Afterward, they never heard another word about the terrorist attacks.

Wellspring didn't use the term *deprogramming*. Survivors voluntarily underwent two or three weeks of intensive counseling. Many suffered from anxiety and post-traumatic stress disorder, as if they had been soldiers in combat, or victims of violent crimes.

Shana learned from experts that what happened at Word of Faith Fellowship wasn't her fault, that cult leaders like Jane Whaley are masters at manipulating the people around them.

But it was hearing other people tell their stories of survival that really helped Shana to find herself. She spent three weeks at Wellspring, and came to believe that there was "no difference between Word of Faith Fellowship and Jim Jones."

Shana learned something else at Wellspring: a lawyer reviewed the custody agreement, and said it was not legally binding. Meantime, a television news program reached out to Shana to tell her story. When Shana returned to Spindale, she arrived with a camera crew and Mary Alice Chrnalogar, a cult deprogrammer and author of the book *Twisted Scriptures: Breaking Free from Churches That Abuse*. Chrnalogar believed the Word of Faith Fellowship was "one of the most dangerous cults in America."

When the group arrived at the Rutherford County Sheriff's Office, Sheriff Dan Good, the longtime Word of Faith Fellowship supporter, refused to speak on camera. He invited Shana into his office.

"I want my kids back," Shana said. "I need your help."

"Look, Ms. Muse, we spent a lot of man-hours helping you get your kids back last time, and you just turned around and gave them right back. And you signed a custody paper."

"Yeah, but that agreement is not valid. I had a lawyer look at it. A judge has to sign a custody agreement for it to be legal in North Carolina."

"Well, there's just not much I can do."

"The last time, you made me prove that the kids were mine. So let's go to the Covingtons right now and see if they can prove that they have custody of the kids. Put them through the same thing you made me do."

Good refused.

"Nope. It's a civil matter now," he said. "You have to go file a civil case."

"But this is not right. They are my kids."

"I'm sorry, Ms. Muse. There's nothing else I can do for you right now. I suggest you get a lawyer and work with the courts."

It was December 2002, and a man named Edward Smart was on the news, pleading for the safe return of his fourteen-year-old daughter, Elizabeth. The girl had been abducted at knifepoint from her bedroom in Salt Lake City, Utah, on June 5, 2002.

Nobody knew at the time, but Elizabeth was being held in the wilderness by a maniac who thought he was God. Shana saw the story was getting a lot of attention. Images of Elizabeth Smart flooded the airwaves. The Smart family had been making regular TV appearances for months to keep attention on the case. It had worked. People across the country were captivated.

That's it, Shana thought. She called the local news media and arranged a news conference. From the steps of the Rutherford County Courthouse, Shana pleaded for help getting her children back.

"My kids have been programmed, so I cannot get them to

leave without assistance. But they will obey the sheriff or Kent or Brooke Covington," she said.

The Covingtons fought back, coaching the children for an interview with a reporter for the *Daily Courier*. Sarah, the oldest, said the kids wanted to stay with the Covingtons.

"They are the best thing that has ever happened to us," she said. "Mom has told her story, and no one has seen our side and what all we've gone through. When we first got here, our lives were a mess. This is a better way of living."

Shana did anything she could to bring attention to her cause, even joining a dozen protesters on the road leading to the church before a Wednesday night service. They held signs with messages like Free the Children and Blasting Is Abuse. Shana stood in the rain, holding a sign that said Jane Whaley, Set My Family Free.

Inside the compound, Jane Whaley was planning to counterpunch. She summoned Suzanne to her office.

"What do you think about going to court to fight for the kids?" Whaley asked.

Suzanne knew what the church was doing was wrong. She had nightmares about what she'd done to her sister. She had followed Jane's orders when she told sheriff's deputies that she, not her sister, had custody of the children. She lied when she said Shana had abused her kids. But this was going too far. Perjury was too much to ask.

After all these years, Suzanne was still looking for Jane's approval, still the ninny who didn't have courage enough to leave the church or her marriage. But that day, she tried to change Jane's mind.

"Please don't take her kids," Suzanne said. "Let the kids stay with Shana, and when they get older they can decide for themselves if they want to be a part of our church."

Whaley's eyes narrowed. "Suzanne, this could have been

you." She brought up the time Suzanne had tried to leave the church. Had she not "submitted to God," Whaley said she would have taken Jeffrey and Lena and raised them as her own.

Suzanne lowered her head in shame. She had always suspected that. The message was clear: obey Jane Whaley, or she'll tear your family apart. Suzanne didn't say another word about giving back Shana's children.

Jane rallied her followers to the cause. "We are going to fight for these kids. I've talked with the aunts. I've talked to Sarah and Rachel, and they want their brothers to serve God with them," Whaley said. "We are going to court."

Throughout the weeks leading up to the 2003 custody hearings, Brooke held daily meetings with Suzanne, Cindy, and Shana's children to prep them to lie under oath and paint Shana Muse as an abusive mother.

Sarah testified that her mother once hit one of the boys so hard "it threw him five feet across the room and left red marks on his face."

She also defended church practices: "A blast is a strong prayer from God. I love strong prayer. It has changed my life."

North Carolina Superior Court Judge Randy Pool didn't buy it. He blamed the church for the abuse. In October 2003, Pool said there was "clear and convincing evidence the children were abused and neglected by isolation, excessive corporal punishment, and blasting." He ordered the Muse children placed in foster care.

For Shana, it was bittersweet. If the children couldn't be with her, at least they would not be stuck in a cult. But the church wasn't going to give up without a fight. Before the Covingtons handed the children over to social services, they slipped cell phones in with the girls' belongings.

The children were sent to live in Lexington, North Carolina. The boys were placed with a foster family, while the girls were put in a group home. When Shana visited, they did not want to see her.

Jane hatched a new plot. The girls were sixteen and seventeen, old enough under the law for a legal proceeding that could "emancipate" them. If they could prove to a court they were mature enough and had enough financial backing to survive on their own, a judge could declare them adults. Then the girls could choose where they wanted to live.

It was an expensive legal process, but that was no problem for Sarah and Rachel. The church had its own legal team. The court didn't need to know the details.

The girls followed a carefully written script, and convinced a judge to release them from foster care. They returned immediately to the Covington house. An appeals court overturned Judge Pool's ruling, and their brothers were sent back to Kent and Brooke, too.

It was another victory for Whaley, but it paled in comparison with what came next.

14

RELIGIOUS FREEDOM

Danielle Cordes slipped her favorite dress over her head and
tied the white ribbons at the waist, just so. It was a pink-and-
white-checkered Bonnie Jean with a splash of tiny pink flowers. Matching socks, white flats. Perfect.

This could be the day, she thought. The ten-year-old brushed
her brown hair.

Every Tuesday for weeks, the social workers from the Rutherford County Department of Social Services had come to
talk to Danielle. If she did everything perfectly, she thought,
maybe they'd take her away with them.

Shana Muse gave the Covingtons a full-on custody battle.
Shana told the social services agency everything, including the
names of every child she'd seen abused and placed in isolation,
including her nieces and nephews. She recounted the terrible night when Rick and Suzanne tried to leave, when Lynn
Millwood held down the screaming young Stephen Cordes
and shouted into his ear.

It wasn't long before agents arrived at Cindy's door. That

was how Danielle, one of Stephen and Cindy's four children, met the social workers.

Once alone with the social workers, Danielle said she had been abused for as long as she could remember. She was eighteen months old when her family moved to Spindale in 1995. One of her earliest memories was Jane Whaley stopping Cindy in a church hallway, pointing at Danielle, and calling her "wicked."

If only that was the worst of it.

Memories of beatings started when Danielle was about three years old, when Whaley spanked her in the church nursery. Still, Danielle said nobody tormented her like Lynn Millwood, a minister assigned to oversee her family.

Millwood was from Savannah, Georgia, raised by a deeply Christian mother. Lynn and her mother met Robin Whaley and Rusty Millwood, two Word of Faith stalwarts, at a "deliverance conference" when Lynn was still in high school.

One Sunday morning mother and daughter drove two hours from their South Carolina home to visit the Word of Faith Fellowship. They found the young people there "on fire for God," so they joined the church and moved to Spindale in 1990. It was there that she began "walking out a relationship" with Rusty Millwood. They married years later and eventually had a daughter.

Lynn Millwood became a trusted church leader. For years she had served as the Cordes family minister, and she'd proven herself in the difficult days that followed the Cordes and Cooper families' 2001 escape attempt. Her job now was visiting the Cordes family almost every evening to ensure they "stayed within the will of God."

It was during one of those evening visits that Danielle suffered one of the worst beatings of her life. She was six years old then. The children were playing when Millwood arrived.

"OK, kids, it's time to pick up your toys and get ready for bed," Millwood told them.

"Can we just have five more minutes?" Danielle asked.

"No."

"Please?"

"That's back-talking," Millwood snapped. "Go upstairs. You're getting a spanking."

Millwood grabbed the family's paddle. It was painted white, fifteen inches long, and an inch thick, carved by Stephen Cordes from an old dresser drawer. It thinned down into a grip on one end. Danielle couldn't count the number of times it had been slammed against her body. The sight of it made her shiver.

Lynn grabbed the child by the arm and led her up the stairs and into a bathroom. She bent Danielle over her knees, then rained down five hard licks.

"Now repent," Millwood said, pulling the child to eye level.

"I'm sorry. I'm sorry," Danielle pleaded. "Please forgive me."

"That's not good enough," Millwood snapped, pushing Danielle back over her knees. She whacked the child again.

"Please forgive me," Danielle screamed. "Jesus. I'm sorry."

"That's still not good enough," Millwood said, swinging the paddle harder. "We have to get those demons out of you."

The scene was repeated, over and over, for what seemed like hours. Danielle thought it would never end.

The next day Danielle woke up with deep black-and-purple bruises from her lower back to her knees. She dressed herself and limped downstairs. She curled up on the couch.

"Why don't you go outside?" Cindy said. "Go and play."

"I can't, Mom. I'm bruised."

"No, you're not," Cindy said.

"Mom, you weren't in the bathroom. You didn't see what she did to me."

"Go get a shower, Danielle," her mother said. Cindy walked in behind her, but quickly turned her head.

"See the bruises?" Danielle said. "I don't lie."

Cindy turned away. Danielle knew that pressing the matter would mean "going against the church authority." And probably another beating.

Her parents wouldn't save her. There was no one to tell this to, no one she could trust, and no one willing to listen. Until the social workers arrived.

They were gentle, and asked questions Danielle could understand. They never screamed or shouted or even raised their voices. It was clear the church leaders were afraid of them.

Jane Whaley knew that some of the children might talk, so she held countless meetings with parents and children before the DSS investigators showed up. The social workers were part of a satanic attack, she said. God wanted the families to lie.

Whaley had a list of questions they thought the workers would ask, and they peppered children with "correct" answers. Children were told never to speak to social workers without another church member present. If they found themselves alone with one, they should "throw a temper tantrum" and demand to go back to their parents.

Church leaders told Danielle that her aunt Shana was evil, that God had turned her over to the devil and marked her for death. At church services, Whaley quoted Scriptures about obeying God's Word, suggesting that her congregants would die, too, if they said anything negative about church practices, or left Word of Faith Fellowship.

Whaley left nothing to chance. During a visit to the Cordes home, she said the investigation was "more than a fight to save the children, it is a war of good and evil."

She warned the Cordeses "they are going to be looking for any reason to take our children away. Satan is working hard against us. We need to hide our paddles. And I really hate to say that because I like that white paddle you have. I wanted to get one like it for the church, but we have to be prepared now. So get rid of the paddle."

If children needed a beating, parents should use a wooden kitchen spoon, Whaley said. "DSS won't think anything about people having a wooden spoon in the kitchen. But do not leave marks on the children. No bruises. They will be looking for that," Whaley warned.

Some of the children were forced to sign affidavits that said they only got "strong prayer" when they wanted it, and that spankings were "well deserved" and not hard.

When social workers began interviewing children, most were afraid to tell the truth, including Jamey Anderson and the Coopers. A minister told John Cooper that he'd go to hell if he didn't answer the questions their way.

Some children were interviewed inside the church, where they were least likely to speak freely. Jamey Anderson was interviewed in Jane Whaley's office.

At first, ministers moved Anderson from house to house, trying to hide him from social workers. He'd filled many empty hours rehearsing what he'd say, telling the workers about the Five Boys' long year of isolation, the beatings that had marked his childhood right back to when he was a toddler.

But when the moment arrived, he was frightened into silence. He suspected Jane had recording devices in the room, so he kept quiet. When he walked out an hour later, he saw his mother there, "white as a sheet," worried her son had cooperated with the child welfare workers.

Danielle's interviews took place at her house, in her bedroom, just her and the social workers. They worked hard to gain her trust, and soon realized that Danielle was wise beyond her years.

She told them about isolation, being put in a closed room and left there indefinitely. She said she was told to lie about it, to call it "a time for solitary religious study."

The social workers were baffled. "Danielle, are you saying that someone told you how to answer my questions?" one of them asked.

"Yes, ma'am."

The more Danielle opened up, the more the workers wanted to talk to her. They came back, week after week. Her parents and church leaders were suspicious. After each interview, Brooke Covington interrogated Danielle, and a church typist took notes. The transcript was put in a file along with pictures that Mark Doyle had surreptitiously snapped of the social workers.

As weeks turned into months, Cindy complained that social workers were disrupting her family's life. She told them to stop bothering them at home. Soon, child welfare workers began interviewing Danielle anywhere they could, including in their cars. Danielle didn't care where the meetings took place. They broke up the monotony. Someone listened to her, paid attention. They gave her hope.

But Danielle's mother finally put an end to the interviews. One Tuesday morning Cindy cornered the social workers in their car outside the school. She pulled her daughter from the car and informed the workers they were violating her First Amendment rights.

Whaley was fed up, too, and ready to take action. She hired the same big New York law firm that represented the Church of Scientology, and filed suit against the Rutherford County Department of Social Services, claiming the church was being harassed because of its religious beliefs.

That was it. They would turn it around. They could say they were being persecuted, that their practices, abusive or not, were protected by the First Amendment.

Whaley and a dozen church families, including the Coopers and Cordeses, were plaintiffs in the lawsuit that said worshippers were entitled to "practice their religion free from unwarranted government interference."

The fight invigorated Jane Whaley. She used their victim status to rally her followers.

As he listened to Whaley rail against DSS, Rick Cooper had a sense of déjà vu. Whaley had invoked similar references to spiritual warfare in the aftermath of the *Inside Edition* episode.

Whaley reminded her followers what was at stake. If they lost the lawsuit, their children would be taken away. Without Word of Faith Fellowship, their kids would lose their moral compasses. The boys would fall into drugs and alcohol, and the girls into fornication and harlotry. All hope of eternal salvation would be gone.

His kids were why Rick joined the lawsuit in the first place. Through those long meetings, with Suzanne by his side, Rick and the entire congregation promised Whaley all their support. They'd fight to the end. With their unity, Rick was sure they could defeat Satan, save the church, and keep their families safe and pure.

15

"WE WON. WE WON!"

By early 2005, the church's civil lawsuit had slowed to a crawl. As with most legal proceedings, deadlines for a trial were set, then reset, motions and countermotions were filed and refiled. Attorneys for the Rutherford County DSS asked a federal judge to toss out the case, saying social workers were only doing their jobs. By law, they were required to investigate all child abuse allegations, and that was what they did. They had no bias against the church.

But Judge Lacy Thornburg refused to dismiss the lawsuit. If everything went right, maybe the trial would begin in November. No one was optimistic.

Meanwhile, Jane Whaley was facing another legal challenge, this one in criminal court.

A longtime Word of Faith member named Lacy Wien said she tried to escape the church in February 2002, and was seized and beaten. Jane Whaley, she said, repeatedly slammed her head into a wall. It took months for Wien to recover from the trauma and manipulation, and she didn't feel emotionally fit to file the criminal complaint until nearly eighteen months later.

It was only a misdemeanor assault charge, but the case wouldn't go away, in part because Jane wouldn't let it go. In March 2004, Judge Robert Cilley heard evidence in a Rutherford County courtroom and found Whaley guilty.

After years of allegations of abuse, Jane was finally convicted of a crime. She shrugged it off and dug in. Her lawyers quickly appealed, and asked for a change of venue. The appeal was on the docket for early February 2005 in neighboring Polk County. This time, she'd go before a jury. She was confident she'd be vindicated.

With so much chaos, uncertainty, and negative publicity, church leaders took extra care to hide questionable practices. They relaxed a few of the more punitive rules, and the Cooper family felt the benefit.

Jeffrey finally started college in 2004. He and a group of young church members enrolled at Wofford College in Spartanburg, South Carolina. They couldn't live on campus, so the group commuted nearly eighty miles round-trip each day. When Jeffrey returned to Spindale in the afternoon, he still had to work for free at a business owned by a church leader.

Jeffrey studied to become a certified public accountant, but law school beckoned, too. Why not? It seemed that everyone was becoming a lawyer. Whaley's son-in-law, Frank Webster, had just graduated from the University of North Carolina law school, as did Joshua Farmer; his wife, Andrea; and Mark Morris. When the Farmers and Morris passed the state bar, they opened a law firm across the street from the Rutherford County Courthouse. Webster landed a job as an assistant prosecutor in a district that tried cases in three neighboring counties.

Over the years, Jane began viewing Jeffrey as the de facto

head of the Cooper family. She kept him at her beck and call, and he served as her eyes and ears in the Cooper household.

A few years earlier, when Benjamin went to live with Mark Doyle, Jeffrey was the one who broke the news to his grandmother Wanda. Even after Rick and Suzanne's escape fiasco in 2001, Wanda tried to keep in touch with her daughters and grandchildren. She still hoped that someday they'd break free and enjoy a normal life.

Contact between Wanda and Suzanne was sporadic and tense. Suzanne didn't return calls. When they talked, it always ended with Suzanne slamming down the telephone.

The last time Wanda paid a visit, she was greeted by all her smiling grandchildren but one... Benjamin. When she asked where he was, neither Suzanne nor Rick would answer. Wanda felt panicky, wondering if something terrible had happened to him.

She was about to call the police when Jeffrey stepped in. "Benjamin doesn't live with us anymore," he said. "He was having trouble. He needed spiritual guidance that only a minister could provide. He's right down the road. We see him all the time. He's happy where he is."

Wanda was appalled. One grandson sent off to live with a preacher, and another one talking to her like a robot. How could Suzanne be OK with that? These children were her daughter's whole life.

"Suzanne, how could you?" she asked. "What's going on here?" But Suzanne didn't answer.

With that, and Suzanne's betrayal of her sister Shana, it was one of the last times the mother and daughter spoke. Suzanne didn't answer Wanda's calls anymore. Wanda was heartbroken, but determined, too. This was her family. She would never give up on them.

In the middle of the legal mess, Suzanne discovered she

was pregnant. She was rarely intimate with Rick, and the one time she was, she conceived. Rick was happy. It would be the couple's ninth child—the first since Adam was born in 1996. The church's reaction was predictable. This time, Suzanne was prepared for the criticism, but it still stung. She gave birth to a girl in February 2005, and named her Jacklyn.

One bright spot was that Benjamin was back home now, at least for as long as the church was under scrutiny for separating children from their parents.

His brothers could see he wasn't the same Benjamin. He was distant and distrustful. John picked up on it right away. Benjamin had always been John's protector, the one who looked after him, the one he could talk to without fear of judgment. Now Benjamin seemed on edge, shifty, like he was hiding something.

One morning John heard Benjamin singing as he swept up the kitchen, a song that John had never heard before, an upbeat tune remarkably different from their usual round of worship choruses and the dreary, flat, angry spiritual warfare songs composed by Jane.

Benjamin's song was catchy. "I used to stand so tall, I used to be so strong," Benjamin warbled. "Your arms around me tight, everything, it felt so right."

"What are you singing?" John asked. "That's not a song we sing."

Benjamin had to think fast. Just about everyone in the house played an instrument, so it was plausible that he could have written it. "I made it up," he said.

"No, you didn't. You couldn't have."

"Yes, I did."

"Ben, I know you didn't make that up."

"God gave me that song."

John shook his head. He knew his brother was lying. Benjamin had to be sneaking around, listening to unauthorized music, maybe secretly turning on the radio in someone's car.

"It's really good," John said. "You oughtta teach it to me."

Benjamin arched an eyebrow at his brother. Nothing more was said.

What John didn't know was that Benjamin was dealing with his first heartbreak. Benjamin had a crush on a girl in the church. They'd never dated or even spoken to one another. But she was attractive, and there was something about her that made Benjamin feel a way he'd never felt before. Maybe that meant she was the one.

Two weeks before his high school graduation, Jane and Brooke called Benjamin to a meeting.

"We know you're thinking about a girl. It's unclean," they said. "Repent, Benjamin. Give it up. Forget about this girl, or you will not graduate from high school."

Benjamin was crushed. He had to graduate. It was his only chance to go to college, like Jeffrey. His only shot to get away. He promised them he'd put the girl out of his mind.

But he couldn't.

Looking for solace, Benjamin sneaked into his parents' attic. He and his brothers had done that for years, mostly looking for books. Suzanne had been a voracious reader before joining the church, and when the Whaleys banned books, she had stuffed some of hers into boxes and put them in the attic.

The attic was a secret treasure cave. There was an FBI series about the exploits of J. Edgar Hoover, and *The Adventures of Huckleberry Finn*. The boys sneaked the books into their rooms and read them under the covers with a flashlight. They'd even read encyclopedias, just for something fresh to think about.

But it wasn't books drawing Benjamin to the attic now. It was a little transistor radio he'd found buried with relics of his parents' past. It was a connection to the outside world like he'd never had before.

When the house was quiet, Benjamin liked to sneak into the attic, turn the volume down low, and press the radio to his ear. That was where he first heard "Behind These Hazel Eyes," a Top 40 Kelly Clarkson hit. It reminded him of his forbidden love. The lyrics spoke to him: "Broken up deep inside, but you don't get to see these tears I cry."

Benjamin found himself sneaking into the attic more and more, waiting for the song to crackle over the airwaves. It was the only way he'd found to soothe his broken heart.

Silence fell over the second-floor courtroom. It was February 9, 2005, and Jane Whaley was about to take the stand.

Because of the publicity, the assault case had been moved to Polk County Superior Court in Columbus, North Carolina, a half hour west of Spindale. Lacy Wien didn't shy away from the publicity. She'd taken her story to *Inside Edition*. She explained that she'd endured "at least one thousand sessions of being spanked" between the ages of five and eighteen, sometimes being pinned down by her arms and legs.

The gallery was packed with Word of Faith Fellowship members. They were dressed up in their Sunday best, and they hung on to every word.

Wien recounted what had happened to her three years earlier. She was eighteen years old then, she said, and was caught passing notes to a boy during a church service. Afterward, nearly twenty worshippers surrounded her and began blasting her.

She asked them to stop, but instead, Lynn Millwood took her into a storage area called the "holding room," and told her to bend over a table for a paddling. Wien said no, and sat on a table so Millwood could not hit her. Frustrated, Millwood stormed out of the room.

Moments later, Jane Whaley rushed in, grabbed her by the neck, and slammed her head against the wall, Wien testified.

"She kept screaming, 'Did you fornicate with him? You're a fornicator,'" Wien said.

In that moment, Wien said it became clear she had to leave. She was tired of the abuse that began soon after her parents joined the church when she was five years old. So that night, when Whaley wrapped her skinny fingers around her neck, Wien glared into Whaley's contorted face and had a revelation. She knew once and for all that Word of Faith Fellowship was a farce.

And a few days later, Ruben Wien, the friend she would eventually marry, pulled into a parking lot across the street from Lacy's parents' house. He backed the car in, hoping she'd see him there. When she did, she slipped on her shoes, grabbed a coat, and ran for freedom.

Now it was Jane's turn to tell her version of the truth. She was dressed as sharp as ever, but she moved slowly to the stand, appearing weak and frail.

It was calculated. But would it work? Would the jury see a thin, elderly woman who was too weak to attack anyone? Whaley was sworn in, and spun her tale. Whaley said she did not grab Lacy Wien by the neck or slam her head into the wall. She claimed she had not rushed into the room, but simply walked in and asked Wien what was wrong. Whaley said she was surprised to hear Wien say in court that she was in love with the man in question.

"It literally shocked me when she said that because she had told me...she wanted absolutely nothing to do with him; she was so afraid of him," Whaley testified. She said she had coun-

seled a lot of young Christians and warned them that fornication would tempt them.

Whaley said she was only worried that Wien was struggling with the fact that she'd had sex. "That was the reason I
asked her if she fornicated with him."

Whaley said she laid her hand on Wien's shoulder and
prayed for her. That made Wien happy, she said.

"She said, 'My mind is the clearest it has ever been,'"
Whaley said. "The life of God was in her face, her cheeks
were rosy, and she was very happy, and it was like the torment had gone off of her."

Jane was finished. She stepped down from the witness stand
and over to her attorneys' desk. It didn't take long for the jury
to deliberate.

As they came into the room, Whaley glanced around the
courtroom and smiled at her followers. They filled the seats;
Wien sat alone.

The verdict was read: guilty. The Word of Faith members
let out a collective gasp.

Polk County Superior Court Judge Dennis J. Winner
handed Whaley a thirty-day suspended sentence, unsuper-
vised probation, and a $468 fine.

But the case was far from over. Whaley appealed, and several years later, after the North Carolina Court of Appeals
overturned the conviction—and Wien grew tired of fighting—the case just disappeared.

John Carroll, director of the Rutherford County Department of Social Services, and the agency's attorney, Brad Greenway, had for years been looking into child abuse allegations
inside the church. They ran into nothing but roadblocks and
resistance: parents didn't want to talk, children were clearly
coached in advance or spirited away.

Now a lawsuit was accusing them of religious discrimination. The agency was already understaffed and overworked. In a poor, rural county, the agency's dozen or so social workers had more cases than they could handle. The Word of Faith Fellowship allegations were the last straw.

Rutherford County law enforcement tried not to get involved in domestic matters at the church. It was too much work, too much he-said, she-said, and way too much pushback from above, recalled Michael Davis, a Rutherford County Sheriff's Office investigator for fifteen years. If sheriff's deputies appeared near the church, Ray Farmer would get on the phone, or sometimes Jane herself would call, and it would turn into one big clusterfuck.

At the child welfare agencies, most of the social workers strove to do their jobs, despite the obstacles. But their bosses were starting to crack under the pressure.

Kirk Randleman, a lawyer in the North Carolina attorney general's office assigned to the state department of health and human services, found the lawsuit worrisome. Under North Carolina's child welfare system, county agencies are responsible for providing services and investigating allegations of abuse. The North Carolina Department of Health and Human Services provides oversight and training, but generally leaves the day-to-day operations up to the county agencies. Church attorneys had been trying to reach a settlement, and DSS Director Carroll appeared to be wearing down. Randleman feared Carroll might negotiate a deal with the church that could have a "far-reaching impact" on social services departments throughout the state.

Randleman fired off a letter to the state DHHS. He said the county didn't have authority to negotiate legal policy, but they were doing it, anyway.

Randleman said the church wanted protections for blasting. He noted that Judge Randy Pool had found blasting to be abusive in two different custody cases. He also said the church had sought out a big New York law firm to press their case.

"These people are very serious and have very competent counsel, and if they succeed, this case could have far-reaching impact on DSS throughout North Carolina. The areas they are attacking are set by state policy. I have cautioned them that Rutherford County does not have the authority to negotiate policy decisions, but they are proceeding full steam ahead," he wrote.

Despite Randleman's warning, Carroll and Greenway buckled. In June 2005, a year and a half after the church filed its lawsuit, the agency signed a settlement favorable to the church.

Word of Faith Fellowship received guarantees that abuse investigations could no longer be solely based on objections to such core practices as blasting.

Under the existing law, if a child was in imminent danger, social workers had to show up within twenty-four hours to investigate, and could pull a child out of a home if they substantiated the complaint. But the new ruling turned that protocol upside down. If the agency received a complaint involving the church, they'd have to run it by DSS officials first. They'd have to tell the church they were coming to investigate. In effect, it restricted social workers' ability to protect children. It was a groundbreaking decision, and Rutherford County DSS was the only child welfare agency in the United States bound to operate under those conditions.

The agreement also placed limits on where social workers could interview children, and banned them from interviewing kids in cars, as Melanie Taylor had done with Danielle Cordes. In fact, it singled out two social workers and banned them from ever investigating the church again.

The deal also prohibited social workers from asking questions about the church's religious beliefs or practices. Social workers were forbidden to mention exit counseling or cult deprogramming centers like the one Shana Muse attended in 2002. If that wasn't enough, DSS agreed to pay the church $300,000.

Whaley rejoiced. Not only had she won, her first grandchild, Brock, was born in the middle of the chaos. Someone who could carry on the legacy. She was truly blessed.

The service that night at Word of Faith Fellowship was electric.

"We won. We won!" Whaley shouted from the pulpit. "God is so good! I told you we would get through this."

The congregation exploded in celebration. Rick Cooper hugged Suzanne. People all around them embraced, jumped up and down, and shouted praises to God.

Jamey Anderson watched the rejoicing. He knew there was no hope for him getting out anytime soon. They had beaten the system again.

The news was crushing for Danielle Cordes. Nobody would save her, after all. No one had listened. She wanted to weep, but held back the tears, afraid she would be punished.

16

THE "SLAVES"

Luiz Vargas sat back in his seat and closed his eyes. Jane had finally finished up the sermon, and Sam was stepping up for the appeal for "tithes and offerings." Luiz relaxed and set his features in a suitably contemplative pose.

"Let us bow our heads and close our eyes in prayer," Sam Whaley said.

Luiz fell asleep instantly.

Luiz was eighteen, youthful enough to take it, but living on two or three hours of sleep per night was wearing him down. He'd come to North Carolina from Brazil on a student visa, but classes at the local community college weren't nearly as important as coding an electronic inventory system for Kent Covington's plastics factory. Luiz snatched five-to ten-minute naps here and there throughout the day. It was the only way he had the energy to keep going.

Deep asleep, Luiz was no longer in the Spindale worship center. It wasn't the summer of 2006. In his mind he was back in the suburbs of Belo Horizonte with his parents, brother, uncles, and aunts. He was a kid, playing soccer in the dusty fields.

He grew up outside one of Brazil's most impoverished cities, but Luiz was blessed. His grandfather hadn't owned a pair of shoes until he turned eighteen, but the old man had clawed his way to wealth by buying and selling land. His son, Luiz's father, consolidated their position by opening a string of pharmacies.

Luiz and his brother, Samuel, were the beneficiaries. In a world of grinding poverty, they had a nice house, clothes, and access to a good education. But their father knew there was more to life than material possessions. He wanted his family to "walk with God." In the 1990s, he joined Ministério Verbo Vivo, "Living Word Ministry," one of several Brazilian evangelical churches with ties to Word of Faith Fellowship.

Spindale became a place of pilgrimage for hundreds of Brazilian Pentecostals. They traveled by the dozen on tourist visas to attend church seminars, sometimes several years in a row. Some decided to settle in permanently.

Luiz first saw Word of Faith as a nine-year-old child, attending a weeklong children's Bible seminar. It was a big deal. Luiz was wowed. It seemed that everybody in America—especially in the North Carolina church—had "nice things." They drove new cars—Mercedes-Benzes, BMWs. They lived in big new houses with neatly manicured lawns and kitchens with granite countertops and marble floors. They dressed up to do yardwork. Luiz was hooked. When he got back to Brazil, he was "one hundred percent Word of Faith."

The fascination didn't last. He came back in 2000 and 2002 for weeklong seminars, and started to notice the church's dark ideology: the world was an evil place, full of demons that wanted to take over your soul. Luiz, like most kids, was afraid of monsters coming into his room at night. That fear was only exacerbated by ministers screaming in his face that demons were taking him over. He was older now and more sensible, but every time he saw a child blasted, he felt scared and resentful.

During seminar weeks, he counted down the days until the sessions were over. On the last day he breathed a sigh of relief, and headed for the shopping mall.

Luiz had graduated from a Christian high school, and his pastors recommended he attend college in the United States— they knew just the program! Young Brazilians often did "work-study" stints at the Spindale church, and Luiz had heard a few guys his age complain privately about being "worked to death" by church leaders there. But Luiz wasn't worried. His dad was a big supporter at Verbo Vivo. His $90,000 yearly tithe ensured his boy an easy ride. By 2006, their church was six hundred members strong and was growing fast.

The Whaleys' involvement in Verbo Vivo began with John Martin, an American missionary who moved to Brazil in the late 1970s. Martin married a Brazilian woman, Marialva, and took a job as pastor at a Baptist church near Belo Horizonte, a sprawling city in the shadows of the Espinhaço Mountains.

Martin's ministry began to change in 1986, after he met Sam Whaley, adopted the Word of Faith model, and opened Verbo Vivo. Sam and Jane made regular trips there, and slowly introduced the congregation to their way of worship. In 2005, the church moved to São Joaquim de Bicas, a small city about forty-five minutes outside Belo Horizonte.

Over the same period, the Whaleys began taking control of another congregation in Brazil, this one about three hundred and fifty miles to the south. The Whaleys planted those seeds with Solange Granieri and Juarez de Souza Oliveira, married pastors they met at a religious conference. In 1988, de Souza Oliveira founded Ministério Evangélico Comunidade Rhema, or Rhema Evangelical Community Ministry, in the city of Franco da Rocha, near São Paulo.

In the early 2000s, Whaley ordered a third church, Comunidade do Evangelho Pleno, or "Community of the Full
Gospel," to move wholesale to Franco da Rocha. The merger
bumped the Rhema Community church to nearly seven hundred members. The Whaleys and other American ministers
made regular "missionary outreach" visits. And with each
visit, they exerted more control.

Luiz Vargas could remember when his church was the usual
Sunday school, songs, and a sermon by the local pastor, but
now congregants passively watched videos of Jane's sermons.
Over time, Living Word began instituting the same totali-
tarian rules Jane Whaley had imposed on believers in North
Carolina.

Fundamental Brazilian traditions were taken away. The
country's national anthem was banned, because Whaley hated
the "blasphemous, idolatrous" lyrics. Peteca, a traditional game
similar to badminton, was banned. Even Guaraná, a soft drink
as ubiquitous as Coca-Cola in the US, was prohibited.

By the time Luiz moved to North Carolina, Jane Whaley
was in complete control of the Brazilian branches. When his
minister suggested he go to North Carolina, Luiz knew he
had no choice. His brother, Samuel, was already there.

Still, Luiz vacillated as he boarded the flight to North Carolina in 2006. *I can go to school anywhere I want in Brazil. What am
I getting myself into in Spindale?* he asked himself. The screaming, the demons, the strict rules… Luiz was a positive guy.
He was an excellent musician. He played several instruments
and loved all kinds of music, but he wondered if Jane would
let him continue playing. Then there was the "ultrareligious
stuff" he had been taught his whole life. If he didn't submit
to Jane and her rules, he was doomed to eternal damnation.
So Luiz decided to conform, eliminate his negative thoughts,
continue being the good son, and obey every rule. It wasn't

forever. By the time the plane landed in Charlotte, he was OK with that.

But trouble started straight away. He and nearly a dozen other young Brazilians were sent to live with Kent and Brooke Covington. Once they were shown their sleeping bunks and shared bathroom, Brooke demanded their passports.

"I'm not giving you my passport," Luiz said.

"You need to turn it in to the office. Nobody is to keep them at home," Brooke said.

"But I might need my passport to get around."

"It's for security reasons. We don't want young people losing their passports. The safest thing is to keep them in the church. It's for safekeeping."

Most of the Brazilians complied, but Luiz stood firm. He'd call his father if necessary, he said.

Brooke relented. She could deal with him later.

Brazilians were scattered all over the Covington house. At least a half dozen were crowded into the basement. But Luiz did see two familiar faces in the house: Benjamin Cooper and his brother Peter.

Once the big lawsuit was settled, Whaley had pulled Benjamin and Peter out of the Cooper household and placed them under the Covingtons' "ministerial care." It was the Cooper diaspora. Jeffrey was sent to live with the Millwoods.

For Luiz, the rules at the Covington house were unbearable, and his father's standing at Belo Horizonte made no difference at all. Restroom time had to be scheduled. They had to ask for permission to do anything. The Brazilians had to clear out of the kitchen by 6:30 a.m. sharp. They weren't allowed the company of women or girls.

Luiz's student visa required him to go to school, so he enrolled at Isothermal Community College. Luiz wanted to become an engineer, but Jane said no.

"There are no engineering jobs around here," she said. It wouldn't do the church any good to educate a member, only to see him move away in search of a job. The whole point was to keep them close by and under control.

As soon as he arrived, Luiz and several other Brazilian men were assigned to work for elder David Caulder, a successful real estate developer. The "students" hauled and placed heavy riprap—jagged rocks up to two feet square—on the sides of mountain roads to prevent soil erosion. They toiled from sunrise to sunset, with a thirty-minute break for lunch. No one on the crew was paid for his work.

Caulder often rode up the mountain on his four-wheeler to check on their progress. The workers would murmur, but then get back to work. By the end of each day the crew was exhausted, blistered, and aching.

It was modern-day slavery, Luiz thought. The Brazilian churches were providing Word of Faith Fellowship businesses with an endless source of free labor. It was flat-out wrong, but Luiz was too afraid to tell anyone. His phone calls home to Brazil were monitored, and he had no idea who to complain to in North Carolina.

After Luiz started at Isothermal, he took a job at Kent Covington's plastics factory. Luiz had excellent computer skills, so Kent had him catalog every pipe, fitting, screw, and object the company made or sold. He took photos and wrote detailed descriptions of each and every item, and entered them into a comprehensive database. It was a massive, skilled undertaking, a project that could take a year or more. At the end of each workday he was sent down to sweep the factory floor.

Luiz hated working for Kent, but at least he wasn't breaking his back on the road crew, or pounding nails and slinging paint with the guys assigned to remodel houses. A blessing, he thought. Between everything he had to do—classes, work, and church services—Luiz caught a few winks whenever he could.

He and at least a dozen of his fellow exchange students snoozed in the sanctuary while Sam Whaley prayed and ushers passed the collection plates. They only hoped they didn't snore.

Jamey Anderson turned eighteen. No one could stop him from leaving Word of Faith Fellowship. All he had to do was walk out his mother's front door.

But where would he go? What would he do? The questions paralyzed him. He wanted to go to college. Almost all of the congregants began their higher education at Isothermal. Several church members worked at the school and helped fellow congregants with their applications and financial-aid forms.

Jamey wanted to aim higher. He could go to the University of North Carolina in Chapel Hill or Charlotte. But he'd have to get his transcripts from the Word of Faith school, and fill out the paperwork himself. He didn't know how. Asking for help would trigger an avalanche of prying questions.

Jamey was alone. Most of his close friends had already fled. Benjamin Talley and John Blanton were gone. And Jay. Jay Plummer was the worst loss of all.

The Plummer family had left a year earlier, July 4, 2005—a true independence day. They'd made a dramatic escape in the middle of a church service. Congregants had surrounded the family and tried to separate Jay and his three siblings from their parents. Somehow they'd all hung together and pushed through the crowd. The family jumped into their car and sped away. Jamey wished to God they'd taken him along.

Losing the Plummers was a big blow to Jane Whaley. Jay's dad had lived two doors down from Jane in an exclusive Tulsa neighborhood, back when they were young. Jane recruited the family to join her church, and Jay's aunt Andrea eventually married Josh Farmer.

Jamey and Jay met at a summer Bible seminar. Jay's family moved to Spindale in 2000, and Jamey introduced his friend to the other members of the Underground. Jamey and Jay had the same sense of humor and formed their own nonverbal communications signals. If Jamey walked into class with one shoelace tucked in and the other hanging out, Jay knew that meant High Alert: someone was coming to interrogate them. They exchanged skewed glances, smirks, eye rolls. They might mean trouble, or something good, or boredom. Or a wish to be someplace else, far away.

They just knew.

Over the years, Susie Plummer had become a surrogate mother to Jamey. She taught eighth-and ninth-grade science at the church's Christian school. She did what she could to protect him, but Jamey and his friends were always being singled out for punishment.

A week before her family left, Susie invited Jamey along on a family trip to Concord Mills, a big shopping mall north of Charlotte. It was a way for the family to say goodbye.

It was a wonderland. Susie let the children run loose and explore. She took Jamey and Jay into a music store. They didn't know anything about most of the artists. Susie thumbed through the compact disc rack and made some suggestions. "Oh, you should listen to this," she'd say, remembering songs from her pre–Word of Faith Fellowship days.

Jamey bought Backstreet Boys and Madonna albums. He'd have to hide them when he got back home, but the freedom was exhilarating. There wasn't time to see a movie, but they went into an arcade to play video games.

Jamey was seventeen years old. It was the first time he'd

ever been to an amusement arcade. Here he was, shooting down virtual alien ships like a normal teenager, talking to his buddy without having to worry about who might see, or what words he used. It was the first time in his life that he could be himself.

Just before it was time to go back to Spindale, Susie pulled Jamey aside.

"We're leaving the church, honey," she said.

Jamey was silent. He didn't seem to understand. "We're leaving the church," she said again. Jamey's eyes welled up. "If I could take you without being arrested, you'd go with us, Jamey. But because you're underage, I can't," she said.

He bit his lower lip, but told her he understood. "It's all right. I want you guys to get out of here."

"You know they're going to cut off communication with us, you're not going to be able to talk to us," Susie said. "But we're going to try to call. Just remember, we'll always be here for you. You're family."

Anderson nodded his head. "When I turn eighteen next year, I'm leaving. I don't know how I'm going to do it, but I'm getting out. We'll see each other."

Now here he was. He was ready.

He thought about Tulsa. The Plummers would take him in until he figured out his next move, but Jamey really wanted to stay in the area. He hoped that he'd be able to keep in touch with his grandfather Dr. Pat Pagter, the most important male figure in his life.

Jamey couldn't understand how a man who had graduated from the prestigious Duke University School of Medicine, and had been a Navy officer, could've been sucked into this nonsense. But the old man had always been good to him.

And as much as he disliked his mother for bringing him to this hellhole, Jamey still wanted to protect her from Jane and the other ministers. A few weeks earlier, he watched her break down after his stepfather died. Yes, John Dolan was abusive—often beating Jamey with a paddle. But he saw how much his mother loved John, and took care of him while he was dying of a rare disease, amyloidosis, an abnormal protein that attacks the body's organs. When he passed away, John, a tall strapping man, was barely a hundred pounds. And after his death, while his mother was grieving, Jamey watched Jane remove his mother's wedding ring from her finger. "You won't need this anymore," she'd said. Jamey's mother was crushed. His stepfather hadn't even been buried yet, and she was doing this?

For a moment, Jamey was too angry to feel fear. He stormed after Jane and told her she was wrong to do that to his grieving mother. "You should give that ring back," Jamey said. To his surprise, Jane did. And Jamey wasn't disciplined.

Maybe Jane knew the young man was weighing his options, and she didn't want to push him out the door.

But Jamey had checked out long ago. Jane Whaley didn't care about him. It became clear to him a couple of summers before, when he and Jay were sent to paint a patio wall at the Whaleys' home.

It was a blistering summer day, a week before seminar.

The boys had worked at the Whaleys' house before, mowing the lawn and cleaning up. The weeks leading up to seminar were always hectic. Jane wanted the church—and her house—to be immaculate. Everyone kept busy, or well out of the way.

Jane wanted a back wall painted and the patio spruced up around the swimming pool. She picked Jamey and Jay to do the job. They started from the top. Jay held the aluminum ladder while Jamey scuttled thirty feet up with a bucket of paint and a brush. The sun beat down.

After a while, Jamey felt his arms getting heavy. His feet

ached on the top ladder rungs. The boys were dripping sweat, but taking off their shirts was out of the question.

"Let me take a turn up there," Jay said. "You need a break."

"I'll just finish this section," his friend called down.

The patio door slid open, and Sam Whaley walked outside carrying a big glass of lemonade. He was wearing suit pants, a dress shirt, and alligator shoes. He settled into a patio chair under a parasol and adjusted his sunglasses. His face was beet red in the heat. He rattled the ice in his cold drink and watched the boys work, like a trusty watching prisoners on a chain gang. He did not speak to them.

Jamey glowered at Jay. Jay made a face back. The boys were hot and tired, but the cool waters of the Whaleys' big swimming pool might as well have been a million miles away. It was off-limits.

And just when things couldn't get worse, they did.

Jamey leaned too far to the left, trying to reach the far edge. The ladder wobbled, one of the legs shifted. Jamey knew he should have gotten down and moved the ladder first, but he was tired, and cutting corners.

Jay threw his weight against the ladder and quickly stabilized the situation. But Sam had seen it all, and shouted at them.

"Jamey, make sure if you fall you don't hit the house!" Sam yelled. He wasn't joking. He was dead serious.

What the hell? Jamey thought, anger boiling up inside him. He hung on to the ladder and locked eyes with Jay for at least thirty seconds. Clearly, their lives and safety meant nothing to Sam, their minister.

What could they answer back to the thoughtless old buffoon? What good would that do? The boys turned their attention back to the project.

About ten minutes later, Jane stormed onto the patio. She

glimpsed at the boys, then at Sam sitting and watching, doing nothing. Her face went red with anger.

"YOU ARE JUST… LAZY!" she screamed at Sam. He didn't say a word. Jane was building up a real head of steam, and rounded on her husband.

But there were witnesses. Jane stopped herself and turned to the boys. "Take a break," she said. Then she turned her attention back to Sam.

Jamey and Jay exchanged a glance, then made a beeline for the big garage, where the Whaleys and others parked their cars. They found one with the keys in the ignition, jumped in, and cranked up the air-conditioning. They switched on the radio, but kept the volume low.

They didn't say a word. They leaned back in the cool semi-dark and listened to a song that seemed to speak to them. They had never heard "Drift Away," an old R&B ballad by Dobie Gray. But they were touched by the melody and lyrics about how music could erase their pain.

Maybe that was why Jane hated music so much—it felt happy or sad with you. It could soothe your soul or inspire you to do great things. She taught her followers not to feel any emotion at all. How else could you explain a mother turning on her child? A husband turning on his wife? You only do that when you're devoid of feeling.

Music cut through all that control. And that song, "Drift Away," made Jamey and Jay feel hope. They had to keep fighting. Somehow, some way, they were going to make it out, and everything would turn out all right.

Jamey smiled. Did it really matter if he didn't have a place to stay? Even if he slept in his car, it was still better than this place.

He headed to his room to pack, whistling the melody. It gave him inspiration and courage as he walked out the door and into a new life.

★ ★ ★

From the beginning of her ministry, Jane had her followers confess the most intimate details of their lives. Over time, she learned all of their predilections. If men liked women or if they were attracted to men. If men were attracted to children. If a woman had lustful thoughts. If a congregant spent too much money on makeup, or lusted after a movie star, or any issue at all.

Jane kept an index card for each congregant, stored in a box in her closet. And when a congregant asked too many questions, or didn't pay sufficient tithes, or was thinking of breaking free, she'd use their confessions as blackmail.

Sexual desire was the worst sin of all, she'd say. Lustful devils. The unclean. Over the years, Jane had created edicts to control libidinous thoughts and behavior:

—Congregants needed permission from Whaley and other ministers to get married. Months or even a year or more could pass before the newlyweds were allowed to have sex.

—Unmarried people were not allowed to date without permission. Most relationships and marriages were arranged by Whaley and ministers.

—On their wedding night, couples were permitted only a "godly peck on the cheek." When they got into bed together, they must roll over and go to sleep.

—Marital lovemaking was limited to thirty minutes, no foreplay allowed, the lights needed to be turned off, and only the missionary position was sanctioned.

—Couples needed permission from church leadership to have sex. Pregnancy was not allowed without church consent. Couples with permission to have sex were given condoms to prevent unauthorized pregnancies.

For years, the church "counseled" married couples in private and in classes. Rick and Suzanne had been going to those sessions for more than a decade. Couples were expected to disclose their secrets, and eventually, inevitably, Jane revealed their sexual confessions to everyone present—much to the members' embarrassment.

Suzanne Cooper hated that violation. During one class, Jane pointed to a woman and said, "This one is lustful." Once, she singled out a man who'd had a wet dream. When a man's hand was crushed while working on Whaley's garage door, Whaley told the church "it was the judgment of God" because he'd admitted to masturbating.

In the summer of 2006, Jane called a special meeting about sexual activity.

Karel Reynolds and Brooke Covington were the leaders of Suzanne's group. Karel and her husband, Todd, were some of Whaley's earliest followers. Karel had become a spokeswoman of sorts, speaking to the media on different occasions, praising Word of Faith Fellowship and its practices.

Now Karel was a top leader in the church, and a de facto sex educator for married couples.

Suzanne knew nothing could save her marriage. She and Rick hadn't had sex in more than a year, and she had no desire for intimacy. Suzanne had been reporting Rick's "unclean thoughts" to Jane Whaley for months. When Karel announced that someone in the room was refusing to have sex with her husband, Suzanne knew her number was up.

"We're going to deal with that in this meeting," Reynolds said. "And this is how your sex should be. We're going to show you how God wants you to do it."

Oh, my God, Suzanne thought.

Karel and Brooke embraced and rocked back and forth, two middle-aged ladies in twinsets and pearls, simulating godly intercourse.

"When you're together you should cry out to God," Brooke

said. With her eyes closed and her arms still around Reynolds, Brooke demonstrated.

"Oh Jesus, oh Jesus, oh Jesus," she said slowly. But as they rocked faster and faster, Brooke's voice got louder and louder. "OH JESUS, OH JESUS, OH JESUS, OH JESUS, OH JESUS," until it sounded like she had reached an intense orgasm.

Everyone was silent.

Jane reminded everyone they should "hear from God" before having sex. It couldn't be spontaneous. They'd still have to get approval. As Jane told Suzanne, intercourse was no different than "going to the store and getting a loaf of bread," something to put on your to-do list, get it over with, and move on. You weren't supposed to enjoy it.

Most pastors preach that sex within a Christian marriage—of one man and one woman—was a beautiful thing, a gift from God that should be freely shared and enjoyed.

But in Word of Faith, married couples were expected to fight their sexual desires, or they could risk possession by sexual devils.

The "ideal sex" demonstration didn't help Suzanne. She wanted nothing to do with Rick. She held him accountable for the unhappy way her life was turning out.

A few weeks later, Suzanne made up her mind. Without asking for permission first, she told Rick to leave. He had no place to go but next door, to his mother's place.

Jane confronted Suzanne a few days later.

"It just wasn't working," Suzanne said. "I have tried for so long."

"I understand," Jane said. "Rick has been struggling to have a breakthrough. You are going to need help with the kids. I'll have Kent come by your house and talk to the children about what we are going to do."

Suzanne nodded. She knew this was causing upheaval in her home, but she didn't care, as long as Rick was gone.

Jane Whaley stood tall in the pulpit and scanned the congregation. Almost every seat in the sanctuary was full.

She said she had a story to tell, about a longtime follower that everybody knew: Joe English, the former drummer for Paul McCartney and Wings. All eyes turned to Joe.

English was still wrestling with his demons, even after all these years, she said. He kept trying to leave the church. He'd pack his bags, make it as far as an airport, then call his wife or someone else in the church to pick him up.

"Joe was full of demons. But he could not get a breakthrough," Whaley said. "Well, you know what happened this week?"

Everyone in the congregation shook their heads.

"The spirit of God embraced Carla Pederson," Whaley said.

All eyes turned to Carla.

Whaley said Carla grabbed Joe and tossed him across the room to expel his demons. That was what it took for Joe to get a breakthrough. A dramatic step indeed. But sometimes that was the only way to cast out devils.

This was a pivotal moment, an announcement. If blasting didn't work to stop unacceptable behavior, it was now acceptable to slam the sinner to the ground. It was the will of God.

Blasting had evolved over the years to something more violent than shaking fists, screams, and shouts. Congregants were often now held down by other members, and slaps, punches, and kicks were becoming common. Now they had Whaley's permission to take it to the next level.

By 2006, worshippers began tossing bedeviled congregants to the floor and beating them in the name of the Lord. "Demonic deliverance" resembled a gang initiation, with congregants hitting a subject so many times they'd get tired, take a step back, and let someone else take a turn. Sometimes so many people were involved in a blasting they'd jump on top of the subject in "dogpiles." The end of a lively Sunday service sometimes resembled *WrestleMania*.

The members still did not view blasting as violent. They believed they were genuinely helping one another, even children, get rid of their demons.

The practice spread to classrooms and homes. It could happen anytime, in any place within the church confines.

Whaley split her congregation into groups she called "classes," with separate groups for schoolchildren, middle-aged married couples, older singles. Each group was assigned a pastor. Kent Covington and Rusty Millwood were put in charge of John Cooper's group of young ministers in training.

Rusty Millwood was born and raised in the Rutherford County area. He was a bodybuilder who had abused steroids, drugs, and alcohol before he joined Word of Faith in 1986. He said the church had saved his life, and now, twenty years later, he was a trusted minister and a tough enforcer of the rules.

The Young Ministers classes were essentially long blasting sessions with a growing level of violence. Nobody wanted to become the focus, and that created an "incentive to take stuff out on others," John Cooper said.

During one of the classes, somebody called out John Cooper for "not having his heart in it." John's peers circled him, inching closer, screaming at Satan, and throwing their fists. The circle got tighter, the voices more frantic.

"Devil, we beseech you. Get out!" they screamed. Suddenly, someone grabbed John and slammed him to the ground. The screaming stopped.

"What is it, John? What is the sin in your life?" someone asked.

John knew the drill. He had to make something up. "I talked to a friend without a guard present," John replied.

"No, that's not it. God is telling me you have given in to the unclean."

The blasting resumed, but with pushing, slapping, and screaming. The men swayed and waved their arms, screaming and groaning. Exhausted boys peeled off their suit jackets, their dress shirts drenched and sticking to their bodies. John's ears were ringing, his head pounding. He was slammed to the floor again.

"John, what is the sin in your life?" Millwood shouted.

"I had an erection," he said, wiping away tears.

It worked. Now it was time for celebration. Loud music blasted over the speakers. The men raised their hands to the heavens, and John got up, cleared his head, and quickly joined in the hopping and singing. If you weren't as enthusiastic as the others, you would be next.

17

THE LONELIEST DAY

Love came quick in the spring of 2008 at Word of Faith Fellowship, or at least commitment did. With a joyful flourish, Jane Whaley announced that high school students could now "walk out relationships" among themselves.

In Word of Faith Fellowship parlance, that meant single members were now allowed to have relationships with members of the opposite sex, as long as they followed the rules: no kissing or touching. No talking without a chaperone present. And every pairing must be approved by church officials.

Jane Whaley told the congregation one Sunday that a younger member had changed her mind about teenage romance.

"He said that God put it on his heart that he should walk out a relationship with a girl, but this girl is still in high school. The more I thought about it, the more I prayed about it, I realized that this is what God wanted," she said.

John Cooper knew Whaley was talking about his brother Chad, newly graduated, eighteen years old, and now working at the school as a helper. Chad had fallen for Lauren Caulder, the daughter of a top minister. Whaley had never hesitated to bend her rules when it favored her family or her favorite ministers, but now she'd leveled the playing field for everybody.

This is interesting, John thought. *This opens things up for my grade, too.* John was sixteen, a junior in high school.

At the end of the service, Jane encouraged her young followers to "come see me and tell me what God is putting on your heart."

A large portion of the high school lined up to speak to their leader. The afternoon turned into the Word of Faith Fellowship version of the dating game. Jane was delighted. She'd struck a nerve.

Whaley had years of practice playing matchmaker. If she didn't arrange a couple herself, she had to approve the relationship before it went anywhere. Whaley decided when it was time for a commitment. She'd buy an engagement ring and have the couple and their parents meet in her office. She asked the man if God wanted him to marry the woman, and the woman was likewise questioned. If everyone agreed, Whaley then handed the man the ring. And just like that, they were engaged.

This night was different. As older congregants prayed that Whaley's young followers would find the right match, others—including John Cooper—approached Jane Whaley with their hopes and dreams.

When John got in line, he knew his options were limited when it came to partners. There were only about ten girls his age in the Word of Faith Fellowship. Of those, John liked Jessica Fields the most.

A month or two before, while helping a teacher move desks in the girls' classroom at the school, John and Jessica had locked eyes. She was a petite, pretty girl with long brown hair, deepset brown eyes, and an engaging smile. They didn't speak, but he felt nervous and excited at the same time. Since then, he had fantasized about kissing her and holding her hand.

When his turn came to speak to Jane, John took a deep breath and told her, "God is putting it on my heart that I want to walk out a relationship with Jessica. Maybe even marry her someday."

Whaley beamed. "Oh, wonderful! That's what Jessica told me about you."

John was stunned. He had no idea Jessica even liked him. He didn't know anything about girls. Kids on the outside would probably be experts by his age, having learned about sex and dating through school, movies, and the internet. On drives into Spindale, John often saw local boys and girls his age hanging out. He suspected the boys probably talked a lot about "scoring."

But at church, "scoring" for guys like John meant making eye contact. Just a steady gaze or a smile could be incredibly validating. When that happened, John would tell his friends, 'Hey, that girl noticed me!' In their world, being noticed was right up there with being loved. And the slightest physical contact, like an accidental brushing-up-against in the hallway, made for a raging boner.

The young people were sexually repressed. When the inevitable happened, some adolescent boys looked down at their pants and freaked out, thinking a devil was inhabiting their bodies. Health and anatomy textbooks at the Word of Faith school were carefully censored. Images of breasts, penises, and reproductive organs were blacked out.

Girls in the church were expected to downplay their beauty. Makeup was forbidden. When they bent over, girls placed a hand over their chests to hide their cleavage.

John returned to his seat, excited and a little embarrassed.

Whaley was excited, too. Her next move took everyone's

breath away. She began calling the newly matched couples to the front of the church: Chad and Lauren, then another couple, and another. John lost count. Then he heard Whaley calling for him and Jessica to come to the front of the church.

Wow, he thought, *is this really happening?*

Whaley was euphoric. "God has put in the hearts of these young people that they should be married," she said. "It's God's will."

And just like that, at age sixteen, before so much as a first date, John David Cooper was engaged. Although they had grown up together, he didn't know Jessica at all. By creating tight family ties among church members, Whaley made sure no one could leave the fold. John's older siblings were on a similar path. By 2008, all of them had found partners in the church.

Jeffrey had married a woman who was raised in the church, and Peter was engaged to another whose parents joined when she was young. Only weeks before, Benjamin had promised to marry Micah Carlson, a third-generation church member. Micah was a "Word of Faith poster child," a sweet girl who never broke a rule or stepped out of line. She and Benjamin seemed an unlikely pair.

Benjamin was "always pushing the envelope," which was what caught Micah's attention. He was ambitious. He wasn't like a lot of the other men in the church, who simply focused on following the rules. Benjamin asked why. He looked beyond the walls. He had an eye on his future.

He had just finished community college and started at Gardner-Webb University as an accounting major. He planned to go to law school. He was driven, and didn't let manipulative church officials hamper his progress. If he was going to get out, he knew he had to bury his anger and play the game for a while longer.

Even though they were forbidden to talk about their feelings, Benjamin sensed that Micah was a lot like him. She wanted more from life than a teaching job at the church school. She wanted to go to college and have a career independent from the church. Right out of high school, Micah started doing paralegal work for Josh and Andrea Farmer.

With Whaley's approval, Benjamin and Micah began walking out a relationship. Soon after, Jane announced to the congregation that she was going to Atlanta to buy engagement rings. She warned that she wasn't going back anytime soon.

Benjamin had to act fast. He had to take his relationship with Micah to the next level. He rushed to the bathroom and scribbled a note: God wanted him to marry Micah. Then he bolted from the bathroom and handed the note to Jane. She glanced at the paper, then smiled at Benjamin. She said she'd buy the ring.

John Huddle slumped in the plastic booth of a McDonald's restaurant. He sipped his Diet Coke and stared at his computer screen. An email, to his mother. It was July 14, 2008. He didn't know where to begin.

Music was playing, rock and roll oldies—"Betty Lou Got a New Pair of Shoes." It reminded him of growing up back in Virginia. A simpler time. What would Jane Whaley think if she knew he was listening to music?

He didn't care. Not anymore.

The cursor blinked. So much had happened in the six years since he moved to Spindale in 2002. His mother knew some of the details, but he couldn't tell her everything yet. The story was still unfolding.

"I've just left the house," he wrote. "Martha is there alone. The children don't want to see me. Before I left, Martha asked me, 'Why are you doing this?'

"But I didn't answer the question. She already knows.

"It's been an emotional day," Huddle wrote.

He had wanted to leave Word of Faith Fellowship for years. He'd finally made the break, but the price was terribly high.

Huddle had arrived from Greenville in 2002, thinking he was one of the "chosen," that living in Spindale would bring him into the presence of God in a community of supportive believers. Instead, he joined a group he now saw as a network of deception, exploitation, and manipulation. It took years to realize that he and his family had been duped, and the pain and shame were overwhelming. He had to get away, even if it meant leaving his family behind.

The humiliation and isolation began soon as they arrived in Spindale. Jane Whaley made Huddle quit his job with the Spartanburg Credit Union. He went to work for Ray Farmer and his son, Josh, who owned Two Mile Properties, LLC, a company that managed rental properties. He didn't understand why, but he accepted the decision. It came from Jane, his leader. She knew best.

But there were other changes, too. In Greenville, the church didn't control every aspect of their lives. While his world revolved around church activities, his family could still come and go as they pleased. Huddle had privacy, and hours each day to spend with his family.

In Spindale, all his time outside work was spent in church, fund-raising, praying, and doing work projects. His relationship with Martha deteriorated.

He worked long hours for the Farmers, but he didn't make enough money to keep up their standard of living. Martha taught at the church, but she wasn't paid much, either.

Still, Huddle was a good soldier. Over the years he tried hard to align his thinking with church practices. He knew every Bible passage that justified "strong prayer," chapter and

verse. He accepted blasting as a God-given method of healing, protection from threats like legal investigations, or for
help with financial needs.

"Let's blast those devils attacking the finances of God's people," a minister would say during a service or prayer meeting.
"Let's hit the heavens for the will of God for the businesses in
the church," another would implore.

Huddle had believed everything Jane said. He was sure the
church was being attacked by the godless DSS for their beliefs, not for abusing children or assaulting worshippers. He
witnessed members being disciplined for not being "locked
in," for making decisions without clearing them first with
church officials. He'd never experienced such control at the
Greenville church, but he saw it every day in Spindale. For
years, he looked the other way. But as he told his mother, he
couldn't take it anymore.

Mild-mannered Huddle was his own man, and that had
landed him in trouble almost from the time he moved to
Spindale.

When he was property manager at Creekside Apartments
in Gaffney, a salesman from a cleaning chemicals company
told him they had several part-time openings. Huddle called
and was interviewed, but decided against accepting the job.
He mentioned the job interview to his wife. She reported him
to the church officials.

The next day at church, someone tapped Huddle on his
shoulder. "Step outside, please," the usher said. "The elders
want to have a word."

Out on the front lawn of the church, Ray Farmer scolded
him, "I heard about the job interview. The interview was not
gotten ahold of in God."

Jane Whaley was visiting her churches in Brazil, but Karel

Reynolds told Huddle she had just gotten off the phone with Whaley.

"Jane was very grieved that you would do something like this… We don't do things like that out from under authority. You need to find a place of repentance for even allowing the thought of going to that interview," Reynolds warned Huddle.

The pressure grew too strong. John began to weep. The church leaders assumed he was repenting, but Huddle was crying for another reason. He couldn't believe he was expected to ask for permission to look for a better job. He was expected to pay a tithe of his income and work for a low-wage church-owned business. He was finding it hard to provide for his family, and he found this treatment terribly humiliating.

Huddle's children were getting older. He wanted to start a college fund, so they could do better than he had. Savings accounts weren't part of the Word of Faith Fellowship world, but meeting the church's financial needs was a major feature of worship service. Offering plates were passed three or four times on Sunday morning, for missions or weddings, teacher salaries or property insurance, whatever the crisis happened to be that week.

Sam Whaley exhorted everyone "to hear God the first time so we don't have to keep passing the plates." Brooke Covington once said, "Why don't you just give it all the first time?"

It was never enough. After the offering, the service paused while an elder read out announcements. Workers in the office counted the money. If there was not enough, a messenger hurried back to the sanctuary and told whoever stood at the podium that another go-round was needed to reach the day's target figure. "We need another $15,000 to $25,000," Jane called out at one service.

"OK. We are going to pray. Since the church budget is not

met yet, someone is not hearing God." The prayers went on until the figure was met.

During one $25,000 drive, Jane Whaley said, "God told me that some folks are saving money for their children. God said to give that."

The idea made Huddle shudder. But sure enough, that night, when the money was counted, the church had collected $50,000. Jane returned to the microphone and shouted, "We have a miracle!" She cried big tears. Her followers had obeyed, and gave up their children's inheritance.

What happened to that extra $25,000? Huddle believed he already knew the answer. He surmised it was probably funding Jane's lavish home, international trips, jewelry, and designer clothing. While the Huddles counted pennies and were scolded for looking for part-time work, Jane and her cronies were living it up.

Sam Whaley made it a point to bring up finances—something from his "prosperity gospel" days at Rhema. "If you are not being blessed financially, you are not tithing," he'd say.

During certain services, people stood up and testified how God was blessing them financially, describing their new cars and houses. All these purchases had to be approved by the Whaleys. Sam attended auto auctions and bought cars for members—they had to buy their cars from him. When member Douglas McDonald bought his own car, he was rebuked from the pulpit for cutting Sam out of the deal.

No one was immune from humiliation.

Huddle had asked Whaley for permission to work part-time at a credit union to make more money "for my family and the church." They agreed.

But on April 9, 2008, Huddle was asked to a meeting in Ray Farmer's office. He knew it had to be serious when he saw his wife standing outside the office door, "as nervous as a bridled filly waiting to jump and run."

When he walked inside, the powerful people were there: Ray and Josh Farmer, Brooke Covington, even Gerald and Linda Southerland.

Josh told Huddle that he was spending more time at the credit union than at work at Two Mile Properties. He would have to quit working at the credit union, or he'd be fired from his Two Mile job.

"I have a real problem with that," Huddle said. The leaders surrounded him and began to blast.

"There must be unclean in your life since you could not immediately accept and embrace the will of God for the job change," Covington shouted at Huddle.

Another minister screamed, "What is it, John? What is the sin so deep which you have hidden for years that is taking you over?"

Everyone in the room took turns berating Huddle, trying to force him to confess something. Huddle drifted into a dreamlike state. The noise continued around him, but time slowed down. He knew this was wrong, but he was powerless to stop it.

Finally, to end the nonsense, he confessed to something, some obscure sin. But that wasn't enough. Jane Whaley stormed into the room, poked her finger in Huddle's face, and screamed, "YOU ARE FULL OF THE UNCLEAN!"

Jane turned and glared at Martha. "And you let him be this way."

Before Martha could respond, Jane wheeled around and left the room, muttering. She had other meetings, she said. The others continued. Martha turned on her husband and joined in the blasting.

Finally, when they were worn-out, Josh Farmer told Huddle he was fired. When Martha and John got home, she told him they could no longer share the same bed. That day was their twentieth wedding anniversary.

John Huddle knew he was done with the church.

In late June, Jane Whaley told Huddle he was no longer welcome. Whaley was used to seeing congregants beg for forgiveness when she said such things, but Huddle didn't give her that satisfaction. He wasn't playing her game anymore.

He contacted his mother, brother, and old friends. He knew he would need their support. On July 10, Huddle moved into his new two-bedroom apartment in Marion, a small town near the credit union. He sat down to write an email to his mother, to bring her up to date on the change in his life.

Friends had given him a sofa and love seat for his new place. "I now have more places to sit than friends to use them," he wrote.

He stopped, took a deep breath, and fought back tears. He realized just how alone he was.

By late 2008, Jane Whaley had built an empire. Her two churches in Brazil and the one in Ghana were thriving. She had several thousand followers on four continents: North America, South America, Africa, and Europe.

But something happened that Whaley couldn't control: America's worst economic crisis since the Great Depression.

The problems cut across all economic sectors. Banks and insurance companies failed. Tens of thousands of businesses across America were shuttered. Companies and consumers had trouble borrowing money. No one was spared, not even the "chosen" of Spindale, North Carolina.

In addition to tithing at least ten percent of their incomes, members had historically showered Whaley with "love offerings"—gifts of property, jewelry, or cash. But the recession was cutting deep. Some of the business owners pleaded with Whaley for relief.

Cutting back on tithes was not an option. So Whaley and her lieutenants discovered a solution. They called it "God's plan."

Randy Fields's construction company was in deep financial trouble. Fields hated asking Jane Whaley for anything, but his family's well-being was at risk. Over the years, he had seen many Word of Faith Fellowship members file for bankruptcy. Leigh Valentine, one of the most high-profile members, had asked for bankruptcy protection in 2006, listing more than $500,000 in assets and more than $1 million in debts. Josh and Andrea Farmer were bankruptcy attorneys. They had filed hundreds of cases. (The couple would later file for bankruptcy protection themselves.)

Fields couldn't stomach the thought of that, but if he didn't do something fast, he'd lose his business, and probably his house, too. His daughter, Jessica, was engaged to John Cooper, and the couple planned to move in with the Fieldses after the wedding. He could tithe thousands of dollars a month during good times, but not now.

Fields was a gruff, no-nonsense guy with big calloused hands. So when he walked into Jane's office, he blurted out the words "Jane, I'm having financial trouble."

Jane stopped him. She said they had found a way he could continue tithing and keep his company in business. Kent Covington would explain it all. When he did, Fields saw that "God's plan" was an unemployment scam.

Covington told Fields they could make it look like they laid off their workers due to the poor economy. Their employees would be eligible for unemployment benefits.

Laid-off workers could receive up to ninety-nine weeks of unemployment with a maximum weekly check of $535. Em-

ployees who were members of the church could quietly continue working while collecting unemployment. The business
owners wouldn't pay the employees their usual salaries even
though they continued to work. Bottom line: their unemployment checks would replace their paychecks, Covington said.

Fields was skeptical. Workers would have to show proof to
the North Carolina Division of Employment Security that
they were actively looking for another job.

They'd thought of that, Covington said.

Church members owned nearly two dozen businesses in
Rutherford County and the surrounding area. Employees
"laid-off" from Covington's businesses could simply say they
looked for a job at a company owned by another Word of Faith
Fellowship member. They all would cover for one another.

Covington and his bookkeeper, Diane Mary McKinny, had
already implemented the scheme at Diverse Corporate Tech-
nologies, his plastic plumbing parts plant. At first, some of his
employees were afraid of getting in trouble for breaking the
law. But Covington used his church position to "coerce the
employees to comply." It worked so well that Covington was
using it at his other companies. Other Word of Faith Fellowship business owners were putting it to work, too.

Fields didn't know what to do. God's plan was illegal. But if
he didn't sign on, he'd go out of business. "I'll do it," he said.

God's plan kept public money flowing into the church for
years. Jeffrey Cooper was uneasy about it from the beginning.
He knew all about economics and the law. He was a CPA,
in his second year of law school at the University of North
Carolina. He planned to become an estate planner after he
passed the bar, and for now he was working part-time for
Kent Covington.

He knew Covington and McKinny were keeping two sets
of books. He had heard Jane talk about God's plan from the

pulpit. She said it was helping the church's bottom line. But Cooper suspected the scheme had to be illegal. Why would a prophet encourage such ungodly behavior? Maybe Jane and the others didn't know it was against the law.

So Jeffrey decided to do a little digging. He called the North Carolina Division of Employment Security and asked them a "hypothetical question."

"Can an employee file for unemployment while they are still working for a company?" Jeffrey asked.

The agent on the other end of the phone was quiet. "I hope that was a hypothetical question because that's illegal. The people involved could face serious charges," the man said.

"Thank you," Jeffrey said. He hung up the phone and tracked down Covington in the parking lot outside the factory.

Jeffrey said he had called a state official and asked if what they were doing was legal. "He told me..."

Covington cut him off. "YOU ARE WICKED!" he screamed, his eyes narrowing to slits, his face turning beet red. He ripped into Jeffrey, calling him every name he could think of. Covington was out of control, and Jeffrey was too scared to move.

Once he caught his breath, Covington wheeled around and bolted into the building. He knew he'd just made a big mistake.

Jeffrey was still Jane's favorite Cooper. He was being groomed for leadership, and was not rebuked often. But that night at church, she criticized him harshly during the service. Then he was placed on discipleship, separated from his wife, Natalie, and isolated from everyone in the church. Church leaders knew Jeffrey's punishment would send a clear message to everyone: keep your mouth shut. Don't question authority, or you could be next.

Jeffrey was crushed. He was just trying to do the right

thing, to keep Covington from getting in deep legal trouble. Now, he was worried that Jane would make Natalie leave him, like she'd done to other couples. If Jane was really feeling vindictive, she might make him quit law school.

He was chastened, but he knew one thing: if they pushed him too far, he'd protect himself. Covington didn't know it, but Jeffrey had transferred most of DCT's important documents, including payroll records and spreadsheets with tax information, to a thumb drive. He'd share that information with investigators if he had to. Jeffrey prayed it wouldn't reach that point, but he'd have the damning ammunition just in case it did.

The Lower Building was hidden from sight behind a thicket of trees. It was the most dreaded place on the Word of Faith Fellowship grounds, a one-story, four-room structure reserved for the worst sinners.

The building had first been used as a school, then it was converted to storage. But in 2010, the structure was reborn as a place where men and boys were sent to deal with their sexual demons.

No one wanted to go there.

In late 2009, Jane discovered a new spiritual crisis that was threatening the foundation of church: too many men and boys were having sexual thoughts. She said their demons were deep-seated and needed to be exorcised using long-term prayer, Bible study, isolation, and blasting.

Her rants began after a worshipper confessed to having erotic thoughts about Jane's daughter, Robin. He said he had seen her exercising, and the sight of her "bouncing breasts" turned him on.

Jane placed the man on discipleship. He was forbidden to speak to his family and attend church services. Usually those punishments could be served at home, but Whaley decided to make an example of him. She sent him to the storage building. The man would have to clean it up and live there until ministers felt he had repented, she said.

He spent more than a year inside.

The Lower Building seemed like the perfect place to put other men whose "thoughts were consumed with sex," Jane said. The problem was "epidemic," she said, so ministers started separating men and boys from their families and sending them to live at the Lower Building. Word spread. Many wives reported their husbands to ministers. If a husband made unwanted sexual advances, or tried to have sex without being "locked in," they were sent to the building. It wasn't only married men. If a minister believed a young single man, a teenage boy, or even a child was having erotic thoughts, they were sent there, too.

It was an odd mix of young and old.

Michael Lowry knew all about the Lower Building. He'd been there for three months during late 2010. He was choked, smacked, punched, and kicked countless times by the others before church leaders sent him home. Michael's parents were told their boy was "hopeless."

In August 2011, he was sent back again. His clothing was in a small bag, his stomach was in a knot. For most of his twenty years, Michael, the boy with cherubic cheeks, blond hair, and thick glasses, had been the butt of abuse at Word of Faith Fellowship because he was purportedly too effeminate. He spoke too slowly, in a high-pitched voice. He sounded more like a girl instead of a young man, so he must be gay.

Michael didn't know what *gay* meant. He suspected it had something to do him never having a girlfriend. He wasn't physically attracted to boys or girls. He knew nothing about sex. He knew that "gay" was something terrible, and it made people at church surround him and scream at the top of their lungs, "Come out, homosexual devils!"

As bad as it was inside the school and church, nothing had prepared Michael for the Lower Building. It was an over-crowded jail without bars or guards, a place where he ner-vously waited for the next brutal assault by the other "inmates."

There was little oversight, and no locks on the doors. The prisoners policed themselves, with the help of ministers. Dur-ing his first stay, Michael learned quickly that he'd have no contact with his family. No one knew how long he'd be there. He also learned the rules:

—Read your Bible all day.

—No talking.

—No eating without permission.

—If you have an erotic urge, start blasting.

—If you have a sexual dream, wake up and do the same.

—If you hear someone blasting, join in and, when neces-sary, beat the sinner to drive out their demonic spirits.

Michael was still haunted by his first night in the building. When he walked inside, he could hear the yelling and scream-ing of "strong prayer." The ministers there told Michael he was going to hell, that he'd be hit by lightning, die of cancer, that he'd "better confess to everything." He feared for his life.

And for good reason. Michael saw boys thrown against walls and pounded onto the floor by groups of men. It would usually start with someone accusing someone else of "giving in to the unclean." The sinner would be surrounded. Noth-ing could stop the inevitable violence.

Michael was targeted right away. He soon found himself in the middle of those deliverance circles, being blasted, told he was the "most evil of all, the worst one down here." He deserved the punishment, just by being himself.

One night he was forced to sleep outside the building with

no coat. The temperature dropped into the low forties. He shivered all night, his feet went numb, but he didn't run away. He stayed, even though they made him feel "lower than dirt."

He saw many things he just wanted to forget, like an eight-year-old boy sent down to the building. What could a little boy have done that was so bad? Michael thought.

When Michael was released, he returned to the room over his parents' garage. He used to hate that room, but now he welcomed the solitude and privacy. But his parents—Robert and Marcia Lowry—continued blasting him. They were quick to tell ministers about their son's flaws.

Why couldn't he be more like their oldest boy, Jonathan, who was a dentist? Or David, the middle son, who was so successful? Michael was slower than his brothers, mentally challenged from birth. Jane said that was the outcome of the Lowrys conceiving him without church permission. Michael took longer to learn in school, but he was really just a shy, kind, goofy kid. But at Word of Faith Fellowship, those were liabilities.

Now his parents had sent him back to the Lower Building. Sweat rolled from his forehead and down his face. Mark Morris stood by the door. He was one of the church's attorneys, a firebrand of righteousness, the man in charge. Morris grew up in a religious family in suburban Los Angeles, active in a megachurch. When he learned about the Word of Faith Fellowship, he drove across the country to experience the church for himself. The sound of "every single person in the room crying out to God with everything in them" changed his life. He believed God spoke to him, saying, "This is the place you are looking for."

Morris moved to Spindale for Bible school. Morris married a fellow church member in 1994. His daughter, Elizabeth, would later be groomed as a mate for Jane Whaley's grandson, Brock. After law school, Morris joined Josh Farmer's firm.

Now, Morris was one of Jane Whaley's most trusted enforcers, in court and in the church.

Michael entered the building and did a double take. Inside were some of his friends, young men who had "vanished."

The lost boys were sitting in chairs with their heads bowed, Bibles opened, deep in prayer. Some were rocking back and forth, chanting over and over: "Come out, devils" and "Forgive me, Jesus."

All of the activity was taking place under the watchful eyes of a minister or two who made sure there was no "tomfoolery."

The place was even more crowded than he remembered. There were four boxed-in areas turned to bedrooms. Twelve sets of bunk beds were crammed into the rooms. There was a small common area with a couch, one bathroom, and a powder room. People slept on the couch and the floors—there had to be thirty people in the building, he thought. Michael saw some of his old tormentors, including Shana Muse's son Patrick Covington.

After being released from foster care, Patrick and his brother, Justin, had moved in with the Covingtons with Sarah and Rachel, their "emancipated" sisters. All four of the Muse children had dropped their surnames, and now used Covington.

Michael was given a bunk, and told to read his Bible and pray. He didn't sleep the first night. How could anyone sleep with all the men around him blasting demons? Some of the inmates were let out of the building during the day to work, but when they returned there was a rush to use the bathrooms and showers.

Michael got up early in the morning to use the shower. He had to be quick, only a few minutes, and he'd have to clean up for the next person. If someone found a pubic hair and reported it, he could be in trouble.

When Michael stepped out of the bathroom, a group of congregants were waiting for him at the door.

"Why did you take so long?" one of them asked Michael.

"I wasn't in there—"

"Were you masturbating?"

Michael didn't know what that meant, but he knew how to answer. "No. I was just taking a shower."

They didn't believe him. He had demons, and was going to hell. They jumped on him. They threw him against a wall, punched him in his face, punched his body. Others pushed their way into the bathroom. Then Michael blacked out.

When he opened his eyes he was alone on the floor.

He pulled himself upright, braced himself against the wall to get to his feet. He was wobbly. He stared at the image in the mirror. His face was bruised and swollen. His body was dotted with red welts he knew would turn to bruises. It was hard to breathe. He couldn't complain. He couldn't say a word. He picked up his shampoo and soap, and dragged himself to his bunk.

Years later, Patrick Covington recalled the bathroom beating. He said Michael was a frequent target.

"We beat him like a dog. I know it's hard to understand, but if you didn't take part, they'd target you. It was how you survived," he recalled.

But for Michael, this was it. He had to get out. He didn't know how long he'd be in there, or how many other beatings he'd endure, but he promised himself one day he'd find a way out. Then he'd tell the world about the Lower Building, and the brutal church behind it.

PART THREE

THE ADVOCATES

18

SAVING MICHAEL LOWRY

John Huddle got a tip: a young man named Michael Lowry had left the Word of Faith Fellowship on November 19, 2011. Now, two days later, he had just walked into a store to buy a cell phone. A former member of the Word of Faith Fellowship spotted him and sent word to Huddle.

"Lowry?" Huddle said. He searched his memory. Yes, he knew him, but not well. Huddle called Michael, who was still in the store. They talked briefly. Michael had been staying at a motel in Forest City. He didn't have much money. Huddle could sense Michael was in trouble.

"Can we meet now? I can pick you up," Huddle said. Michael said yes.

Huddle had been out of the church for three years, but it seemed that he couldn't leave the place behind. Not when so many former members turned to him for help. Not when he felt compelled to warn people about the church and its evil ways.

His life had been a roller coaster since that day in the summer of 2008 when he said goodbye to his wife and children.

He got divorced, beat cancer twice, continued working at the credit union, and launched a blog about religious cults, focusing on the Word of Faith Fellowship. He formed the Faith Freedom Fund, an organization dedicated to helping people leave the church.

Huddle's blog put him on Whaley's shit list. A few times a month, he disclosed all the latest developments inside the church's walls. He shared his experiences and disclosed some of the church's dark secrets.

The words got under Whaley's skin, former members told him. She'd regularly attack Huddle from the pulpit, calling him Satan, the anti-Christ, and a few choice words in between.

When Huddle pulled up, Michael jumped in the car. Then they headed to the Super China Buffet, a restaurant in a strip mall in Forest City.

Huddle had asked the Reverend Billy Honeycutt, a fellow member of the Faith Freedom Fund, to join them at the restaurant. He didn't know what Michael would say, but he wanted a witness.

As Michael picked over a plate of fried rice, he recounted how church leaders had berated and abused him for most of his life. After all the years of torment, he finally found the courage to leave. The tipping point, he said, was the Lower Building.

Huddle looked puzzled. "Lower Building?" he said. "The building down the hill from the office?"

"Yes," Michael said. For the past several months he had been held there against his will, with about thirty other men and boys. The "tenants" endured constant blasting and frequent beatings.

Huddle and Honeycutt listened in disbelief as Michael matter-of-factly recounted the disturbing details. "It was like jail," Michael said. "They wouldn't let me leave and they wouldn't let me talk to my family."

"I know the building, but I don't think they used it like that when I was there," Huddle said, pulling out a pen and yellow legal pad. He drew a rectangle on the paper with lines that represented each room. "Can you describe it?"

Michael nodded. "That's where the bunk beds were," he said, "and that's where I slept. That's where they did the blasting."

He wrote the names of all the people he saw living in virtual imprisonment during both stays. He couldn't remember everyone, but by the time he had finished, Michael had jotted down close to seventy names.

"How long were you there?" Huddle asked.

"I'm not sure about the first time. But the last time, I was there from August to just the other day, when I left the church," he said.

Huddle was stunned. Things were bad enough before he'd left, but locking people away in an old storage building? That was over-the-top, even for Jane Whaley.

If Michael would go public, maybe this would finally be enough to end her reign of terror, Huddle thought. But he didn't want to get ahead of himself. First, they contacted Michael's brother, and had him drop off Michael's clothing and personal necessities.

Huddle stayed with Michael that night to help him adjust. Michael's behavior was odd. He watched cartoons and Disney movies and wouldn't clean up after himself. *Maybe he's just rebelling after years of strict rules*, Huddle thought. He arranged to house the young man at a Faith Freedom Fund member's home forty-five minutes away.

Huddle thought about his own children. Would they ever leave the church? He hadn't seen them in a year, and they didn't like spending time with him. He accepted that he'd likely lost his family forever, but the painful truth set him free to fight back. In January 2010, he started a blog about his life in the Word of Faith Fellowship. He called his website *Religious Cults Info: Resources, Answers and Hope.* He started with his own experiences in the church.

At first, he only had a few followers, but it made him feel better, bringing the church's practices to the light. It also brought him grief. Reverend Gerald Southerland, the pastor he had followed to Word of Faith Fellowship, called him to complain. His ex-wife knocked on his door, and scolded him in the hallway outside. "You are printing lies," she said.

"Everything I wrote is true. You know it's true."

"They're lies. I don't understand why you are doing this, John."

Forget reasoning with her, Huddle thought. *She's brainwashed.* Huddle tried to move on with his life, his "new normal," but he couldn't walk away from what had happened to him. He underwent cancer treatments, worked his job, and spent the occasional afternoon on the side of the road near the church, holding a sign that said WOFF Is Not Safe.

He read everything he could find on cults. The more he learned, the more Huddle realized he was going to need help to expose Jane Whaley. He soon found that partner—a woman who didn't shy away from trouble.

Nancy Burnette was a court-appointed advocate for foster children. She had never heard of the Word of Faith Fellowship until she investigated a strange couple who wanted to adopt a pair of young brothers.

There was just something off about the couple. They were older, originally from Europe, and stiff. Their home was not outfitted for young children, and the couple didn't seem inclined to cuddle or interact much with the boys. And when

Nancy visited their church, she had a disturbing run-in with their pastor, Jane Whaley.

Nancy was the children's guardian ad litem. She tried to remove the foster children from the home. When that didn't happen, she started digging. Nancy called Wellspring, the cult deprogramming group in Ohio, to see if they had any information. They told her to call the Faith Freedom Fund. And in December 2011, she met with the group at Adaville Baptist Church in Spindale. Nancy showed up with her husband, Chad, a police officer.

Nancy introduced herself as a child abuse survivor who had devoted her life to protecting children.

The members could see that she was passionate, but they didn't know just how driven Burnette could be. As a child, Nancy was molested by an uncle and physically abused by family members. At fourteen she went to live with her school bus driver, who had noticed Nancy was bloody and bruised.

She'd grown up, raised three children, worked as a police dispatcher. When her children were grown, she went back to school for a criminal justice degree, and became a guardian ad litem. Her childhood had been hell. She wanted to help others break free from similar situations.

Nancy peppered the group with questions about the Word of Faith Fellowship and later called Huddle for a follow-up meeting. They met at a restaurant where alcohol was served. Huddle knew they'd be safe there because no one from Word of Faith would ever dine at a place that served beer and wine.

"What do you know about Werner and Hetty Trachsel?" Nancy asked. "They are trying to adopt two foster boys."

"I know them," he said. "She's from Holland. He's from Switzerland. He works on cars in a garage behind his house. They've been in the church for years, but I don't know anything about the boys. I was gone by then."

"Something's not right. The Trachsels did not go to social services in Rutherford County, where they live, to become foster parents," Nancy explained. "They went to Cleveland County, where I work."

"Well, there's a woman from the church who is a social worker in Cleveland County. Maybe that has something to do with it," Huddle said. "Her name is Lori Cornelius."

Nancy jotted it down. The whole thing was strange, she told Huddle. Werner seemed to enjoy the boys, but Hetty appeared indifferent. Their house was like a museum, with fancy furniture and tea sets, but no toys in sight. The boys' play area was a closet. The children seemed to be regressing emotionally. When she'd met them, the boys were full of energy and fun. But at their new home they seemed "out of it," like they were medicated. The couple gave conflicting accounts of how they would raise the boys.

The older boy was four, the younger not quite two. Nancy explained to Huddle that her job was to ensure they were in good hands.

"I wanted to see it for myself," she said. So one Sunday, Nancy said she and her supervisor, Dawn Scoggins, went to a service.

As soon as they sat down, people began staring, asking why they were there. Burnette said they were there to see the Trachsels.

Soon, Hetty and Werner arrived. Hetty was carrying the younger of the two boys. The boy looked lethargic. Strange, she thought, both boys were naturally energetic.

"I'm going to take him next door to the children's church," Hetty told Nancy. "I'll meet you back here in a minute."

Werner carried the older boy to the front of the room and took a seat. Nancy could see Werner and the child from her seat. Music was blaring and people were jumping up and down, but the little boy in Werner's arms "seemed out of it," resting his head on Werner's shoulder.

"Something is off," Nancy whispered to her supervisor. "It's so loud in here. How could he seem so tired, oblivious to all this noise?"

The music suddenly stopped. There was "some kind of ruckus near the pulpit." Werner scurried out the door with the boy. Jane Whaley and a group of her followers headed toward Nancy, scowling.

"My daughters have heard from God that you are here to cause strife in our church," Whaley said. "You can come here to visit, but you can't be here if you're not here with a pure heart and good intentions."

"I'm sorry that they heard that, but they're wrong. I'm here to observe the boys," Burnette said.

"We played songs specifically for you and your supervisor because we knew everybody knows those songs. You didn't even bother participating."

"Ma'am, I'm not here to participate in your service. I'm here to observe," Nancy said. "That's my job. I'm sorry if you're offended, but I'm not here to worship. I'm here to observe the boys."

Cornelius, the church member and social worker from Cleveland County, exchanged some words with Whaley. Then Whaley turned back to Nancy.

"God gave us these boys. DSS gave us these children," Whaley said, pressing closer, jabbing her finger in Nancy's face. "You are wicked. You are here to cause strife. You are here to judge us. You don't think these kids are supposed to be here!"

Nancy extended her arm to block Whaley. "You need to take about three steps back," she said. "You are entirely too close to me right now."

Whaley's eyes widened, but she retreated. That didn't stop the others. They circled Nancy and Scoggins. A man walked by and flipped open his coat to expose some sort of badge.

"We have to get out of here," Nancy said.

"I agree," Scoggins replied.

Nancy glanced at her supervisor. "We have to go now," she said. "But I'm not leaving until I see the boys."

The congregants could see Nancy was serious. Hetty appeared, pushing her way through the crowd with one of the children.

"We're going right now. This is out of control," Nancy told Hetty. "But we'll be back."

Then the little boy lifted his head off Hetty's shoulder. "Ms. Nancy, please don't leave me," he said in a pitiful voice. Burnette felt her heart break.

"Buddy, Ms. Nancy has to go right now, but I'll be back. I promise."

Members of the church's security team followed them out. Cornelius approached. "Let me explain to you what just happened," she said.

But Nancy was angry. "I don't need you to tell me what just happened. I am forty-three years old. I don't need you to tell me what I just saw."

The children were usually active and alert, but now they seemed out of it. Nancy was convinced they had been drugged, that they were "sedated." The children had been neglected by their biological mother. They needed special care to develop physically and emotionally. Nancy and Scoggins agreed that the boys should be removed from the Trachsels' home. The next day, they met with a child psychologist and made plans to pick them up the following Friday. Instead, Nancy got a call from a high-ranking Cleveland County official saying she was being taken off the case. She was "too personally involved," and her protests were "more personal than professional."

Bullshit, she thought. Cleveland County officials were afraid of facing a religious discrimination lawsuit like the one the church had settled in Rutherford County. The children were allowed to stay with the Trachsels, who eventually adopted them.

Months later, Nancy left her position as a guardian ad litem in protest. But she wasn't walking away from Word of Faith Fellowship. Far from it. She bought a subscription to the federal court website and printed off hundreds of pages of documents related to the lawsuit the church settled with Rutherford County in 2005. The more she read, the angrier she became. *This is crazy*, she thought. How could the county limit child abuse investigations?

As Burnette recounted the story to Huddle, he nodded, knowingly. "The church has a lot of power," Huddle said.

"Well, it's time for somebody to stand up to them," she snapped. "They don't intimidate me."

Huddle knew he could trust her. "Let me tell you about someone who just left the church."

He told Nancy about Michael Lowry, who had then moved to an aunt's home in Michigan. Burnette was appalled. "How have these people gotten away with this for so long?" she asked. "We need to get police involved."

"Michael wants to go to the police," Huddle said. "He needed some time to recover. Maybe he's ready now."

By the end of dinner, Burnette vowed to fight with Huddle to seek justice for Michael and others inside the church.

Nancy called Michael and introduced herself. She seemed genuine, sincere, and Michael opened up, just like he had with Huddle and Honeycutt. By the time he finished, Burnette was both shocked and angry. It was one thing hearing the story from Huddle, another listening to the details from the victim.

"Michael, you need to file a police report about this," she said. "I will be with you every step of the way."

Michael agreed. So on January 11, 2012, he called Sergeant Billy Scoggins, an investigator with the Rutherford County Sheriff's Office. Michael disclosed what happened to him and others. He said he wanted to press charges—the people who did this needed to be held accountable.

A month later, Huddle went to the department and learned that Scoggins never filed an incident report. Nothing had been done. Scoggins was blunt with Huddle.

"Look, [Lowry] is just not durable or credible enough to take the pressure of cross-examination at a trial," Scoggins said. If Huddle insisted, Michael could go to the local magistrate and file misdemeanor charges there against the church. "That's his best option," Scoggins said.

North Carolina law allows citizens to initiate criminal charges. They have to go before a magistrate and show there's probable cause to issue an arrest warrant. And even if a magistrate issues one, the sheriff's office doesn't have to investigate.

But Michael didn't think misdemeanor charges were fair after what they had done to him. He called the sheriff's office again on February 20, 2012. This time, a deputy created an incident report. It didn't mention the Lower Building, or how he was held there in 2010 and 2011 and beaten almost every day during both stays.

Instead, the report said that in August 2011, a group of church members held Michael down, hit him "about the face and chest area," then let him go. The officer wrote that Michael said the reason they did this was "because he was a homosexual and they were trying to get him to stop being homosexual."

The report named six church members involved in the attack, including a church attorney, Mark Morris. That alone should have been enough to trigger a major investigation, but Huddle could sense the sheriff's office was reluctant to do anything.

Why didn't they take an incident report on January 11? Why did the sergeant suggest Michael go to a magistrate? Huddle expressed his frustration in an email to his mother: "I am mad and sad at the same time. This fight is just not for Michael Lowry—but all the others who have been or will be wronged under Jane's practices."

Lieutenant Jamie Keever was assigned to the case, but by the end of March 2012, Keever told Michael the investigation was over. The report had been turned over to District Attorney Brad Greenway—the same DSS attorney who helped settle the agency's lawsuit with the church in 2005.

Keever refused to disclose details, including whether he talked to any of the witnesses on Michael's list, or even if he had visited the Lower Building. Michael was sure the church was still holding people there.

Nancy became a familiar face around the Rutherford County courthouse, gleaning any information she could about the church. But she ran into one roadblock after another. And then she met Robynn Spence, the clerk of Rutherford County Superior Court.

"I'd like to talk to you about the Word of Faith Fellowship. But I can't do it in my office," Spence told Nancy. "Can you meet me in the parking lot of the Dollar General?"

"Just tell me when and I'll be there."

Spence was friendly and outgoing. She was also a beer-drinking, chain-smoking Republican who wasn't afraid to buck the system. More important, she had a soft spot for people in need.

Originally from Charlotte, Spence moved to Rutherford County in the early 1990s. Since then, she had worked for the courts, the sheriff's department, as a social worker, and at a law office. She lived with a sheriff's deputy. Her blond hair was always perfect, her makeup and outfits impeccable. She loved bright orange clothes and big earrings.

Spence detested the Word of Faith Fellowship. She knew people were abused inside the church. She also knew that Jane Whaley was a street fighter.

She discovered just how hard the church would fight not long after she won a special election in 2008. She'd refused to reappoint two assistant clerks who were members of the church: Ramona Hall and Laura Bridges. Spence believed Hall had been using her position to supply information to church leaders, including her husband, Wayne Hall, a private investigator and former sheriff's deputy.

In early 2010, Hall filed papers to challenge Robynn for the office. She ran a dirty campaign and lost in the Democratic primary. Spence went on to win the general election, but Ramona Hall didn't go away without a fight. In November 2010, she sued Spence in federal court, accusing her of religious discrimination. The North Carolina Department of Justice settled the case for $375,000 in June 2012.

When Nancy pulled into the dollar store parking lot, Spence was already there, her red Lexus parked by the side of the building. Nancy parked in the opposite direction, so they could talk to each other without getting out of their cars.

Spence got right down to business.

"I used to work for a lawyer. He was one of the first people to win a custody case against the church," Spence said. "The church is dirty. They are abusing people inside that place. And when somebody challenges them, they will fight to the end. They'll do anything to get their way."

"That's what I've learned," Nancy said.

"In that custody case, even after a judge ordered them to hand over the kid, they drove him around in a car, blasting him for twelve hours. That boy was just distraught when they finally handed him over."

"Well, I will tell you this," Nancy said, "nothing pisses me off more than someone mistreating children."

"Me, too," Spence said. "I have to stay professional because of my position. There's only so much I can do. But you seem to have the balls to stand up to these people. And I hope you will stick with this."

"I'm not afraid of them. I promise you that."

Spence smiled. "Well, I can help you, but I won't break the rules. I can tell you where to go and where to look. But you need to be careful. These people have money and connections. They have a bad reputation about harassing people. You have to watch your back."

"I always do."

The two agreed to talk again. Nancy was feeling confident, determined. Now she had a powerful ally.

On a sweltering day in August 2012, a man named Kevin Logan walked into Robynn Spence's office.

It wasn't unusual for people to stop by. Attorneys, court reporters, even judges liked to talk to her. But this was different. The man had a troubled look on his face. He asked if he could close her door. He had something important to tell her.

Spence was a little uneasy, but she knew he didn't have a gun. Otherwise, he couldn't have gotten past the metal detector by the front entrance, the only way into the building.

He pulled up a chair.

"Somebody hired me to kill you," he said. "They offered to pay me $10,000."

Spence was stunned. She didn't know how to respond. Before she could say a word, Logan elaborated.

"Don't worry. I am not going to do anything to you," he said.

"So why the hell are you here?"

Logan said he was contacted by a "middleman" who asked him to do the job for a Word of Faith Fellowship member. They wanted her out of the way, he said. They wanted to run one of their own for clerk of courts.

Spence stared at Logan. She had good bullshit detectors, and this guy seemed to be telling the truth.

"Why are you telling me this?" she asked.

"Because I remember you. You used to be a social worker, right? I remember you helping my family. I know you are a good person. That's why I came here to warn you. People are out to get you. You need to watch your back," he said, then left.

Spence drove straight to Michael and Amanda Davis's house. Both were in law enforcement. Spence sobbed as she recounted Logan's visit. Over the years, Spence had been trailed by people in her car, she'd had her vehicle run off the road into a ditch, but this crossed the line.

"I have to make sure that people I trust know what's going on, so if something does happen to me, I know y'all will push it," Spence said.

"You need to report this to the sheriff," Amanda said. Spence winced. Sheriff Chris Francis supported Word of Faith Fellowship. They held a fund-raiser for him when he ran for office in 2010.

Spence knew the sheriff's office had some good people, but the sheriffs themselves were a different story. Dan Good was

sheriff from 1990 until he resigned in 2005. Over the years
he'd strongly supported the church. His longtime lieutenant,
Philip Byers, another church supporter, filled out the rest of
Good's term. Byers was defeated in 2006 by Jack Conner.
Over the years, Conner got close to Spence, and was poised
to help her when he was defeated by Francis.

Spence knew she had to tell Francis. She hoped he would
investigate. How could he ignore it? It was serious when someone tried to hire a hit man to kill a public official.

Spence told Francis everything she knew, but Francis waved
her away, saying she needed to "stop being so damn thin-
skinned." He wasn't going to do anything about it.

Upset, Spence went home and told her boyfriend, Chad
Murray, the sheriff's deputy. Soon two sheriff's investigators
contacted the State Bureau of Investigation.

When Francis found out, he decided his office would handle the case, after all. A few weeks after Logan's visit, Spence
met with three sheriff's office investigators for several hours,
but she remained on edge. Every time she left her office or
house, she'd look over her shoulder. She became hyperaware
of her surroundings. She couldn't take the chance of being
caught off guard. Her life depended on it.

19

A LITTLE HELP FROM HIS FRIENDS

Jane Whaley was obsessed with knowing what everyone around her was saying and doing. Ironically, communication technology was making it ever more difficult to shadow her followers' lives.

Mobile phones made life easier for many congregants who ran businesses or scheduled mission trips and church activities. When encrypted messaging services like Viber began replacing expensive long-distance telephone calls, high-ranking members were allowed to use them to keep in touch with members in Brazil and Ghana.

It was a common practice for ministers to grab congregants' phones, to check on their call histories, and see which applications they used. If they had a smartphone, they'd check their emails, and see if the follower had used the phone to search the internet.

But Viber made it harder for ministers to snoop, and church members were apparently downloading the app without prior permission. Phone users who were "out from under authority"—church-speak for those acting on their own—were punished.

★ ★ ★

By the summer of 2012, John and Peter Cooper had both graduated from the local community college and were both enrolled at Wofford College.

The brothers were majoring in biology with hopes of continuing on to medical school. Whaley had already approved their career choices, with one caveat: John and Peter had to be accepted into the same school. Otherwise, neither could go.

The edict made little sense in the real world. Their choice of medical schools was limited to a handful within driving distance of Spindale. Admission was fantastically competitive. What if one brother got in, and the other didn't?

They both worried about it in silence. In the church's paranoid universe, anything personal John shared with Peter would be reported to leadership. Peter felt the same way about sharing his secrets with John. They spent their long daily commutes to Wofford making innocuous small talk.

Both had to fit studying around busy schedules. John helped in the church's Christian school, and was always involved in a carpentry project. Peter worked for his brother Benjamin at Cooper Solutions, a recycling business.

Ever the entrepreneur, Benjamin had created the company after contemplating a pile of abandoned car tires. He found a ready market for them overseas. With Jane's permission, he began recycling not only rubber but plastics, textiles, and metal.

Business was booming, but Benjamin and Micah had just started classes at Elon University Law School, 165 miles east of Spindale, and were stretched thin. Benjamin asked Peter to help him run the company and made him the general manager.

One Friday afternoon in the late summer, Peter and John had just gotten back from Wofford and scrambled to get to church in time for the fellowship dinner. When they got there, Brooke Covington approached them with her usual scowl.

"Come with me. You're in major sin," she said.

The brothers glanced at one another as they trailed Brooke upstairs into the sound room, where the church's video and audio equipment was stored. Jayne Caulder and a few others were there.

"You downloaded that Viber app without authority," Brooke screamed at Peter. "Who do you think you are? You are in sin."

Without warning, she shoved him hard. Peter fell into a clothing rack, disappearing into the wall of hanging garments.

"GET UP," Brooke shouted. "YOU ARE IN SIN!"

Peter recalled lifting himself off the floor as Brooke and Caulder pounced. John watched in horror as they punched, slapped, and screamed at his brother. He wanted to do something, but he just stood there, frozen.

After the blasting session, Brooke called Jane. They decided to track down everyone who had downloaded Viber. Anyone who had the app without permission would be sent to the Lower Building.

The following Monday, Peter and John were summoned to the church for a meeting of young congregants being groomed for leadership. They met in one of the fellowship halls. They arranged the chairs in a circle.

It was the same routine as ever. One by one, the members of the group spilled their secret sins. But John and Jessica didn't have much to say. They couldn't think of anything they'd done wrong. Neither had smartphones.

"What's going on with y'all?" someone asked. "Y'all haven't said much. What sin is in your life?"

Jessica didn't say a word. John hesitated.

"There's unclean between you two," someone said. "What have y'all been doing?"

In an instant, the group pounced, dragging John and Jessica from their chairs to the floor.

John couldn't see what was happening to Jessica. He didn't realize that she had been dragged to another room for a separate blasting session. Eight or ten people were right in his face, screaming hysterically.

Chris Davies sat down on John's legs. Others held his arms. Another grabbed his head and began shaking it, pounding it against the floor. Davies punched him in the chest. John couldn't catch his breath. Davies punched again, and he didn't stop. Blow after blow, his heart was racing, gasping for breath, screams rattling through his brain, John finally lost consciousness.

When John opened his eyes, it was silent. The room was spinning.

"What is the sin in your life, John?" someone asked. "What unclean have you and Jessica given in to?"

John finally had it. He had seen plenty of people break, admitting to things they didn't do. John wasn't going to feed their appetite for lurid sexual lies. He refused to implicate Jessica in something she did not do. He was willing to "go to war."

"We didn't do anything wrong," he insisted.

"I have been talking to Jessica in the other room," Brooke said. "She told us what you did. She told us everything. If you don't tell us what she has been telling us, then you are going to be kicked out."

"There's nothing to say, because we haven't done anything. Nothing."

The beating resumed. When Chris Davies tired out, John's cousin Brent Cordes straddled John and punched him in the chest. John desperately tried to curl up to protect himself from the blows.

Now it was Peter Cooper's turn to take a stand. When they started at Wofford, Peter was put in charge of his little brother. He was responsible for his life. If they didn't stop hitting him, he believed John could die. He'd never tried to stop an attack before, but he couldn't stand this anymore.

"Brooke, this is wrong," he shouted. "They're hurting my brother. You have to stop it."

Brooke ignored him. But tonight, Peter wasn't going to give up. "I'm calling Jane," Peter said. "This is wrong. They're hurting my brother."

Peter stormed out of the room, phoned Jane, and told her his brother was being savagely beaten while Brooke cheered. When Peter returned, Brooke was on the phone. She hung up and ordered the beating to stop.

The men retreated. John stayed on the floor, too weak to move. Peter helped his brother up and took him home.

John took himself to the bathroom to clean up. He looked at his body in the mirror. His chest was bruised from his collarbones to his sternum. It hurt to touch or move or breathe. He wondered if a rib was broken, but he knew he couldn't go to the hospital. Nobody did. That was the ultimate sin. The ministers would go nuts. He pulled out his phone and snapped a picture, not sure what he'd do with the image.

The next day, Peter and John headed to Wofford like nothing had happened. They usually commuted with other congregants, but this time they were alone. John swallowed his distrust.

"Thanks for saving me," he said.

Peter smiled, but kept his eyes on the road. "How do you feel?"

"I'm having a hard time breathing without it hurting," John said.

"That wasn't right what they did to you," Peter said.

"I know. Things got out of hand. They really hurt me this time," John said.

And at the moment, John realized he was having an actual conversation with his brother. He was expressing emotion. But then, John began to worry. Was this a trick to get him to say something bad about the church? Would his brother run to Jane? To the other ministers? Could he really trust him? John took a deep breath. The night before, Peter showed he cared. That felt real. So John decided to take a chance. What he didn't know was that Peter felt the same way. And from that day on they began to open up, a little at a time. And for the first time for as long as he could remember, John didn't feel so alone.

Meanwhile, Brooke Covington hadn't forgotten.

A few days later, just before another nighttime service, Jane called John into her office. Brooke and most of the other top leaders were there.

"How are you feeling, John David?" Whaley asked.

"My chest is all bruised and it hurts to breathe."

"Yes. I understand some of the young men probably took it a little too far. But are you sure there's not something you need to tell us? Something about the unclean?"

John couldn't believe it. They just wouldn't let it go.

"Like I've been saying, we didn't do anything."

Whaley wasn't going to back down. She repeated that God told her that there was sin in his life. When she pulled out her wooden paddle, the one that was an inch thick and three inches wide, John stopped fighting.

"You are going to repent. Maybe you didn't do what we

thought. But there is sin in your life. That's why God was speaking to us," she proclaimed.

Standing there in the middle of the room, in front of everyone, John swallowed his pride. He bent over, and Whaley swatted him. All John wanted to do was get out of there, so he uttered the words they all wanted to hear: "I'm sorry. I repent."

Jane stopped and put away her paddle.

Rick didn't look up from his Bible, but he could see Benjamin, Peter, and Jeffrey walk into the building. He wanted to greet them, to tell him how glad he was to see them, but talking was forbidden. If he did what he wanted, the others would surround him and start blasting.

It was like that in the Lower Building.

Jane had given Benjamin permission to use Viber for his business, but she suspected he gave others the download link. It was probably Benjamin's fault that unauthorized apps were found on so many members' smartphones—even Peter's and Jeffrey's.

So Benjamin, Peter, and Jeffrey were sent to the Lower Building to consider their sins. Unlike the others, they only had to stay one night. They were too valuable to the church to stay any longer.

On their way to a room, the brothers saw a familiar figure. Then it hit them—it was their father. No one said a word. But Rick could see his sons looked uncomfortable in the Lower Building. And why not? This was rock bottom. Rick had been inside for, what…six months? A year? It was hard to tell. There were no calendars. Days blended into weeks. No one told him when he could leave, and he was too afraid to ask.

His only "break" was going to work each morning. After a few months in the building, ministers told him he'd have to work for free at businesses owned by church leaders. Rick didn't care. Anything was better than being stuck indoors.

Seeing his sons brought back the darkness to his soul. Rick hung his head over his Bible and let the whole sordid newsreel run again: bad decisions, pride, arrogance, unbelief. He'd lost his wife, his children, his home. It was clear he had taken a wrong turn on the road to salvation.

How could I have been so stupid? he thought.

The sun was going down, men were coming in from their shifts at work. Rick braced himself for another night. He had never seen so much violence, men and boys pinned to the floor and beaten. Young Alan Eiss was accused of masturbating. Chris Hall and several inmates had beaten him bloody.

Rick didn't take part in the violence, but he did nothing to stop it.

Michael Lowry, that poor kid. No one was brutalized more than he was. Rick thought Michael must be dead; he hadn't seen him in a while. He turned his attention back to his Bible, but he couldn't focus.

Rick and Suzanne had been separated for years now. They were still legally married, but they hadn't been "husband and wife" since before their daughter Jacklyn was born. In the weeks leading up to his exile, Rick had been repeatedly blasted for having erotic thoughts. At first, Rick defended himself to church leaders. He said that everyone had those thoughts, even King David, but it wasn't a sin unless you acted on them. That only made it worse. And after one especially brutal deliverance session, ministers gave Rick an ultimatum: go to the Lower Building or they'd kick him out of church. He'd never see his family again.

After he got settled in the building, he asked attorney Mark Morris when he could leave.

"When you get a breakthrough," Morris told him.

"How do I know when I have a breakthrough?"

"When we tell you," Morris snapped.

Rick used some of his military training to help himself and others survive their time in the building. When the ministers weren't around, he told the others that he had read all the Scriptures and that thinking about women wasn't a sin, "no matter what they say." He couldn't find their justification anywhere in the Bible.

Rick felt like he was making a difference. Still, he couldn't help but feel depressed. He didn't know how long this could go on.

Michael Lowry slumped in the passenger seat and stared at the mountains in the distance. They were only a few miles from the Rutherford County line.

"Are you OK?" the driver, Jerry Cooper, asked.

Michael nodded yes, but he wasn't sure. It had been nearly a year since he'd fled his parents' home, the church, and the Lower Building. He had been living with his aunt far away in Michigan, while pressing North Carolina law enforcement to reopen his case.

Huddle, Nancy, Spence, and others had been pushing the police, but Sheriff Chris Francis had refused to budge, as did Greenway, the district attorney. Greenway saw firsthand how the church threw all of its money and political connections into every case. Life was a lot easier when he just ignored "the crazy church."

Michael was headed back to the county for a long-awaited meeting with the sheriff's investigators. Faith in America, a national nonprofit group that fights religious bigotry, had intervened on Michael's behalf after Huddle contacted them. For Brent Childers, the group's executive director, this case was in their wheelhouse. The North Carolina–based nonprofit was founded in 2006 by Mitchell Gold, the chief executive officer of a furniture company. A gay man, Mitchell understood the pain caused by religious leaders who used the Bible to justify hostility toward gay, lesbian, bisexual, and transgender people. His group was created to educate the public about "misguided religious teachings."

Faith in America charged the United States Department of Justice to investigate Michael's allegations, which they considered "hate crimes." In his request, Childers said Michael's was the "most disturbing case" his group had encountered.

Suddenly, the local DA and sheriff realized their stonewalling might become an embarrassment. Greenway and Francis contacted Michael and asked him for an interview. Michael agreed to meet them. But he was scared.

Huddle and Nancy told him they would stand with him. Jerry Cooper, a former Word of Faith Fellowship member who was not related to Rick Cooper's family, said he'd drive Michael around during his stay in Rutherford County, to keep him feeling secure and supported.

Days before the scheduled interview, Jerry picked up Michael in Charlotte, then headed west to Rutherford County. They would avoid the church and Michael's home. The last thing they needed was to be charged with trespassing. But as they headed into Forest City, Michael's heart began racing. What if his parents—or anyone from the church—spotted them?

"You're going to be fine," Jerry assured him.

But a few minutes later, Jerry realized he'd spoken too soon. In his rearview mirror he noticed two cars tailing him. They were members of the church's security team.

Jerry didn't want to scare Michael, but he had to tell him. "We've been spotted."

Michael panicked. His legs began shaking. Jerry saw the blank, shell-shocked look on Michael's face. He knew he had to calm him down.

"Nothing is going to happen. I promise," he said.

Jerry turned into the parking lot of a nearby mall. One of the security team's cars boxed them in. Jerry was angry. He knew following former members was a form of intimidation, a church tactic. It wasn't going to work on him. Cooper bounded out of his car, shaking his fist. Randy Fields jumped out of a car and approached him.

"Why are you following us?" Jerry shouted.

"We're not following you."

"Yeah? Then why are you here?"

"We have every right to be here."

"OK. You want to play games?" Jerry said. He wheeled around, got into the car, and revved the engine. Cooper was going to get out of the parking spot even if it meant bashing into the security team vehicles.

Sensing that something bad was about to happen, Fields waved for the cars to let Cooper go. As he backed up, Jerry nearly hit Fields, who jumped out of the way.

Jerry headed straight to the magistrate's office. He walked inside and told the people there that he and Michael were being followed. He said the Word of Faith security men blocked his car and wouldn't let him out. The judge issued misdemeanor stalking and false imprisonment complaints against Fields and three others.

In the car, Cooper turned to Michael. "Don't ever let them intimidate you, Michael. Sometimes you have to take action," he said.

A few days later, Michael met with investigators and told them everything, all over again.

Mark Morris stormed into the Lower Building. He didn't usually appear there at night, so Rick knew it had to be important. Jane wanted to see everyone in the sanctuary for an urgent meeting.

Jane and other church leaders stood in the front of the big auditorium, looking grave. They didn't waste any time. Jane said that God told her everyone had a breakthrough. They were all going home this very night.

Rick was stunned. He no longer believed that God talked to Jane Whaley. But he also knew Jane never did anything without a reason.

Whaley was certain the sheriff's department knew people were being held in the Lower Building. She didn't know why Faith in America didn't include that information in its news release, but with all the nosy journalists snooping around—and with Huddle, Nancy, and Jerry Cooper causing trouble—it was just a matter of time before they discovered that juicy detail. When they did, law enforcement couldn't continue to ignore Michael's complaint.

After releasing everyone from the Lower Building, Whaley met with church leaders and ordered a complete makeover of the structure. The work would have to be done within forty-eight hours. No excuses.

The day after Whaley released the men, ministers scrambled to assemble a team of the best church workers. The crew, many of whom had been living in prison-like conditions in the building themselves, worked around the clock ripping out the woodwork in the common area, installing a new kitchen with granite countertops, laying down a hardwood floor, and replacing old couches and bunk beds with new ones. Whaley spared no expense. They painted the walls and hung up pictures with bucolic scenes of the English countryside.

Then Whaley called an emergency meeting of all the men who had ever been held in the building. Everyone had to get their story straight.

As a trusted member of Whaley's inner circle, Jeffrey Cooper was one of the first to arrive. Ever since Faith in America asked for the federal investigation, Whaley had been meeting regularly with her closet advisers: her daughter, Webster, the Covingtons, the Caulders. Jeffrey was in most of the meetings, too, along with other church legal team members and Chris Back, an assistant North Carolina prosecutor who worked in the same office with Webster.

Whaley wanted to derail the police investigation. For months she used Jeffrey and other church attorneys to pass messages to Greenway, the county prosecutor. She pressed Greenway to find out what was going on in the investigation. She didn't want to be blindsided.

She used "her" attorneys to remind Greenway that the church would never hurt anyone. Word of Faith Fellowship was a kind, loving place.

Jeffrey was the go-between for some of those messages, a job he detested. He knew he was interfering in an active investigation, and if someone outside the church found out, he could lose his law license and face criminal charges.

He and everyone else at the meetings knew that everything Michael said was true. Jeffrey found Webster's and Back's behavior especially repellent and viewed them as actively obstructing justice by giving Whaley advice.

Under North Carolina law, prosecutors cannot provide legal advice or be involved in outside cases in any manner—including offering legal advice in an ongoing criminal investigation to help a person avoid prosecution. Every attorney in the church had a legal and moral obligation to report Michael's abuse, as well as the ongoing mistreatment of children.

One at a time, Jane began grilling them. When were they there? Who did they see in the building? Were they there at the same time with Michael Lowry?

When a member said he saw Michael being struck, Whaley

screamed at the top of her lungs: "STOOOOOOOP IT! YOU DID NOT SEE THAT! THAT IS WITCHCRAFT! THAT IS THE DEVIL."

The man's head dropped. "You're…you're right, right," he stammered. "I didn't see anything."

Jeffrey was emotionally torn. He had believed for so long that Whaley was a prophet, his guardian. But the corruption was undeniable. He realized the Word of Faith Fellowship operated more like a crime family than a church. He was becoming more and more disgusted by her behavior, but like the others, he went along with it. Breaking from the church was too costly, too complicated. He risked losing his family.

Faith in America called the eyes of the evangelical world down on Spindale. Childers was sending out news releases with the latest developments. Now local and national media organizations were calling, asking if it was true: Did the church beat Michael to expel his so-called gay demons?

Using her Southern charm, Whaley presented herself as a sweet grandmother. She called the allegations nonsense. She said the church had been under attack from jealous former members for years. Now they were being aided by crazies, troublemakers, and outsiders, people like Huddle and Nancy. "You hope it goes away, and it gets worse," she told one reporter between tears.

She invited reporters to Sunday service to see for themselves. The church had nothing to hide. Her strategy of burying reporters in a blizzard of kindness had worked in the past. She was sure it would work again. She just hoped nobody popped in unexpectedly.

Jane despised surprises.

20

THE RUSE

Christina Bryant pulled her car into the church parking lot. She pulled out a small rectangular-shaped Olympus digital tape recorder from her handbag, pressed the record button, and stuffed it in her bra. It was 6:25 p.m. She was supposed to meet Jane Whaley in five minutes. This was the first time Christina had been back in six years. When she left in 2006, her mother, two brothers, and two sisters stayed behind. Since then, one of her brothers, Daniel, had left. Now he was in the US Air Force, stationed in Monterey, California. But the rest of her family was still in the church and didn't want anything to do with her. They didn't attend her graduation from college or nursing school. They were no-shows at her wedding. Same at the hospital, when her daughter, Ava, was born.

Christina heard what happened to Michael Lowry and wanted to help. She had called the church a few days earlier, telling the receptionist that she was considering rejoining and arranged a meeting with Whaley.

And Michael was the reason she was here on a Friday night in late October 2012. Christina knew exactly how the church destroyed lives. She lived it. For years, she had wanted "to expose the lies and deceit." Now she saw her chance. If she could prove that Michael was telling the truth about his imprisonment and abuse, people would be forced to reckon with what was happening inside the church. She told Nancy Burnette her plan. Christina wanted to talk to Whaley and secretly record the meeting. Maybe Whaley would say something incriminating. If she did, Christina would turn the tape over to police.

"How are you? How is Ava?" Whaley said with a big smile.

"Fine," Christina said.

They hugged and Christina followed Whaley to her office, passing congregants along the way. They sat down and made small talk. Bryant disclosed that she was getting a divorce and that her four-year-old daughter was having problems with her eyesight and weight. It was all a ploy. She knew Whaley loved gossip. If Bryant opened up about her life, Whaley would feel comfortable and offer advice.

Whaley chastised Christina for negative Facebook posts and associating with "attackers" like Huddle and Nancy. Christina apologized, then asked Whaley if it was possible for her to have a relationship with her mother and siblings.

Maybe, Whaley said. But first, she'd have to change. Stop criticizing the church. And she needed to delete her Facebook posts.

"You equated me as a crazy religious nut killing people in the name of Christ. I wouldn't let anybody hurt anybody, much less let anybody get killed," Whaley said.

The posts were "enough for your family not to have anything to do with you," she said, then used Scripture to justify her position. "If you attack, the Word of God says we are to have nothing—absolutely nothing—to do with you. So, we're going to do what the Bible says. And the Bible says Jesus came for the sword to divide, to divide families. He came to divide the righteous from the unrighteous."

Christina saw an opening to broach the subject of Michael and her brother's abuse, but Whaley stopped her before she had a chance. The pastor had been inspecting Christina's face since she walked in the building.

"You have too much makeup on."

"Huh?"

"You need to go into the restroom and wash it off," Whaley said.

Really? Christina thought. She took a deep breath and went to the bathroom. She soaked a paper towel with water and wiped off her makeup, including her black eye shadow.

When she returned, Whaley nodded.

Christina asked what was going on with Michael and Whaley unloaded. She said he was lying about being abused—and being gay. She said the church had set him up with a girl from one of their Brazilian churches and he never complained.

She said Michael was so rebellious his parents kicked him out. So they "made an apartment in this building right down here."

Ah, the Lower Building, she thought.

But then Whaley brought up Christina's brother Daniel. She said at one time he was a troublemaker just like Michael. Christina knew her brother had been beaten for years—she'd seen the bruises. Christina brought that up. Whaley said yes, Daniel had been spanked. But he was never beaten. Even though he had bruises, it didn't mean a thing, she said.

"DSS says you can have bruises, as long as they're not such and such and such and such," she said. "Now, if I spank you, you won't get a bruise," Whaley said, trying to raise her limp right arm. "Anytime I try to use this arm, I can't."

Then Christina asked a question that had been bothering

her for a long time. Years earlier, her brother had been disciplined for horsing around with a friend. A minister saw Daniel tickling his buddy and the two boys were laughing. They said if he didn't behave, they'd tell authorities, insinuating that he had somehow abused the boy. But if Daniel had really inappropriately touched his friend, why didn't they call police?

Whaley avoided answering the question, saying she didn't have to report sexual abuse because of "ministerial confidentiality." (Christina knew that was wrong. In North Carolina, anyone who has any information about a child being sexually abused is required to report it to authorities. No exceptions.)

Whaley then opined about the handling of sex abuse allegations in the church. She focused on Crystal Taylor, the girl who left the church so many years ago.

Whaley said when she heard the girl was sexually abused by a minister, she went to the district attorney's office. (The sheriff's office was already investigating the allegations.) Whaley said she blamed the girl for seducing the minister. She told that to the prosecutor, too. Crystal Taylor "was thirteen but she looked twenty."

"I went to the DA at that time and told him what happened, that it was as much her fault because she had been molested as a child by her grandfather and others," she said.

When a congregant comes to her with sexual abuse allegations, Whaley said she explains to them what'll happen if they file charges.

"Now if a child wants it told, they've got to understand that it will go before the court, it will go in the newspaper, [you're going to have to tell] every detail, which hurts you both. Now if this has stopped and you have forgiven, you got deliverance, do you want to go back to it again and let the whole world know?"

Christina sat there in stunned silence. She wondered how

many children had been sexually abused, the cases hidden because Whaley didn't want any negative publicity. Whaley got up. The meeting was over. She escorted Christina into the fellowship hall, where everyone—including her mother and siblings—was eating. Christina took a deep breath. It was the first time she had seen her family in three years, the first time she had ever met her niece. She gave her mother a brief, awkward hug, then reached down and touched her niece's hand. But the reception was cold. They wanted nothing to do with her. Christina could see the hurt in her mother's eyes, the pain of a woman convinced her child would burn in hell. And she knew that what she was doing would be considered the "ultimate betrayal." Once they found out that she recorded the meeting with Whaley, the damage would be irreparable. But she'd already mourned the loss of her family. She had nothing to lose.

Jeffrey Cooper waited quietly for church leaders to arrive. Voices in the hallway, through the door: Josh Farmer, and the other attorneys—Morris, Webster, Back—and other church leaders filed into the room, looking grim. They took seats around the conference table.

They're as miserable as I am, Jeffrey thought.

It was the middle of November. Whaley was on a rampage, pressing Jeffrey and the other church attorneys for any scrap of information related to the police investigation.

A month earlier, Michael had met for several hours with Rutherford County sheriff's investigators. This time they asked questions and took notes. Chris Francis and Brad Greenway were under pressure to do something. People—voters—wanted to know why they hadn't launched a full-scale investigation back in January, when Michael first asked for help.

Huddle and Nancy had records showing all the times they

had called, and the times Michael was there in North Carolina, ready to meet with investigators who never called. And
when Michael finally sat down with investigators again, he
told them the same thing he did in both January and February. Nothing had changed. His story was consistent.

"They treated me like I was dirt," he said. "I don't know
if anyone is still being held there. But you should find out."

Investigators had no plans for unannounced visits. Even if
they had, the building was now pristine. Police were hesitant
to interview potential witnesses, especially if they were still
in the church.

Greenway came up with a plan. He decided to use a rare
North Carolina legal proceeding called presentment. Essentially, it was a mini-trial. Greenway would present evidence
to a grand jury. And if jurors said there was enough evidence
for a "presentment," he'd be required by law to investigate
the allegations. If the jurors said there wasn't, the case would
be dropped.

The proceeding would give Greenway and Francis cover.
Whaley wouldn't be able to blame them for a grand jury decision, and Michael and his supporters couldn't blame them
for not doing their job.

When Michael had first approached the Rutherford County
Sheriff's Office, investigators told him to go to a magistrate, a
civil officer for more minor offenses. Michael had refused, re-
minding them he was kidnapped, beaten, and tortured. These
were not misdemeanors.

Whaley knew that, too. That was why she had been holding so many meetings—to discredit Michael. But Jeffrey was
worried about something else: it was only a matter of time before someone discovered the church's unscrupulous practices.
The church's many secrets, including its unemployment benefits scheme, were impossible to cover up completely.

More voices in the hallway. Jeffrey's body stiffened. Whaley walked into the room with Brooke.

"We have a crisis," she said. The Federal Bureau of Investigation had assigned an agent from its Asheville office to dig into the Michael allegations. Four church members were already facing stalking and harassment charges for trying to intimidate Michael and Jerry Cooper. Now, with federal investigators involved, they had to go on the offensive. Whaley passed around folders with personal information about Michael, including his medical and educational records, as well as photos from his time inside the church. They began putting together bullet points on how to discredit him.

They decided to say they had no idea Michael was gay because the girls in the photos were his girlfriends.

They focused on Michael's intellect. His records showed he had an IQ of 77. Anything below 70 was considered a benchmark for intellectual disability.

Another suggested they say that Michael's parents kicked him out of the house because he was addicted to pornography. In return, Michael decided to get revenge by making up stories he knew would hurt the church.

Everyone in the room nodded their heads. They liked the idea. They decided to start planting bogus stories about Michael's pornography addiction. Then they discussed how the church would handle questions about the Lower Building.

Webster had an idea.

"When I was younger, I went to a Baptist church and they held weeklong men's retreats. So maybe we could say the building was being used for retreats."

Jeffrey immediately shot down the idea. "Frank, Baptist retreats are for a week. Some men were in the Lower Building for a year. How are you going to explain that?"

They decided that since the men had been released and the

building renovated, they'd invite sheriff's investigators and the district attorney for a tour. That would forestall any questions about prison-like conditions.

On November 29, 2012, Greenway, Keever, and another sheriff's deputy visited the building. Jeffrey showed them around. He told them the building was used to house visitors from the church's Brazilian branches, as well as men in Word of Faith Fellowship's prison ministry. Greenway and the others inspected the fresh paint and new bedding. Before leaving, the district attorney thanked Jeffrey and the others for letting them see the place for themselves.

As he watched them leave, Jeffrey could tell they didn't want to investigate, that they hated dealing with the church. He got the impression that the quicker they could close the case, the better. The probe appeared to be all but over.

Michael was sitting on the bench outside the room where the grand jury was about to meet.

"You OK?" Huddle asked.

Michael nodded. He didn't want anyone to know he was scared to death. He was glad Huddle and Nancy were with him. They wouldn't be allowed in the courtroom, as the proceedings were closed to the public. But they knew he'd need support. In a traditional grand jury hearing, a district attorney lays out the facts and the jury determines whether to issue an indictment. But the presentment hearing required Michael to testify, and the deck was already stacked against him. Spence had discovered that Greenway had met with Michael's father and with attorneys for several people who were named in Michael's complaint. He even talked to Mark Morris, the church attorney named in the police report.

"That never should have happened," said Spence. "The church is trying to influence the case."

Meanwhile, Greenway had refused to meet with Michael to discuss his case or prepare him for his grand jury appearance. And Jamie Keever never talked to any of his witnesses.

Nancy sensed that Michael was uneasy. She had four children of her own. She put her arm around Lowry's shoulder and whispered encouraging words. "We're here for you. We'll be waiting right outside the door. Just go in and tell the truth."

Michael nodded. When he spotted people entering the grand jury courtroom, he began sweating.

This is it. Stay calm, he thought.

But then he saw a familiar face among the grand jurors: Rodney Moore, a Word of Faith Fellowship member.

He immediately turned and told Huddle and Nancy. "There he is," Michael said, pointing to a clean-shaven man in a leather coat.

"Holy shit," Nancy said. She couldn't understand how a Word of Faith Fellowship congregant was allowed to serve on a grand jury panel that would vote whether to investigate allegations against the church. It was a move a Mafia boss would be proud of.

When they told Greenway, he refused to stop the proceedings. He said Michael could still have a fair hearing. Then Spence jumped into the fray. She insisted that the process should be shut down.

"Do your job," she told Greenway. "You know this is wrong."

Greenway could see she wasn't going to back down. He relented. He said he'd schedule a hearing in January 2013, after a new grand jury was seated.

Spence approached Michael just as he left the courthouse. An FBI agent was in town, she said; his name was Wilfredo Molina and he was investigating his allegations. He had already talked to Spence about the murder-for-hire plot. Now he wanted to talk to Michael.

"I have a good feeling about him," Spence said.

Michael, Nancy, and Huddle followed Spence into a courtroom where the FBI agent was waiting. He didn't look like an FBI agent is supposed to look. No suit and tie. He was a clean-shaven, barrel-chested guy, about five-ten, one hundred and eighty pounds with muscular arms. His black hair was slicked back, and he wore khaki pants and a pale blue sweater. He asked Michael to share his story.

"I've seen things with my eyes that I wish I would never have seen before," Michael said. After two and a half hours with Michael, Molina had more than enough to keep him busy. Before he left, he promised he'd keep everybody updated.

The Rutherford County Courthouse was set up for a big trial. The defendants had four attorneys, and their table in the small courtroom was cluttered with thick binders filled with photos and documents. Sheriff's deputies paid close attention to people walking through the metal detectors.

But this wasn't a high-profile first-degree murder case. It was a simple misdemeanor case involving four Word of Faith Fellowship members accused of stalking, harassment, and false imprisonment.

Misdemeanor cases rarely attract attention. Most people charged with minor crimes agree to a plea bargain. A judge usually fines the defendant or assigns them probation, depending on the charge.

But Whaley saw the misdemeanor charges as yet another battle of good against evil. For over two months, Whaley and her team of lawyers, including Jeffrey Cooper, Mark Morris, and Josh Farmer, prepped for Jerry Cooper's defense. Whaley expected a full acquittal. It would show the public that the church would spare no cost to fight attackers.

She also had help from Webster and Back, the two assistant

North Carolina district attorneys. This time, they did more than just provide legal advice in strategy sessions. On January 1, 2013, while the rest of the county was celebrating New Year's Day, they gathered in the sanctuary for the mock trial to prep the defendants.

Jeffrey Cooper recalled watching Back play the role of prosecutor, trying to trip up the defendants, Randy Fields, Gilbert Carmona, Jason Gross, and Chris Hall, during cross-examination. Webster was the technical adviser, halting the rehearsal whenever a defendant veered off point or made incriminating statements, specifically when it came to whether they stalked Jerry Cooper or prevented him from backing out of his parking space at the mall.

They created a narrative that would exonerate the defendants. They were going to tell the judge they began following Jerry after he drove down a private road leading to the church. He had done so several times before, and everyone was worried he was planning to vandalize church buildings or harass members. So they drove behind him, just in case, and they never blocked his car at the mall. They parked nearby, but Jerry, in a fit of rage, backed up and hit Fields. On the morning of January 4, Whaley and her team of lawyers felt confident going into court.

To Huddle, it was clear neither the judge nor the district attorney had been briefed on past cases involving the church and the lengths they would go to defend its reputation.

At the end of the daylong trial, the verdict was no surprise. The judge acquitted the remaining defendants. The church won.

After Jerry Cooper mustered the strength to leave the courthouse, he told reporters that he was discouraged.

"It proves that nobody can get a fair trial in Rutherford County when that church is involved... It's just the way they are. It's a mind game," he said.

He paused for a moment.

"I will say this…they may not get it in this life, but they will get what's coming to them in the next."

While the church celebrated its victory, Whaley was already planning her next move. She knew Michael was subpoenaed to appear January 9, 2013, before the grand jury. According to her law enforcement sources, Michael had written a letter to Greenway to petition the court for a change of venue.

"The accused in my complaint are members of a 'politically powerful' organization in Rutherford County, namely Word of Faith Fellowship, which appears to have some form of 'influence' that perhaps causes the district attorney, Brad Greenway, and the Rutherford County Sheriff's Department to be biased in pursuing every avenue available in the investigation and possible prosecution of my case," he wrote.

Michael gave specific examples how the sheriff's investigators ignored and undermined his complaint. He recounted how Greenway met with his father before the last grand jury. And he said that sheriff's investigators met with the church's attorneys, including Mark Morris, before the grand jury was convened.

Greenway had dealt with Word of Faith Fellowship for most of his public career, first as the attorney for DSS and now as the district attorney. Greenway believed Michael was telling the truth, but what good would it do to talk to any current church members, the witnesses on Michael's list? He knew from long experience that none of them would talk. They were loyal to Whaley.

If minors made accusations, their stories changed several times. And then, "You're going to have twenty people who come in, who are former Navy pilots, schoolteachers, principals, and they're dressed to the nines, and they're going to say these kids are lying." And the people who escaped the church often had prison records, were drug addicts, alcoholics before. They weren't ideal witnesses.

Michael, however, wasn't a criminal. He wasn't a drug addict or alcoholic. He was a young man with a learning disability. All he was asking for was justice.

On January 9, Michael finally appeared before a grand jury. When Huddle asked him how it went, he smiled. "I think I did OK." He didn't know who else was going to testify. Greenway still didn't speak to him. But Michael said he told jurors the truth, in vivid detail, without wavering. Huddle was proud. Michael wasn't the scared kid who'd fled Word of Faith Fellowship a year before. He'd grown up.

Michael now lived in an apartment in Hickory, North Carolina, a block from Brent Childers's home. Faith in America was helping Michael get adjusted to the outside world. A social worker visited him periodically, to make sure he had everything he needed.

The young man loved his freedom. He smoked cigarettes, used an iPad, watched television. He could come and go as he pleased.

Finally the grand jury decided: there was sufficient evidence for the prosecutor to move ahead with an investigation. Indictments would surely follow.

Whaley called an emergency meeting with the church's top leaders and the men that Michael named in the police complaint. Church leaders told them to lie to anyone who questioned them. They were to tell police that nobody was being held in the Lower Building, that it was a place for prayer and reflection. That Michael was a liar, mentally ill, violent. That one day, Michael snapped, started screaming and shouting, and it took several people to subdue him.

But Whaley was still worried. With all the attention—and the FBI investigation—she knew she'd have to do more to derail the investigation.

★ ★ ★

Michael disappeared. His social worker had received a text from Michael saying he didn't need her help anymore. She notified Brent Childers from Faith of America.

"Did he say why?" Childers asked.

"No. There's something strange about this," she said.

"You're right. I'll go to his apartment. I'll keep you updated," he said.

Childers rushed to Michael's place. All his belongings were still there, including his iPad and wallet. Childers called Huddle, Nancy, anyone he thought might have seen or heard from Michael. No one had.

Michael had been doing well. He seemed optimistic about his future. He'd been talking about going back to school. He'd just gotten word that the church members he named in the police report were going to be indicted.

Did the pressure get to Michael? Did he kill himself? They feared the worst.

Meanwhile, Huddle and Nancy worked the phones. They called Michael's family in Michigan. They called his friends, the people he'd met when he left the church. They all said the same thing: they hadn't seen or heard from Michael.

Nancy shared the news with Spence and Molina. They both said they'd check with their law enforcement sources. A few days later, after they still hadn't heard anything, Nancy called an *Associated Press* investigative reporter.

The reporter headed to the Word of Faith Fellowship compound. He knew the church didn't welcome outsiders, but to his surprise, Whaley agreed to talk. First she offered him a tour of the church. She showed him their school, and the holocaust museum tucked in a section of the church's main building. She said she created it in the aftermath of the church's victory over DSS. She equated her "religious persecution" to the systematic destruction of six million European Jews during

World War II. The students learned about the holocaust and worked on art projects for the museum. The museum was a wonderful promotional tool for Whaley. It was sold as a heart-warming expression of Christian kids' love and regard for the Jewish people. She took it on the road dozens of times, and it was featured in exhibitions in synagogues and events honoring Israel. Parts appeared in a special exhibit at the United States Holocaust Memorial Museum in Washington, DC.

Once the tour was over, she made a stunning statement: Michael Lowry was in the church basement. He had something to say. She'd allow the reporter to talk to Michael as long as she and other church leaders and his family were there.

When the reporter got to the room there was Michael, fidgeting on a couch. He said he initially ran away from the church because his parents discovered he was using a computer to look at pornographic images. He apologized for filing charges, hurting his family, and harming the Fellowship.

"I know I'm going to have to pay for the things that happened," Michael said.

He said he felt so bad the week before that he'd texted his brother to come pick him up. He wanted to go home and make things right.

The *AP* story about Michael's recantation set the church in motion. They contacted law enforcement agencies to let them know that Michael wanted to meet with them, to admit that he'd lied about the beatings.

Unknown to the reporter and others, Michael had been tricked into coming back to the church, lured by a text message from his brother that said their mother was seriously ill. Michael hated the church, but he loved his mother. He told his brother where to pick him up.

When he arrived at his parents' home, he discovered his mother wasn't sick at all, and they wouldn't let him leave. They never left him alone. Not for a minute. He had no phone. No transportation. No way to tell anyone what happened, that he was being held captive and being blasted. He was too scared to go. He was too scared to stay.

After the *AP* interview, Michael's father drove him to the sheriff's office to meet with Keever. But then, for a brief moment on the way, Michael changed his mind and decided to tell Keever he was under pressure to recant.

But as soon as Michael walked into Keever's office, he handed Michael a piece of paper. It was Lowry's recantation, prepared in advance. Lowry was made to sign it. If he lied again, he was warned he'd be in trouble with the law.

But they weren't finished. Just to make sure everyone in the law enforcement community knew Michael had recanted, several church members, including Michael's brother Jonathan and their parents, drove Michael to the FBI office in Asheville.

Michael sat in the waiting area while his brother and Farmer talked to an FBI agent in the next room. Minutes later, Michael was asked into the agent's office. He told the agent that yes, he was recanting, and why. Michael followed the script.

On the way out, Michael said Andrea Firpo, a social worker who works with the FBI, noticed how distressed he looked. She handed him her card with her contact information, just in case he ever wanted to talk.

But as soon as Michael got into the car, his brother ripped the card out of his hand.

As they drove back to Spindale, Michael felt hopeless, helpless, and alone. He'd ruined everything. He might as well be back inside the Lower Building, he thought. He wanted to die.

21

MATTHEW FENNER

Matthew Fenner was sixteen years old in 2010, when his family joined Word of Faith Fellowship. Wiry, neatly dressed, with a quick smile and kind eyes, he grabbed Danielle Cordes's attention right away.

Danielle was always intrigued when new kids arrived. She wondered where they came from, the things they'd seen and done in the world outside. Matthew was something special. His soft voice and body language radiated kindness, something Danielle longed for more than anything.

She fell in love. The church approved. But Matthew was not what he seemed to be. Now, three years later, he was gone. Disappeared. And no one in the church would talk about it. Maybe it was because of the vicious beating he'd taken in the sanctuary, a blasting so violent Danielle thought he might be killed.

Danielle had been there; she had done what she could to stop it. But when she didn't see Matthew in class at Isothermal Community College a few days after the beating, she knew something was very wrong. She asked the professor about Matthew. He said the young man had dropped the class.

She was perplexed. Danielle knew how much school meant to Matthew. If he'd escaped, if he was somewhere on the outside, she'd join him somehow. She had tried to escape before, but didn't get far. This time she'd be more careful. She couldn't take Word of Faith without Matthew. He was her hope.

It was February 2013, nearly eight years after Danielle's involvement with DSS caseworkers and the disastrous settlement that ended the church lawsuit. After that, things got worse for Danielle, who was looked on with suspicion by church leaders. Over the years, Danielle figured she'd been beaten by at least forty different adults in her life—her parents, teachers, principals, and ministers—not to mention being slapped and thrown to the floor countless times by her peers during blasting sessions. Danielle never believed the prayers were meant to help her. No, she believed the people in those circles wanted to hurt others, whether they stomped your toes, yanked your hair, or punched you in the chest. Jane Whaley like to say to "do whatever it takes." In Danielle's life, violence "was normal and encouraged." And how could she forget her freshman year of high school, when an accusation of impure feelings for a boy escalated, leading to a confrontation with Jane Whaley? Whaley alternated hands, slapping her on each side of the face "probably fifty times." The violence only fed her determination to someday escape.

And then Matthew came into her life. Danielle was as naive as all of the children born into the church. She had never held hands, or kissed a boy, but she was sweet on Matthew almost from the beginning.

But Matthew Fenner was not interested in girls. His nascent homosexuality was one of the reasons his mother had joined the church. She thought "strong deliverance" could cure her son's proclivity.

Danielle was confused. She was nineteen years old, but no

one had ever explained the facts of life to her. She had little understanding of homosexuality. No one had ever taught her about sexual intercourse. Three years into a relationship with Matthew, she still held out hope that someday they could be together as a couple.

Matthew and his family first attended a service at the Word of Faith Fellowship in 2010. Matthew thought the church was "a wild mess," and he never wanted to go back. He didn't believe in God, so church seemed like a waste of time.

But his mother, Linda Addington, was impressed. When she heard Whaley preach about the sin of homosexuality, she believed God had led her home.

The year before, Matthew had come out as gay to his family. He'd always known he was different. Even as a child, when his friends talked about growing up and getting married, he pictured himself with a man. When actress Uma Thurman's character kissed Robin in the 1997 movie *Batman and Robin*, Matthew imagined himself kissing actor Chris O'Donnell.

Linda tried to ignore the signs. She believed homosexuality was a sin condemned in the Bible. Once Linda joined the Word of Faith Fellowship, the church's teachings reinforced her fears. Matthew was an angry teen, but now he had a bargaining chip. His mother was intent that he go to church. He agreed to attend the Friday night fellowship meetings if his mom would let him go out with a boy he liked.

Matthew knew his mother couldn't accept him for who he was, but he longed for her love and approval. He agreed to keep an open mind about the church. And the first time he attended a Friday night social event, something surprising happened: he liked it.

Everyone was fun and friendly. Nobody asked about his sexuality. For the first time in years, he felt like he fit in. And there was something else: people in the church seemed so much better-off than his family. While his mom and siblings struggled at times, depending on unemployment and food stamps to get by, people in the church had nice clothes, new cars, and beautiful homes.

When Brooke Covington asked Matthew if they could spend some time together, he happily agreed. She picked him up and drove to a McDonald's restaurant. They ordered from the drive-through window. Matthew, a vegetarian at the time, ordered only water. Brooke ordered a drink and fries. They sat in her car in the parking lot and she asked him about his dreams and aspirations.

The longer they talked, the more comfortable he felt. It was "like a therapy session, only less formal," he later said. He told Brooke about how his parents had divorced when he was a child, and how difficult his relationship with his father had become. His mother got sick, he said, so they had to live with his grandparents.

And Matthew had been sick, too, he said. He'd been diagnosed with melanoma when he was a child. It was in remission now, but he worried about it coming back.

She nodded, listening intently as the young man unloaded a lifetime of pain and resentment. When he finished, he felt relieved. Covington seemed to care about what he had to say. He felt important, like his life and struggles mattered.

Over time, Matthew came to believe that the Word of Faith Fellowship was the right place for him. As soon as his junior year of high school ended, he transferred to the Word of Faith Christian School.

He committed himself to the church, attending events nearly every day. It was a "fresh start," his mother said. She hoped Matthew would meet a nice girl and "live a normal life," maybe even give her grandchildren one day.

Danielle Cordes seemed like a perfect match. She was an

energetic seventeen-year-old from a good family. Danielle's brother and sister had both married Brazilians from the church. Linda made a point of bringing her and Matthew into contact, engaging the girl in conversation during big church fellowship dinners.

"Danielle, are you going to marry a Brazilian, too?" Linda asked one evening. Danielle was surprised by the question, but she knew Linda was new to the church and didn't realize those kinds of questions were off-limits. She didn't make a big deal about it.

"I don't have any plans right now," Danielle responded with a smile. But in her head, she was thinking, *No way. I want to get out of here.*

Matthew was observant by nature, watching closely how others behaved and interacted. He made mental notes of what seemed to please the church leaders and what made them mad. *This place is a big, nonstop psychological game*, he thought. Like a method actor, Matthew slipped into character. He dressed the way he was told and prayed the way he was expected. He told on others when he believed they were in sin, participated in blasting, and "dealt with" people who needed it. And when it was his turn to be blasted, he found a dramatic way to signal a breakthrough: he'd pretend to have a seizure, flopping around on the floor. It was over-the-top, but it thrilled the ministers.

Yes, he had figured things out. Listen to what they say, observe everything that's going on, and just play the part. But there was one part Matthew was not ready for. By their senior year, teenagers were expected to start looking for a mate. It wasn't a surprise when Robin Webster announced to Matthew's class that it was time to start "walking out a relationship."

"Is anyone carrying anyone?" she asked. "If you are, raise your hand."

Danielle lowered her head, wanting to be as small as possible, invisible. She didn't know what to say. She wanted to leave the church. Getting paired up with someone wasn't going to make that any easier.

But Matthew raised his hand. He knew that his mother wanted him to be with Danielle, and if he had to spend time with a girl, it might as well be her. She was friendly and outgoing and, best of all, trustworthy. Only a few ministers in the church knew he was gay, and they were convinced God could change that.

"I feel like I should fellowship with Danielle," he said.

Danielle felt her heart beat faster. Matthew was an outsider. She had wanted to leave the church ever since she was a child. Maybe Matthew would be her way out.

And just like that, they were a couple. They sat together at Friday night youth socials, where couples gathered around tables for pizza and salad. Danielle began having Sunday lunch with Matthew's family.

In time, she developed strong feelings for him. He could sense that she was falling for him, but what could he do? He wanted to tell her he was gay, but he was too afraid. So he continued playing the part, hoping his feelings would eventually change.

In the spring of 2012, Whaley said God wanted the Fenners to move into the Covington house. It seemed a natural fit. Brooke had taken Matthew under her wing. He was allowed to travel with her and the Whaleys when they toured the country with the church's traveling holocaust museum, a coveted position among the church youth. It was a perk that gave him a close-up view of the leaders' hypocrisy.

On the road it was easier to see Jane Whaley's hypocrisy. She watched television in their hotel room, and had several well-worn reasons why it was OK. The Whaleys liked to travel with their dog, and would sneak it into their hotel rooms. "We turn on the TV so nobody will hear the dog," Jane would say.

Matthew just smiled and nodded. After a while, the Whaleys didn't try to hide it anymore. Sam channel surfed right in front of him, and Matthew never said a word. He saw Jane hang up the telephone and laugh with scorn, having just sent some "stupid fool" to the Lower Building. She called followers derogatory names, even while bragging about the expensive gifts they gave her.

Matthew's family moved in with the Covingtons. A dozen other people lived there, too, including Shana Muse's children. All but Patrick, who was doing a stint in the Lower Building. He was back home by early 2013, and he and Matthew found they had a lot in common.

Both were "bubbly and excitable, not hypermasculine." When they could steal moments alone, they talked about the outside world. They realized that when Patrick had been in foster care during the custody battle, they had attended the same elementary school. They knew some of the same people. They talked about music and movies they remembered from their time outside the church, and the things they'd like to do someday. There were giddy moments with a "flirty undertone."

That was dangerous. The ministers noticed.

"The way you two interact with each other is not godly," they were told. "It's not what it means to be a godly man."

One day in late January 2013, Matthew was working in the laundry room at the Covingtons' house when Patrick walked in and closed the door. Spontaneously, as if it was something they couldn't control, they embraced. Then they locked eyes and kissed. It shocked them both.

"We need to go," Matthew said. "If they find us here, we'll be in trouble."

For Matthew, it was a pivotal moment. He had been trying to suppress his feelings for Patrick, but now he felt validated. It was terrifying, too. Matthew shuddered to think what would happen if anyone found out.

The following day they were sent together to paint the basement of a church member's house. While one of them stood on a ladder painting, the other grabbed a leg, slowly edging his hand higher, trying to see how far things would go. Eventually they were touching each other's crotches, enjoying the excitement of a new, forbidden romance.

Danielle was oblivious to it all.

When Brooke and Jayne Caulder pulled her aside after a church service, they only confused her.

"We know that you know about Matthew's problem," Brooke said. "You need to deal with his sin. If you don't do something, he is going to leave the church. If that happens, his blood will be on your hands."

Danielle nodded, but she had no idea what Brooke was talking about. She knew Matthew was a little different than other boys in the church, but strict rules forbade any kind of intimate knowledge of his character, much less his sexuality. Everyone worked hard to keep her in ignorance, then expected her to understand it all.

She'd been taught there was a sin called "homosexuality," but that was it. Sexuality was a taboo subject, and homosexuality was beyond the realm of her understanding. Danielle couldn't figure it out exactly, but she knew something was seriously wrong.

Ever since they'd moved in with the Covingtons, Sarah and Rachel, Shana Muse's daughters, were on the fast track to becoming ministers.

They never talked about their mother. After months of rejection, drama, and shunning, Shana had decided to take a step back, trusting that someday her children would realize she loved them and had fought as hard as she could for them. Maybe someday they'd come to their senses. She returned to Florida and moved on with her life.

Years passed, and Sarah and Rachel became Brooke's side-kicks. They sat alongside as Brooke and Jane discussed church business at the dinner table. They were good girls. They followed the rules, and made sure others did, too.

Sarah was assigned to "watch over" Matthew at church and school, so it was no surprise when she approached Danielle after the Sunday morning service on January 27, 2013.

"I think there's something going on with Matthew," Sarah said.

"What do you think it is?" Danielle asked.

"I don't know—he just kept smirking at Patrick. I feel like something is going on between them. I think he has the unclean," Sarah said.

That night after church, Matthew was taken aside by Brooke, Sarah, and Sarah's husband, Nick Anderson. They asked him to "open up about the sin in his life."

At the same time Jayne Caulder accused Danielle of having "perversions" for her sister, meaning their relationship was too personal. "You need prayer," Caulder said.

Danielle knew exactly what to do. She "went through the motions," listened to the screaming, confessed her sin, and "had a breakthrough."

When it was over, Danielle noticed a commotion across the room, where a growing number of people had surrounded Matthew. They were blasting him. She wanted to go over to him, but Caulder waved her away. Matthew started to scream, real bloodcurdling screams.

Danielle bolted to the other side of the sanctuary, where Matthew was seated within a circle of nearly two dozen people. Brooke was pushing on his chest, screaming, "Open your heart!"

Sarah slapped him hard in the face, leaving four red fingerprints on his cheek. Before he knew what was happening, Matthew was being shoved and punched. He weighed only about one hundred and thirty pounds, and a week earlier doctors had taken biopsies to ensure his melanoma hadn't returned.

"The way you hold your hands, the way you cross your legs, that's all homosexual devils. We are going to get it out of you," Brooke screamed. "Did you have homosexual thoughts in a dream? Did your body manifest?"

Danielle had seen and heard many blasting sessions over the years, but this seemed more frightening, more hysterical, and clearly more violent. She shivered when she heard her name.

"Danielle, get over her and deal with your friend," Brooke shouted.

When Danielle approached, Brooke "shoved" her into the middle of the circle. Matthew was crying and pleading, shaking his head, denying he'd done anything wrong. Danielle had to do something or she'd be in the same spot.

"Matthew, you better tell your sin," Danielle wailed.

Others joined in.

"Come out of him, you wicked demon. You're so wicked!"

"You disgust me!"

"You're going to die and go to hell."

"You satanist!"

"You're going to burn in hell."

"He's not saying what his sin is," Brooke exclaimed. Sarah and Patrick's brother, Justin, grabbed Matthew and began "beating him in the sternum." Adam Bartley stood behind Matthew "with his hands wrapped around his neck," shaking hard. With every line of the prayer came another blow to Matthew's chest. Matthew felt "frail." All he could think was, *Is my neck going to break? Am I going to die?*

Danielle thought he might. All the punching, slapping, choking, being thrown to the floor only to be picked up and beaten more. At one point he lost consciousness and urinated in his pants. It went on for two hours.

Danielle couldn't watch Adam Bartley choking him anymore. She slid her hands under Bartley's fingers, "trying to peel them off."

Bartley looked at Danielle with wide eyes, then turned to tell Brooke she was interfering. Danielle knew what would happen if she was accused of "getting in the way of God's will." She had to think fast. She brought up Matthew's biopsy on his neck.

"Adam, wait, wait, wait," she pleaded. "He just had surgery on his neck. Remember?"

Bartley paused and shook his head, satisfied with Danielle's explanation. He pulled his hands away.

Matthew finally got his "breakthrough." He panted on the floor, dripping with sweat. His face was ghostly white, his eyes dark and sunken. To Danielle, he looked "like a dead person."

The crowd broke up. Danielle helped Matthew to his feet and helped him get home.

Matthew felt like he'd been flattened by a truck, but there was no time to rest. He had to get out. He waited until Patrick passed in the hallway, then pushed him into the bathroom.

"Look, Patrick, after what happened tonight, I'm getting out of here," Matthew said. "They're going to get on to me again. It's about to get really bad for me here. I can't do it. I've got to go. If I'm going to be safe, I have to leave. You can come with me if you want. Either way, I have to go."

Patrick didn't hesitate. "I'm coming," he said.

"OK. So let's give it till tomorrow. Tomorrow night we're

out of here," Matthew said. "You just need to listen to what
I say and do it. Just trust me."

Matthew went over the plans. The next night, they'd each
pack a bag, making it look like they were taking work clothes
for a church project.

"Just get what you need. We can't try to take too much.
We won't have time. And we can't make anyone suspicious,"
he said.

Then at 2:10 a.m. they'd sneak out of the house, jump into
his mother's car, and drive to his grandparents' house. He
knew they'd take them in. They had been trying to get him
out of the church for years.

The next night, everything was set. Matthew kept checking the clock, but couldn't sleep. He still had some time, so he
went to his mother's room and crawled onto her bed.

"How are you doing, Mom?" he asked, hugging her.

"I'm fine, Matthew. How are you?"

"I'm fine. I need to get ready for bed," he said. "I just
wanted to say I love you."

"I love you, too."

Matthew palmed the car keys on the night table. He glanced
back as he was walking out of the room. He wondered if he
would see her again. He went to his room, which he shared
with his younger brother, Madison, and chatted to him until
he drifted off to sleep.

Matthew set the alarm for 1:55 a.m., but he didn't need it.
He couldn't sleep. He listened as people came into the house
from working late at church projects. He counted each time
the door closed, trying to account for everyone in the house.
His heart raced.

When it was time to meet Patrick, Matthew grabbed a
backpack and tossed in extra underwear and a stuffed cordu-
roy bear he'd had since childhood. He slipped on his shoes

and began to tiptoe toward the stairs. Suddenly, he heard a bang. He crept down the stairs as fast as he could to the ground floor. It was Patrick; he was coming up another set of stairs from the basement, carrying his trombone. He'd banged it against the wall.

"Put that down and go," he whispered. "Go, go, go! Don't look back," Matthew said. "We've gotta get out of here."

They ran out of the house and down Brooke Breeze Lane, through the woods and finally into Matthew's mother's white Ford Edge.

"Here we go!" Matthew said.

Patrick was excited, like a bank robber making an escape after a daring heist. "I can't believe we're doing this!"

Matthew turned the key, yanked the stick into Reverse, and stomped the gas pedal, nearly slamming into another vehicle parked in the driveway. He took a deep breath and glanced at Patrick.

"This is it," Matthew said. He shifted the car into gear and sped down the winding driveway onto Hunting Drive, past the homes of other church members.

"I'm free. I can't believe it, I'm free!" Patrick shouted.

"I know," Matthew said. "Let's listen to some music."

Matthew pulled out his phone and played the song "Fragile" by John Ralston, soaking in the lyrics he loved before the church took away his ungodly music: "We're so fragile, we're so calm. We are innocent of what went wrong…"

Matthew gripped the steering wheel with both hands, hugging curves and blowing through stop signs. Patrick rolled down the window and let out a long "woohoo."

As they pulled into the driveway of Matthew's grandparents' house, the two looked at one another and let out a sigh.

"We made it," Matthew said. "Let's go inside."

Matthew's grandfather answered the door and wiped the sleep from his eyes. "What's going on?" he asked.

"Something bad happened. We had to get out of there," Matthew said. "Can you please take me to drop Mom's car off? I don't want to get in trouble for taking it."

Matthew drove the car alone. His grandfather and Patrick followed in another vehicle. Matthew left his mother's car just down the hill from the Covington home. Riding back with his grandfather, he stared out the window.

"Are y'all sure you want to do this?" his grandfather asked. "You know what's going to happen."

"Yes," Matthew said. "We had to get out."

"Well, you know they're going to be calling. They're going to try to get you back."

"I know," Matthew said. "It's going to be a big mess. I just can't stay there anymore. A bunch of stuff happened. There's no way I can go back."

"You know I'll do whatever I can to help you."

When they got back to his grandparents' house, Matthew and Patrick told them everything.

It was worse than his grandparents had imagined. They promised to stand by the boys.

"Well, we better get some sleep," his grandfather said. "It's going to be a long day tomorrow."

Patrick and Matthew spent the night in a spare room, whispering about everything that had happened. The next morning, as expected, Matthew's mother and Rachel Covington barged in the door. Linda raced over to her son and got in his face.

"Why are you doing this? Just look at you. I can tell the devil's all over you," she shouted.

"I had to, Mom. Don't you understand? Didn't you see how they beat on me?"

"No, Matthew. You don't have to do this. If you leave the things that God has done for you, you are going to get cancer again and die."

Rachel stood nearby, glaring at Matthew.

"I always thought you were the sweetest person," she said. "Why are you taking my brother away from me?"

"I'm not doing any of that," Matthew snapped. "Y'all know exactly what y'all did to me. What you did was wrong. The things that go on in that place are wrong."

Matthew's aunt, Lynn Rape, had heard enough. "Linda, if y'all are going to come in here and be belligerent, you need to leave."

Linda and Rachel refused.

"Come with me, Patrick," Rachel said. "Let's go talk in the other room."

"No," Rape snapped. "I'm calling the police. I already asked y'all to leave."

As Rape phoned the sheriff's department, Linda and Rachel relented and left.

When a deputy arrived, he asked Matthew what had happened. He told the officer everything. The attack. The escape. The deputy listened, then asked if the young man wanted to file a report.

Matthew shook his head. Not yet. "I just need to process everything. I mean, I've been through all this mess. I haven't had any sleep. Can we do this later? I just can't do this right now. I can't think."

The deputy handed Matthew a card and left.

While Matthew tried to decide what to do, Danielle had already figured out her next move. She'd bolt from the church and track down Matthew. When she found him, she'd tell him she loved him.

22

DANIELLE'S SALVATION

Susanna Kokkonen, a famous holocaust expert, was coming to Word of Faith Fellowship in early March 2013. She would speak at a Wednesday service and tour the Christian School Holocaust Museum. Originally from Finland, Kokkonen now lived in Israel. She lobbied on behalf of Israel, and had served as the director of the Christian Friends of Yad Vashem, the World Holocaust Remembrance Center in Jerusalem.

This was a big deal, and Jane Whaley's prestige was on the line. The compound buzzed with activity. Everything had to be perfect.

None of that mattered to Danielle Cordes. Kokkonen's visit would give Danielle the opportunity she'd waited for.

Danielle was nineteen years old. She had every legal right to leave the church, but she didn't know that. She had hoped she and Matthew might escape together one day, but now he was already gone. She'd have to do it on her own.

It wasn't until she started searching for Matthew and asking questions that someone told her the stark truth: Matthew was queer. He liked boys. He wasn't interested in girls.

At first, Danielle didn't believe it. Maybe it was just another smear by church leaders upset that he'd got away. Was she not pretty enough for him? Was that it?

Then anger set in. He'd duped her. He'd used her to fit in at the church, and didn't care about her feelings. He should have told her. The ministers, too, let her make a fool of herself. But as weeks passed, she finally came to terms with reality: Matthew was gay. They could never be married.

Danielle put on a good show after that, denouncing Matthew like everyone else. "He's in sin," she said. "The devil took him over." She didn't really feel that way at all. Inside, she was still processing what had happened.

Now she had no reason to stay, so she started planning a way out. She had no car or money or place to go, but she knew now that Matthew was still in the area. She might have to turn to him for help.

She had tried phoning Matthew several times after he left, but he never answered, and never returned her calls. Maybe with time he would.

Danielle decided to stay around until the school semester ended, to give herself a little time. Besides, her cousin John David Cooper was getting married in April. She liked John. She wanted to go to his wedding.

But time ran out.

Robin Webster called. The Lord had spoken, and He wanted Danielle to pair up with another boy. Danielle couldn't believe the audacity. Weren't they just telling her that it was God's plan for her to marry Matthew? But Danielle knew she had to keep her cool. She asked who it was, and Robin said it was Nathan, a boy Danielle had grown up with.

"What do you think about that?" she asked.

Danielle wanted to scream. Nathan? He was annoying.

She felt nothing for him but contempt. But she had to hold her tongue.

So for the next few Friday night fellowships, Danielle put on her happy face while she planned her escape. If she stayed too long, they'd do something underhanded to make her marry Nathan. And then her life would be over.

It was time to make a move. The holocaust thing would be her opportunity.

On the morning of Kokkonen's visit, Danielle watched everyone around her scramble. She rode to the church with her mother to make some final preparations. It was time to take the first step in her escape plan.

"Mom, I'm really behind on my schoolwork," Danielle said. "Do you mind if I sit in the car and do some homework? Would that be OK?"

"Sure," her mother said. "I'll be inside."

Danielle did her sociology homework. She knew the next few days would be chaotic, whether she made it out or she got caught trying. Education was her only chance to make it on the outside. She had seen too many people dependent on the church. She didn't want to end up like that.

When she finished, she closed her book. *Stay focused*, she thought. After the event, Danielle went home while her parents stayed behind to straighten up. Danielle paid close attention as she walked up the stairs, trying to commit to memory the boards that creaked. She couldn't risk making a sound when she sneaked out.

She took a shower and slipped on a pair of sweatpants and packed a couple of changes of clothes in her backpack with her computer and schoolbooks. She didn't want to leave behind anything essential. She knew the church would hold her stuff to persuade her to come back, or even throw her books away to make it difficult to keep up with her studies.

Danielle heard the front door open. Her parents and her brother had returned. Shortly before midnight everyone seemed to be asleep. She cracked open her bedroom door. The house was quiet.

She grabbed her backpack and tiptoed down the stairs. She placed the backpack near the front door and then headed back to her room to make the call. Soon as she rounded a corner at the top of the stairs, she looked up and saw her brother standing there. She had to think fast. He was younger than Danielle, so she pulled rank.

"What are you doing up?" she snapped. "Go back to bed. It's late."

"OK," he said. "Good night."

God, that scared the crap out of me, Danielle thought. But she didn't have time to waste. She walked into her room, sat on the bed, pulled out her phone. She was paralyzed with fear. What if he didn't answer? She had to try. She had nowhere else to turn. Matthew answered on the first ring.

"It's me, Danielle," she said, whispering.

"What do you want?" Matthew snapped, expecting her to start with typical church bullshit.

"I wouldn't be whispering if I wasn't in trouble," Danielle said.

He could tell by the tone of her voice she was serious. "Do you want to leave?"

"Yes," she said. "Please, please help me."

"I'll be at the end of your driveway in five minutes," Matthew said.

Matthew turned to Patrick and Jeanna Powell, another former member. They were hanging out at his grandparents' house. Jeanna was born into the Word of Faith Fellowship, but had left in 2008. Her grandmother Sandra Norris was Jane Whaley's first cousin, and a charter member of the church.

Meanwhile, Danielle crept down the stairs, careful to skip the squeaky boards. She looked around one last time. This was it. Everyone was asleep. She grabbed her backpack, quietly opened the door, and slipped outside. Then she ran as fast as she could, as hard as she'd ever run before, sixty yards down the hill and then up the other side, her pack bouncing against her back. She could see the silhouette of a car parked on the road with its lights off. She looked back to make sure no one was following her, then jumped inside and closed the door.

"Let's get out of here," she said.

"Are you OK?" Jeanna asked, stomping the gas.

"Yes," Danielle said. "Just take me to the sheriff's department, please."

"Why? What happened?"

"My parents are going to be looking for me. I just need to make sure they don't think I'm kidnapped. I need to tell the police that I left and never want to go back, in case they come and snatch me."

"OK, Danielle," Jeanna said.

It was well after midnight, so there were few other cars on the road. It took only a couple of minutes to make the four-mile drive into downtown Rutherfordton. Danielle was shaking as they pulled into the sheriff's department parking lot.

She got of the car and looked around. The law firm of Mark Morris and Joshua Farmer was just across North Washington Street, but the place was empty. Danielle approached the first deputy she saw.

"I need your help," Danielle said. "I just left my church. Well, my parents' house. I don't want to go back. I'm scared they are going to come find me."

"What church?" the deputy asked.

"The Word of Faith Fellowship," Danielle said.

"Oh, that place," the deputy said, nodding. "Do you have your ID on you?"

"Yes, sir," Danielle said, her hand trembling as she handed him her cards.

"Ma'am, you're nineteen. You're an adult. You don't have to go back. Nobody can make you. You're old enough to make your own decisions."

Danielle was stunned. She felt relieved, and stupid. There was so much she didn't know about the world.

"What if my parents think I'm missing? Or that I was kidnapped?" Danielle asked. "What if they come looking for me? What if they file a report?"

"I can see that you're fine," he said. "Obviously, you aren't missing."

"Thank you, sir," Danielle said. "Have a good night."

It was almost three in the morning when the group got back to Matthew's grandfather's house. Danielle should have been exhausted, but she was running on adrenaline.

"Do you think they are going to come looking for me?" Danielle asked.

"Yes, of course they will," Matthew said. He recounted how his mother and Rachel barged through his grandparents' front door and told him he was full of demons and going to hell.

"Did the police do anything?" Danielle asked.

"They asked me if I wanted to file a report, but I was just too exhausted. I told him that I needed time to process everything."

"Did you ever go back and file a report?"

Robynn Spence, the clerk of courts, had put Matthew in touch with an FBI agent named Fred Molina. He'd told him about the night he was beaten, the children assaulted in the school, and adults attacked and beaten in church services.

"He said he was going to investigate. He really seemed to care," Matthew said.

He said Molina was the same agent investigating the Lowry case. Even though Michael had recanted, Matthew was optimistic since his case was different.

Danielle didn't know anything about Michael's allegations. She never knew there was a group of people on the outside trying to help. She had never heard of Robynn Spence or most of the names Matthew dropped during his conversation.

"I hope they do something about the church," Danielle said.

Patrick was feeling overwhelmed. He wanted to forget about Word of Faith Fellowship. "I'm tired of talking. Let's watch a movie."

Danielle made an embarrassing confession. "I've never watched a movie before," she said.

"I know the perfect one. It's called *Uptown Girls*," Patrick said, giggling. "There's a sassy little girl in the movie that reminds me of you, Danielle. You have to watch it. It will be fun."

So Patrick popped in a DVD and hit Start.

Danielle was enthralled by the movie. It was a love story. "Are these people together in real life?" she asked. "Like, is this real? Are they really a couple?"

Matthew and Patrick looked at one another and smiled.

"No," Matthew said. "It's just a movie. They're just actors, playing a part."

She focused on one scene, where the main character watches her ex-boyfriend on a music video singing a song called "Sheets of Egyptian Cotton."

"Wow, listen to that. That song doesn't even have anything to do with God," she said.

The others laughed. "Yeah, there's a lot of music that's not about God. And some of it's really good," Patrick said.

Danielle went to the kitchen for a drink. Matthew followed her in, and apologized to her. He hadn't meant to lead her on, he said, but for him, having a girlfriend was the only way to survive. He said church leaders told him not to say a word about his sexuality. Danielle said she was hurt, but she understood. And now they were friends for life.

Danielle's phone startled her awake in the morning. She looked at the number. "It's my parents," she said. "They know I'm gone."

Jeanna offered to take her to the sheriff's office. They would help her return home to collect her things. Danielle was nervous. Yes, the deputy the night before said she was free. But she was still in the emotional grip of the church, and they'd try any manipulation to get her back.

At the sheriff's office, Danielle talked to Chris Atkins, a lieutenant in the department.

"I need to get my stuff from my parents' house, but I'm afraid they will try to make me stay," she said.

"Why would they do that?" Atkins asked.

"They are in the Word of Faith Fellowship. They always try to make people stay."

Atkins nodded. He had been through this more times than he could remember. He told her she had two options: a deputy could escort her, or he could call her father and ask if he'd allow her friends to help her get her belongings.

Danielle asked Atkins if he'd make the call and give her father the options. Stephen Cordes answered.

"Those people are not allowed on my property under any circumstances," Cordes snapped. Atkins told Cordes his daughter had the right to collect her things. He said a deputy would escort Danielle and her friend. Jeanna and Danielle got in a car together. An officer followed them.

"What should I do when we get there?" Danielle asked. She was trembling, terrified her parents would try to hold her in the house.

"Let's trade phones. They can't confiscate mine. I will keep yours in the car with me," Jeanna said. "And before you go inside, call me. While you're in there, you can keep it on speakerphone so I can hear if anything happens."

"That's a good idea," Danielle said, her hand shaking as she opened the car door. "I'm scared."

"I know," said Jeanna, offering encouragement to her friend. She handed her phone to Danielle. "Remember, you can do this. I'll be right here listening. If you need help, just tell me."

As she walked to the house, Danielle relayed every movement like a play-by-play announcer at a ball game.

"I'm walking in the door," she said. "Now I'm going up the stairs to my room."

Danielle piled everything she could onto her bed. She knew it might be her only shot. As she knelt down to pull some clothes out of a bottom drawer, her mother snatched the phone from her hand and hung it up.

"What are you doing, Danielle?" Cindy said. "The demons are taking you over. You cannot do this. If you leave, you are going to die and go to hell."

Danielle didn't want to get into a scuffle with her mother, but she had to do something. She yanked the phone out of her mother's hands and called Jeanna back. Her father walked into the room and closed the door behind him.

"Send the police in," Danielle shouted. "I'm scared."

"You're going to regret this," her father said. "You know they are not allowed to come in our house without a warrant. They have no right. You have no right to do this to us."

But he was mistaken. The officer rushed into the house and stood by as Danielle collected the rest of her things.

Stephen Cordes followed his daughter down the stairs and out the door, chastising her all the way.

"I want that phone back," he said. "I paid for it. It's my phone."

Danielle nodded. It was not unexpected. Jeanna had already wiped the memory clean so that nobody would know who she had been communicating with on the outside. Danielle grabbed the phone from Jeanna, tossed it to her father, and jumped in the car.

"Let's go," Danielle said.

Danielle stared out the window on the way back to Matthew's grandparents' home. She had not slept. She was afraid. But she had a sense of hope, something that had been so rare throughout her life.

Her mind drifted back to her childhood. The spankings, the punches, being dragged around by her hair. She could picture the little girl in the mirror, wearing her pink dress and matching shoes. The child who had to make sure everything was just right so the social workers would take her away. So much had happened since then. More beatings. More isolation. Being paired with a man she could never love.

In the end, nearly everyone in her life had let her down. Her parents, her preachers. The social workers who closed her case and walked away. No matter how much she prayed, nobody had saved her. She had to do that herself.

Did God allow this to happen? she wondered. So much pain, in the name of Jesus.

23

THE WEDDING

John David Cooper donned his crisp black pants, buttoned the studs on his white shirt, and tugged on the shoelaces of his polished black shoes to make sure they were just so. He slipped his arms into his jacket sleeves, and pinned a white carnation to his lapel. His pale skin was shaved smooth; his short black hair was neatly trimmed.

It was April 30, 2013, his wedding day.

The wedding would be like all the others at the church, a carefully choreographed affair. Part Broadway musical, part Holy Ghost revival. Would he remember the lyrics to the wedding song that Whaley had composed for them to sing? Would he recall the vows she helped write for them—words that focused more on devoting their lives to the church than to each other?

If he stammered or blanked out, he knew Whaley and her ministers would accuse him of giving in to the unclean. John didn't want that, not on what was supposed to be the happiest day of his life. John glanced at his watch: it was close to 1:00 p.m. Peter was late.

John had asked his brother to drive him to the ceremony.

He paced in the silent house, wondering why he was doing this. He was only twenty-one. He was about to marry a virtual stranger, a woman who'd never been alone in a room with him. What would they talk about when they were finally together? He had never thought that far ahead, and now he knew why.

John never thought his relationship with Jessica Fields would get this far. Marrying Jessica was Jane Whaley's idea. He'd just wanted to date her. But there was no turning back. Not when Whaley had proclaimed from the pulpit that this was God's will. Now here he was, five years on, dressed in a tuxedo.

What would happen when they were finally alone? He had never kissed a girl before, let alone initiated sex. If it wasn't for his biology books in college, he wouldn't know anything about sex at all. In the weeks leading up to the wedding, John couldn't stop thinking about it.

It didn't do any good thinking about it. They didn't have permission to have sex.

The only good thing he could imagine about getting married was moving out of the Covingtons' basement. He hated everything about their place: the beige walls, hunter green carpet, tiny windows with the miniblinds shut tight. Those awful paintings of aristocrats in red jackets hunting foxes on horseback.

Like most of the older Cooper men, John was plucked from his house as a teenager and forced to live with ministers. It happened to Jeffrey, Benjamin, and Peter. Even now, when his three older brothers and Chad were married men, they didn't have places of their own. They lived with their wives' parents. And that would be John's fate, too. Not even his sister Lena escaped. She married a member of the Brazilian church in 2012 and was living with her husband's parents outside São Paulo.

The doorbell rang. John bounded up the stairs and answered the front door.

"Ready?" Peter asked.

John nodded.

He followed Peter to his white Nissan parked in the long driveway. They jumped in the car and Peter began driving to the church.

"Thank you," John said to his brother.

"For what?"

"For helping me move."

Peter smiled. "You'd do the same for me, right?"

"Yes. I would. You know it."

For weeks, Peter had worked with John to transform Jessica's single bedroom into a marriage suite. Whaley had wanted the couple to live in Jessica's parents' house, so they painted the pink room white and put up bright red curtains. They bought an oak dresser and matching headboard, two nightstands, and a fluffy white down comforter. Only one thing remained from Jessica's past: a four-foot-long pink "body pillow." She didn't want to part with that last vestige of her teenage years.

The brothers had bonded on their daily drive to Wofford College. They scheduled more classes together so it was just the two of them in the car. They didn't hesitate to turn on the radio and listen to music. They talked candidly about the church and their lives. They both hated the church. They knew medical school was their ticket out, but they'd have to broach the subject with their wives, who were deeply committed to the church.

John stared out the car window. It was a perfect day for a wedding, he thought, a pristine blue sky, peach and apple trees in full bloom. As they approached the church compound, John saw the hundreds of cars overflowing the parking lot.

Inside, members of the congregation scurried from one building to the next, carrying trays of food or floral arrangements. Others herded tuxedo-clad children into the church building, where the ceremony was about to begin.

Peter navigated his Nissan past the other cars and let his brother out near the sanctuary entrance. John took a deep breath and then walked slowly into the building, passing well-wishers on his way to Jane Whaley's office. He stopped outside the sanctuary doors to peek at the activity inside. Whaley was standing to the side of the big stage up front, directing traffic and barking orders.

Like a finely tuned production, everyone had a job to do. A team of seamstresses had sewn the bridesmaids' fuchsia-colored dresses and matching jackets. Now they were throwing a few last-minute stitches. Members of the church orchestra were tuning violins, cellos, trumpets, and flutes. Ushers took their spots at the end of the rows of chairs. It was all coming together, from the elaborate floral arrangements—clusters of pink, white, and red carnations—to the matching candles placed strategically around the stage.

As he ran through his lines again, John's head filled once again with questions about what would happen after this. Whaley did her best to isolate the congregation from the world outside, but John knew better. He would soon have his biology degree, and he felt more restless than ever.

He tried to focus on Jessica. She was beautiful. And maybe in time, he'd learn to love her. He'd recently heard that she had tried to run away a year or so earlier, but was caught and brought back. So maybe there was hope that she wanted out, too. Maybe they could find a path together. But first, John had to find out if he could trust her. Maybe when they were alone after the wedding, he would find out.

The music started. John's father approached him.

"Good luck, son," Rick said.

John forced a smile.

"I want you to know that I prayed for you. I want you to have a long and successful marriage," he said.

Rick hoped Jessica was the right one, and that they'd find happiness. But Rick knew eventually Whaley would ruin John's marriage, just like she'd ruined his.

His marriage had gone from bad to worse. After being released from the Lower Building, Rick moved back home, but he and Suzanne were strangers. They hadn't slept in the same bed since 2006. They barely spoke to each other.

Rick had spent more than a year in the Lower Building. During that time, his financial problems had reached the breaking point, so he filed for bankruptcy protection. In the court filing, he listed $382,000 in assets, including his house, and $491,000 in liabilities. Between his credit cards and mortgage, he just couldn't keep up.

But even deeply in debt, he still tithed about $300 a month to the church. With "love offerings" and additional collections taken at multiple weekly services, Rick knew that figure was much higher. He did the math: if every member in just the Spindale church tithed like him—$3,600 a year—Jane was making millions.

He didn't want to think about that at his son's wedding. Rick wanted to talk to John a little more, but his son was on his way to the church office. Rick nodded and watched him go.

When John walked inside, his bride was already there. He stopped in his tracks. Jessica looked stunning in her long white dress. He couldn't compliment her because of all the people in the room. Just before the ceremony started, Holly Morris and Robin Webster asked everyone to leave except John and Jessica. When they did, Morris closed the door.

Morris told the couple they wanted to go over "the rules."

"The rules?" John asked.

"Yes," she said. "When you get home tonight, you can give

Jessica a godly hug and godly kiss. Then you just roll over and go to sleep."

John was stunned, but John and Jessica didn't say a word.

"When you're ready for the next step, let us know and we will talk about it," Webster said.

John and Jessica headed in separate directions. She'd walk in with the women, while John would be accompanied by the men. In the sanctuary, Joe English was up onstage, clean-shaven and tuxedo clad, a far cry from his Paul McCartney days. English was belting out "There's Something About That Name," a sweet hymn written by William and Gloria Gaither, musical legends in the Charismatic Christian world.

The congregation joined in the song, smiling and swaying, some raising their hands to the heavens. When John and Jessica took their seats, Sam Whaley walked to the pulpit and then asked everyone to bow their heads in prayer.

"Father, we're just so honored and blessed to be with John David and Jessica today..." he said. "We know You have a plan for them and a purpose for their lives."

That was the cue for the children to make their grand entrance. Dozens of boys in tuxedos and girls in white dresses moved to the front of the stage to sing. Whaley's grandson, Brock, sang a solo. Then Jane Whaley took the stage in a sparkling fuchsia outfit made to match the bridesmaids' dresses.

John tuned her out. He couldn't stop thinking about what the ministers told him before the ceremony: No kissing. No touching. No nothing.

He was so angry he almost missed the cue for the wedding song. When he heard the opening chords, he jumped up from his chair. He grabbed a microphone, and handed another to Jessica.

"We are expecting a miracle to take place, a miracle where two become one flesh by God's grace," they sang in unison.

Despite his reservations, John belted the dreary Whaley-penned song about Jesus and "darkness" and proving wrong "every tongue that rises up against us."

When the music ended, it was time for their testimonies—a pledge to Whaley and the church. John and Jessica knew these had to be perfect; there were outside guests in the audience. They made it through, but the wedding was far from over.

The children's choir sang another song. Adults sang solos. The ceremony went on and on, an endless procession of music and prayer. When the singing and worship were finally over, the couple recited their vows, but John wasn't told to kiss the bride. Instead, everyone in the sanctuary was invited to come forward and greet the newlyweds. The ceremony had dragged on for more than two hours. For John, it felt like an eternity.

The reception was more like a giant potluck dinner—everyone brought a dish: sandwiches, coleslaw, potato salad, fruit. There was no wedding cake. For Whaley, a wedding cake was too worldly—the little figurines of the bride and groom perched on a pedestal struck her as tiny idols, stealing God's glory.

After the reception, John and Jessica returned to the Fieldses' house, hoping for some alone time. But the house was filled with family and friends. At ten o'clock, John excused himself from the living room. He turned to Jessica. "I'm going upstairs. Are you coming?"

Jessica hesitated.

"Well?" John said.

"OK," she said softly.

She followed John up the flight of stairs. She went to the bathroom to change. Meanwhile, John put on a pair of shorts and a T-shirt. Jessica emerged, wearing a V-neck T shirt and floppy leggings. Before he had a chance to say a word, she crawled into the bed and pulled the covers up to her neck. The big pink pillow was planted between them.

Damn, he thought.

"Can you turn off the light?" she asked.

This was it. If something was going to happen, it had to be now. John walked to her side of the bed. "Look, could we at least, you know, kiss?"

Jessica raised her eyebrows in disbelief. "What?"

"I was just thinking..."

He didn't have a chance to finish the sentence. Jessica jumped out of bed and bolted into her parents' room.

John didn't know what to do. At first, he stood there in stunned silence. He moved into the hallway and placed his ear against the Fieldses' bedroom door. He could only hear the sound of muffled voices.

A few minutes later, Cynthia opened the door and handed her cell phone to John. It was Robin Webster.

Webster told John that yes, he had permission to kiss Jessica. But she added that Jessica just "wasn't ready." She told John to go to sleep.

"Don't touch her. I don't want to hear that you even rubbed up against her elbow," Webster said.

John was confused, angry, and hurt. He hadn't done anything wrong, he'd only asked for a kiss. Was that too much? Jessica was his wife. This was their wedding night.

John had believed that Jessica might be willing to push the rules a little. Hell, she'd run away once, right? So he thought that maybe they'd have a kiss. And in the back of his mind, he thought that maybe they'd have sex, too. And beyond that, maybe, they'd talk about leaving the church.

But now he wasn't sure of anything.

All he knew was that his wife was in their bed with a big pillow parked between them—a perfect metaphor for their marriage. Like his parents, they were married, but they weren't.

24

THE FIGHT FOR JUSTICE

Matthew Fenner was stunned, then distraught. Weeks after he met with FBI agent Fred Molina, he received a letter saying the agency was no longer investigating his case, and Michael Lowry was to blame.

Apparently, the FBI had combined Matthew's and Lowry's cases and linked them together in one case file. When Michael recanted, the FBI simply closed its investigation into the Word of Faith Fellowship.

When Matthew told Nancy Burnette and John Huddle, they were livid. Spence was feeling stalled, too. Someone had threatened her life, but she hadn't heard a word about her case since she made the initial report. She took her concerns to Jack Conner, the former sheriff.

"If I was still sheriff, you know I'd be all over it. It would be priority," he told her. "Have they tried to talk to the hit man? That would've been my first step," he said.

Spence didn't know, but she tried to stay optimistic. "I'm still holding out hope that they'll do something."

Jane felt secure enough to attack the young runaways from

the pulpit. Whaley called Matthew "one of the strongest youth ministers," but he was lost now to the "unclean."

She pointed out the waymarks on the road to perdition: "The next thing you know, they got their Facebook... They're playing their ungodly music. I haven't seen [Matthew and Patrick] in their jeans yet, but it'll come. You watch the devil come to those jeans. It always does," Whaley warned.

"The next thing they do is celebrate their Christmases. They celebrate all their pagan holidays. They go back to their Satan worship full-time... And then the demons possess them, where they can't come out. I don't know if Matthew and Patrick will ever find God again," she said.

It was June 7, 2014, when Matthew Fenner first met with a detective in an unmarked police car in a park in Forest City. He'd asked the Rutherford County Sheriff's Office for a private interview about an assault that had happened four months before. He wanted to meet somewhere far from the prying eyes in the courthouse. Detective Joey Sisk said, "Sure thing."

When Sisk arrived, Matthew jumped into his car. Sisk was all business. He pulled out a notepad. He wanted to know every detail—everyone who was in the room that night and what role they played in the attack.

Matthew named everybody he could remember and also gave names of corroborating witnesses, including Danielle Cordes.

In the months since she fled, Danielle had moved to Florida to live with an aunt. If things went right, she'd start at the University of Florida in the fall. But Matthew said she was willing to talk.

When Matthew finished, he asked Sisk about the next steps. Sisk was poker-faced. He'd have to talk to his bosses, he said, and he promised to work hard on the case.

"We'll look into it," Sisk said.

That was what Sisk told him every time he called, for months. Now it was October. Four months had passed, and Matthew was worried.

"We're getting the runaround from these bastards again," Nancy said.

After Matthew talked to the sheriff's office, Patrick Covington stepped up, too. He told investigators he was beaten in the Lower Building and at the Covington home. At first, Patrick believed investigators wanted to help, but later, when he saw the police report, he noticed they had left out some of the key people involved.

In October 2013, Matthew secretly recorded a phone call with Sisk after investigators told Patrick they weren't going to move forward on his or Matthew's cases.

After pleasantries, Matthew got to the point.

"Patrick said when he came to talk to you today, you asked if we were going to be willing to take charges out on our own."

"Yes."

"And you're meaning, like, we go up to the magistrate's office and take out our own warrants and that kind of thing, right?"

"Yeah."

"OK. I've just been doing my research and pretty much what that means is we're only going to be able to get misdemeanor warrants for what they did. Correct?"

"I met with the DA last week," Sisk replied. "He read over your statement and read over Patrick's and he said the only thing he was willing to prosecute was misdemeanors, anyway."

"So basically what he's willing to do, if I'm understanding correctly, he's willing to look at assault by strangulation, slapping, holding me against my will, and say, 'That's just a misdemeanor'? And just overlook it."

"That's what he's telling me," Sisk responded.

Matthew was outraged, but he channeled that anger.

"I'm not going to let them silence me," he told Nancy. His friends, grandparents, and aunt Lynn promised to help him.

No one in authority wanted to do anything. No one wanted to stand up to the church. "They're too afraid to do their jobs," Lynn told her nephew. Nancy agreed, in her own way: "They're fucking pussies," she said.

In January 2014, Matthew, Patrick, Nancy, Huddle, and Brent Childers of Faith in America met in Charlotte with Jill Rose, an assistant US attorney. They wanted to see if Matthew's beating could be prosecuted as a federal hate crimes case.

Before they started going into details, Rose told them she was familiar with the church. She was an assistant state prosecutor in the North Carolina district that included Spindale in the 1990s.

"We had a horrible time trying to make cases against [Word of Faith]," she said. "For whatever reason, it was always something."

Matthew and the others told Rose everything they could think of, including how the Brazilians were being exploited by the church. They hoped that might spark a human trafficking investigation.

"How did they get hooked up with Brazilians?" Rose asked.

"They have two churches in Brazil and one in Ghana. They mostly bring up members from Brazil to work for free," Patrick said.

"And do they beat up the Brazilians?" Rose asked.

"Most definitely!" Patrick replied.

Matthew explained that some of the Brazilians went to college. "Mostly they bring them up here for free work," he said.

Matthew asked why his case couldn't be prosecuted as a hate crime. He said he had researched the subject and found that the Matthew Shepard and James Byrd, Jr., Hate Crimes Prevention Act stiffened penalties for crimes motivated by a person's sexual orientation or race.

Rose explained that those cases were hard to prosecute because they had to show the attack had an element of interstate commerce, involving the crossing of state lines. It was unlikely she'd move forward on that front.

Rose promised to "take a fresh look" at the case, but after the meeting she didn't follow up. She never responded when they tried to contact her in subsequent months.

The group grew frustrated, but refused to give up. All Patrick Covington had to do was remind himself of what happened to him on January 13, 2014.

Patrick and a friend attended a basketball game between Word of Faith Fellowship and another church in a public building in Forest City. Frank Webster, the assistant district attorney, was coaching the Word of Faith team, while Leon Godlock, a lieutenant in the Rutherford County Sheriff's Office, was coaching the other. Just before the start of the game, Godlock walked over to Patrick. He said he couldn't force Patrick to leave, but if he didn't, Word of Faith would forfeit the game, rather than play in front of him. Patrick left.

The next day Chris Atkins, the lieutenant who helped Danielle get her clothes back, left a warning message on Patrick's cell phone. He said the church was upset at him for showing up at the game, and was considering filing harassment and stalking charges against him. Patrick called Atkins back.

"Can they do that?" he asked.

Atkins said they hadn't, but he was sure the church's attorneys were pushing them to "press charges."

Patrick was angry. He had seen Godlock at the church. He wasn't a member, but he had gone to a couple of services. Others had seen the church attorneys "acting all chummy" with Atkins.

Patrick wasn't going to take it anymore. After he and Matthew escaped, Patrick realized how much his mother, Shana Muse, loved him, and what a mistake it was, choosing the Covingtons over his own mother. He began searching for Shana. He figured his grandmother would know where she was, but Patrick didn't know his grandmother's full name—he only knew her as Mama-Gail. He asked Danielle for help. She and her aunt Trudi drove around the Ocala area trying to find Wanda's house. Patrick finally discovered his mother in a Florida jail, serving time on bad check charges. When she lost her children, Shana lost her anchor. She'd turned to drugs.

Patrick drove down to Florida and visited his mother at a work-release facility in Saint Petersburg. In a dining room they had a tearful reunion. Over time, Patrick disclosed to his mother the brutal details of his upbringing: the Lower Building. Beatings that left him bloodied and bruised. He had a photographic memory, and had written down the incidents along with the dates and locations.

Shana read it and wept. He'd had so many black eyes and bloody noses that he lost count. The main culprits were Kent and Brooke Covington and Jane Whaley. They dealt out violence themselves, and encouraged it in others.

The visit with his mother emboldened him. Patrick went to the sheriff's office and filed a complaint. He wrote that he felt like he was being threatened by Godlock and Atkins. He wrote down everything that happened the night of the basketball game and the next day.

He knew it was unlikely anything would happen. But he wanted to have something on the record, to stop the intimidation.

It had been a year and a half since a man had walked into Robynn Spence's office and told her he'd been hired to kill her.

"It is an active investigation" was all she was told.

In the meantime, Spence suspected someone had broken into her home to plant listening devices and snoop through her things. She refused to talk openly on her own telephone or in her office. It seemed that people were following her. She wondered if she was becoming paranoid, if the frustration was fraying her sanity.

Desperate, she reached out to a group that helps people escape cults. She sent a private Facebook message to Families Against Cult Teachings on January 29, 2014.

"I am an elected clerk of superior court in North Carolina and we have a cult here in my small town. I am the only person (elected, that is) in my county who has tried to help the individuals who have escaped this horrible place. They hate me and have caused me and my family so much trouble because I have tried to help. I currently have a bounty on me. We have gone to law enforcement, SBI, and FBI with no help," she wrote.

"They have endless amounts of money and power… I am about the only elected official that they cannot control. We have nowhere else to turn, no one will help. They have cost me thousands of dollars in attorney fees trying to have me removed from office… If you have never read about the Word of Faith Fellowship in Spindale, North Carolina, please Google it. I am sure you will find them just as scary as the other cults you speak of. If you ever have any advice that could help the survivors of this cult on how to get justice, please let me know."

The group's director, Tibor Stern, studied up on Word of Faith, then contacted Spence. He believed she was in danger. His group would decide what to do to help her.

Meanwhile, Roy Talcott, an executive director with the group, wrote back to Spence.

"Hi, Robynn, so sorry to hear you are going through this horror. Can you send us specific information about what this group has done to harm its members? We can't give advice unless we know specifically what this organization is doing/ how they are treating their followers. Also, how did you find out there is a bounty on you? Are you in hiding because of it?"

"I'm not in hiding," she wrote back. "I won't let them intimidate me. I'm a well-known public figure here so they will have to be very smart on how they will succeed in killing me," Spence wrote.

She introduced Stern and Talcott to Nancy so she could provide more information.

"I spoke with Nancy today," Talcott wrote. "The story is absolutely incredible. These charlatans and abusers must be exposed."

"Great, I'm glad you spoke with her," Robynn wrote on February 5. "She's a wonderful person who has only tried to help… We cannot trust anyone here. Thank you again."

It was her last message to the group. The next week, Robynn Spence began suffering from flu-like symptoms. She died on February 16, 2014. She was forty-six years old.

No autopsy was done, and the official cause of death was acute respiratory distress syndrome. Spence's family asked Francis to investigate her death as suspicious. He refused.

Francis told Robynn's father that Spence never reported a

murder-for-hire plot; she'd only told him the man was hired to "harass her."

Nancy, Huddle, and others knew that was bullshit. Spence was very clear about the threat. She'd warned them all that if she died anytime soon, it wouldn't be an accident.

Spence's death left her community in mourning. It seemed there were few families who hadn't somehow been touched by her work. In March 2014, the Rutherford County Board of County Commissioners voted to have a memorial plaque placed in the courthouse. Her friends did everything they could to keep her memory alive.

For Child Abuse Prevention Month in April, Nancy and numerous former Word of Faith members organized an event on the courthouse lawn. Along with blue balloons and ribbons tied around the columns of the courthouse, Spence's last political sign was hung in her memory.

For Word of Faith Fellowship survivors, it was time to make their voices heard. Nancy and others were making the final preparations when a knot of people appeared, moving together up the sidewalk from Main Street.

"Son of a bitch," Nancy muttered.

A dozen or so Fellowship members were heading in their direction. As they got closer, it looked like some were wired with audio transmitters.

Most troubling, the group was mostly made up of relatives of the former members who were attending the event. John Huddle's wife and daughter were there, and Patrick's sister Rachel.

When Christina Bryant got up to speak from atop the courthouse steps, she could see her sisters in the crowd, standing near the base of the monument honoring Confederate soldiers.

"Finding my voice has cost me a lot," Christina told the crowd. "It has cost me my family." Then, glancing at her family members, she said, "I'm so glad you're here today to support me in my stand against child abuse."

Her sisters began shouting.

"We are not here to support your lies. No, we're not. Lies! Lies! And you know it," they began shouting at Christina.

Nancy knew exactly what was going on. And she wasn't going to let anyone intimidate her friends. She stomped over to confront Christina's sister Meagan.

"You have to go," Nancy said.

"No, I don't," Meagan snapped.

"Yes, you do," she said. "You've embarrassed yourself. And if you want to embarrass yourself further, continue to stand here and yell, and see what happens."

"This is a free country," said Meagan's husband, a church member from Brazil.

"Are you even in this country legally?" Nancy asked. "You're going to go now. You can go yourself or I can walk you."

Meagan dropped her head and walked away.

Back on the courthouse steps, Matthew Fenner held the microphone and introduced Jeanna Powell, who had been helping so many former members escape from the church.

"She's going to sing 'Amazing Grace.' This song is going to represent the struggles she has faced in her life. It represents many of us who are here tonight, who have faced abuse," Matthew said.

With that, Matthew passed the microphone to Jeanna.

But Jeanna wasn't ready to sing. She looked at the crowd and focused on the faces of the Word of Faith Fellowship members.

"First, I wasn't going to say anything," Jeanna said. "I was just going to sing. But then I saw all the people who came out tonight to not support us... We don't care what you say. We don't care what you think. You were our abusers, and we're standing here in front of you. And we're not afraid anymore. At all."

She pointed to church members and let them have it. She criticized the congregants who were sent to record them, video that would surely be watched by Jane.

"You are the adults that allowed it to happen to us, every day. You allowed people to tell us we were harlots, we were going to hell. Everything under the sun. You allowed that to happen. You should be ashamed of yourselves. You should go cower under a table because of what you allowed to happen to us," she said.

The congregants didn't say a word. If they had, they would have been drowned out by the cheers of others in the crowd. People in the square understood what was going on. Many knew there were two sets of rules in the county—one for Word of Faith Fellowship, and one for everyone else.

As the crowd grew quiet, Jeanna sang "Amazing Grace." It took everything for her to hold back her tears, especially when she sang out, "I once was lost, but now I'm found. Was blind, but now I see."

25

THE ESCAPE

John Cooper was running out of time. Jane Whaley was trying to derail the biggest opportunity of his life, and he had to do something, fast.

More than two years earlier, Whaley had given her blessing for John and Peter to attend medical school. But like always, there were conditions. They had to go to the same university, and it had to be in the Carolinas.

In 2012, during his junior year at Wofford College, John had aced the Medical College Admission Test, or MCAT, scoring in the high ninetieth percentile. His options were wideopen. But Peter didn't do as well. They weren't likely to be accepted to the same schools.

Whaley's solution? John should take a year off. It would give Peter time to cram for another shot at the test. John didn't like it, but he agreed. He'd spent a year working for church members, eventually taking a job with his brother Benjamin.

Peter did better the second time, but it was still unlikely that both brothers would be admitted to the same schools.

John's mother-in-law, Cynthia Fields, began peppering him with questions about school.

"What is the best medical school around here?" she asked.

"Duke," John responded. "Then UNC."

"Why don't you go to Duke?" she asked.

"Peter won't get in there with his MCAT score," John said.

Cynthia nodded. She didn't say anything to John, but she repeated his words to others. It wasn't long before Jane Whaley called.

"I hear you are being prideful about the score you made," Whaley said.

John was confused. "Prideful?"

"I'm going to have Mark Cornelius review your med school applications," Whaley said.

Cornelius, a doctor in the church, met with John and Peter in a hallway outside Whaley's office with a group of other church leaders.

"If you are going to go to medical school, you are going to be ministers," Cornelius said. "Why doesn't your personal essay talk about the call of God on your life?"

John stammered. "I just, um, thought…"

Cornelius ripped the papers to shreds. John and Peter quickly found themselves in the middle of a blasting frenzy.

"We're going to help you write these applications the way they should be," Cornelius said. "They need to be written in God's will."

John knew what that meant. It would be more religious manifesto than personal essay. John also knew how important that essay would be. Medical schools look at more than grades. They also consider personality, character, the elements of a good bedside manner. John and Peter knew their essays were critical. They had labored over them for months, and now they'd have to submit religious tracts written by a committee.

John's rewritten essay was exactly what he expected. There was nothing he could do about it. The church had total control over his life.

Despite the meddling, John was accepted to the University of North Carolina School of Medicine in Chapel Hill. It wasn't looking good for Peter.

"You should go," Peter said. "It would be ridiculous for you not to."

"Jane won't let me," John said. "I think I'm going to have to leave the church."

"I think you should talk to Benjamin about that," Peter said. A silence fell between them.

"Benjamin? You think I can I trust him?" John asked. Peter nodded.

What John didn't know was Benjamin and Peter had been secretly rebelling. They'd grown closer since Peter began working for Benjamin's recycling business. And when Benjamin knew he could trust Peter, he began scheduling his brother to come along on work trips. They tried out normal adult things, like seeing movies and watching TV. They visited Luiz Vargas, their Brazilian friend who once lived with them in the Covingtons' basement. Luiz had married a life-long Word of Faith member. The pair left in January 2014 and moved to Charlotte. This time, they had no intention of going back. Luiz had joined the US Air Force six months after fleeing.

Having "outside friends" gave the Coopers courage to consider breaking free. Benjamin, Peter, and Jeffrey began secretly recording conversations they had with Jane Whaley, asking her why couples couldn't have sex when they wanted to. They wanted to catch Whaley making religious proclamations that weren't supported by the Bible, then use her words against her to convince their wives that Whaley was a fraud.

At Peter's urging, John signed up with his brothers to be a "watchman," an overnight security guard. The job was easy. It meant hours of sitting in a car near the church, keeping an eye on the church buildings and calling the security team if something seemed suspicious. It gave them a chance to listen to the radio or talk openly about their frustrations. John signed up for a shift with Benjamin.

That night, parked along Old Flynn Road, John told Benjamin everything about his plan to break free.

Benjamin didn't hesitate. "I'll do everything I can to help."

His answer assuaged John's fears. He really could trust his older brother. All he could say was thank you.

Later, Benjamin and Peter said they wanted to bring Jeffrey into their confidence. John wasn't so sure. Jeffrey was a stalwart church defender, right?

"Yes, he's always followed all the rules. He was Jane's pet," Peter said.

"He's just as fed up as we are," Benjamin confirmed.

John was relieved. Now he had the support of three brothers. All of them wanted out, but it wasn't as simple as all that. They all were married, and they didn't want to leave their wives behind when they left. By the spring of 2014, the Cooper brothers were getting anxious.

"I don't think I have any choice. I have to leave soon," John said, turning to Benjamin. "What about Micah? Do you think she's close?"

"Maybe one day," Benjamin responded. "Sometimes I'll point out something in the church that's wrong and she will agree. And she doesn't tell Jane."

"What about Jessica?" Benjamin asked.

"I don't know," John said. "You know she tried to run away before. Sometimes she doesn't seem like she's willing to do it again. Other times I think she might."

"Amy's nowhere close," Peter said. "I don't think she'll ever leave."

In the meantime, John pestered church leaders about medical school. He had to give the university a yes or no. Finally, Whaley had an idea.

"John David, you need to call the school and tell them you are not going to attend unless they accept your brother," she said.

John was appalled. It was one of the dumbest things he had ever heard. "I don't think that's going to work," he said.

"Of course it will. When Josh and Andrea [Farmer] got accepted to law school, they didn't accept Frank [Webster] at first. You know what I did? I went down there and told them they couldn't have Josh and Andrea unless they accepted Frank. And do you know what happened? They let Frank in. It was the will of God."

John did what he was told. He called the university's director of admissions.

Randee Reid told John there were hundreds of other candidates waiting to get in, and she couldn't do anything for Peter.

John relayed the bad news to Jane, but she wouldn't budge.

"You better do something," Whaley warned. "You can't go without Peter. If you go without Peter, I will wash my hands of you."

Whaley urged John to keep pressing the university. If it was God's will, they'd let Peter go.

John was too embarrassed to keep harassing the admissions office, so he pretended to call, then reported back to Whaley that the school wouldn't budge.

"Well, you just need to drive up there and tell them in person," Whaley said. "Make them understand. Cry if you have to, do whatever it takes to make them understand."

As much as he hated to do it, John called the admissions office again.

"Ms. Reid, this is John Cooper," he said. "Can you arrange a meeting with the dean of admissions?"

"That's not allowed. It could taint the admissions process for the dean to meet with an applicant," she said.

"Oh," John said. "I was just hoping to talk to someone."

Reid could hear the desperation in Cooper's voice. So she decided to dig deeper. "Why don't you come up here and talk to me?" she said.

When John told Whaley that he had arranged a face-to-face meeting, she was pleased, confident Peter would get in. If it didn't work, too bad for John. He'd just have to sit out another year and take the MCAT again.

Peter and Benjamin offered to drive John to Chapel Hill for the meeting. It was a great excuse to get out of church, and even better, a chance for John to hang out with his brothers. Jane agreed to let them go. The four-hour drive was a blast. For the first time in their lives, the brothers listened to music, cracked jokes, and laughed out loud.

But then it got serious. Lying in his hotel bed that night, John rehearsed in his mind what he'd say. Before he knew it, the alarm was buzzing. It was time. His brothers dropped him off at the school and went off to look at apartments for their brother. "Good luck," Benjamin said. John smiled weakly. He was dreading the meeting.

Sitting in the reception area, John's stomach was tied in knots. When a receptionist called his name, John jumped up, took a deep breath, and walked slowly into Ms. Reid's office. She greeted him with a friendly smile. She seemed caring, even motherly.

"Have a seat," she said, motioning to a chair near her desk. "And tell me what is going on here."

John sat down and cleared his throat. He could bullshit her—recite the Jane Whaley–scripted narrative. Or he could tell her the truth. He opted for the latter. "Listen, I don't know how else to say this. I'm in a cult," he said.

The words sounded surreal. John studied Reid's face for her reaction. It was the first time he'd ever used the word *cult* to describe the church. He'd thought it for years. But thinking it and saying it are two different things.

Reid didn't expect that answer. "A cult?"

John fidgeted in his chair and nodded. She stared at him. She could tell he was deeply troubled.

"I knew that something was going on. That's why I asked you to come up here and talk to me. Can you tell me a little more about your situation?"

"They don't let people go to college alone. They want you to have a guard. You watch each other. It's how they make sure you follow the rules. And that way they can make sure you don't leave the church," he said.

"What does your brother think about all this?" Reid asked.

"He's not the problem. He wants me to go to school. We both want to get out of the church. He's not trying to hold me back. And he's not trying to use my opportunity to force the university to let him in. It's the leadership that put me up to this."

Overwhelmed, he buried his head in his hands and sobbed. This was the first time he'd told the truth about his life to an outsider. "This is super embarrassing," he whispered.

Reid stood up, walked over to John, and wrapped him in a tight hug. "It's OK," she said. "I'm glad you are being honest with me."

Then they talked for two hours. John's words spilled out through tears. He told her about a lifetime of emotional and physical abuse. The years of abuse were too fresh—too raw—

for him to describe everything. It was hard for him to even reconcile it in his own mind. He knew it was wrong to beat people, but he had been indoctrinated for years to believe that it wasn't abuse if it was done in the name of the Lord.

"I am a Christian," Reid said. "I can tell you that God loves you. But the god you are describing, the god you are used to, is not the god most Christians believe in. I think you need to find a way to come to school. This opportunity is too big for you to throw away."

John leaned back in his chair. It felt like he could breathe again. He thanked her, and they hugged again before he left her office. Then John bounded out of the building. He couldn't wait to tell his brothers what had happened.

"I told her everything," John said.

"Everything?" Peter asked, incredulous.

"I told her that I am in a cult, and the ministers are making me do this."

Benjamin laughed. "Well, we can't tell Jane that." Peter and John looked at each other and smiled.

"No, we can't tell her that," John said. "So what are we going to tell her?"

On the way home, the brothers came up with a plan. They'd tell Jane what she wanted to hear. He'd say how he told Ms. Reid that it was important to his church that Peter get into school. And John could say with complete honesty that he had made an ally in Ms. Reid. At this stage in their lives, the three brothers were way past the fear that Jane Whaley could read their minds.

As they pulled into the church parking lot, they went over their story one last time.

"Just keep it simple," Peter said. "It will be fine."

When they walked into Jane's office, the brothers could see that Jane was eager to hear what happened.

"How was the meeting?" she asked.

"Great," John said. "I was just really honest with her. I told her how things are. Now she understands where I'm coming from. She was one of the nicest people I ever met. We talked for a long time. She really seemed to care. And she promised that she's going to try to help me. She said Peter is still on the waiting list."

Whaley was ecstatic.

"See, I told you God spoke to me about this," she said. "I knew it was God's will for you to go there today."

For John, it was the moment of truth. He was ready to leave the Word of Faith Fellowship once and for all. Now he had to get his wife to agree.

They had been married for a year, but he and Jessica were still strangers. They didn't talk much about their pasts or their futures. They didn't trust each other, so they were careful what they said. They finally got permission to have sex, but there was nothing fun or spontaneous or satisfying about their relationship.

So John had to figure out a way to broach the subject of leaving. In the meantime, he'd opened a secret line of communication with his cousin Danielle Cordes. As he was getting ready to take a shower before a night watch shift, he stole a few minutes of privacy in the bathroom to text her. Then his phone rang. It was Lauren, his brother Chad's wife.

What does she want? he wondered.

"Hi, John. Can I talk to Jessica?" Lauren asked. "I called her, but she didn't answer her phone."

"Uh, sure," he said.

John stepped out of the bathroom and handed Jessica the phone. Afraid Jessica would see messages from Danielle, he stood nearby, waiting for her to hang up so he could grab the phone back. But the two kept talking. John glanced at the clock. It was nine o'clock. He had to get ready for his shift. He couldn't be late.

He showered as fast as he could. But when he opened the bathroom door, he knew it was too late.

"Who is this person?" she asked, holding up his phone.

John had put Danielle's number in his phone under a business contact name. "It's just somebody from the business," he said.

"Then how do they know about watch?"

"Um..."

Jessica wanted answers. And if she didn't get them, all she had to do was call to her parents in the next room.

"It's Danielle," he admitted. "But please don't tell anyone."

Jessica cocked her head to the side.

"Please don't tell," John pleaded. "Y'all used to be really good friends. She wants to talk to you."

"I don't know, John," she said.

"Just think about it. She's family."

She needed time to figure out what was really going on. "OK. I guess I won't tell for now."

John fretted throughout his shift. Was Jessica going to rat him out? That could ruin everything. For the next week the tension grew between them. Finally Jessica told him yes, she'd talk with Danielle.

Jessica's conversations with Danielle helped open the door for their escape. Danielle told Jessica about life outside the church. She had freedom to come and go, speak and sing, wherever and whenever she liked. No more spying. No more blasting. There was a wonderful world outside Whaley's dark little bubble.

It didn't take much to persuade Jessica. She had wanted to leave for years, but she didn't know how.

A week after her first talk with Danielle, Jessica's husband told her his secret: he was going to medical school, and he didn't give a damn what Jane said. He was leaving the church, and he wanted her to go with him. He didn't know where they would live or how they would make it, but they'd figure it out.

Jessica was quiet, then stared into John's eyes. "Yes," she said. "Let's go."

Those words triggered the next phase: planning their getaway. The first step was getting their car transferred into their names. The title was in Jessica's parents' names, and John made cash payments every week to the church office. If they tried to leave in the car, it could be reported stolen. John took it to Jane Whaley. No detail was too minor for her attention.

"I was wondering if we can get the car in our name so we can start building some credit," John told Whaley. "We're going to need credit to buy a house one day."

To his surprise, she agreed. John talked to the ministers in charge of member finances. Now it was a matter of waiting. John and Jessica would bolt as soon as the title was transferred.

John told Danielle his plans. He started tracking down others who left the church. He was pleased to find Jamey Anderson's number. When Jamey left, Jane had preached long and hard about how he'd "gone over to the dark side." He was a devil, never any good. But Jamey was mentioned less now as other names took his place on Jane's blacklist.

John found Jamey was enrolled in law school at the University of North Carolina in Chapel Hill. They'd be neighbors. Jamey was excited to hear from John. He said he always knew John would leave. He agreed to take him around campus and help him find a place to live nearby as soon as they made the break.

They mapped out the logistics. They'd leave during a Wednesday night service. Pack the car full, hit the road fast, head to Charlotte. Maybe decompress at Luiz's house for a few days before driving to Chapel Hill.

In the meantime, John had to act like everything was normal. His sister Lena was visiting from Brazil, so his mother was planning a big family dinner on Sunday, July 13, 2014. The entire family would be there.

Rick and Suzanne put up a good front. They occupied the same house, but lived separate lives. Suzanne tried to have her children over every Sunday, but with all their busy lives, it was unusual to have all nine Cooper children gathered in one place.

Rick sat at the head of the table like he always had, but in recent years his children had taken over all the key decisions. Rick and Suzanne faded into the background. They had no idea their older children were planning to leave.

John had a lot on his mind, and wasn't in the mood for a big gathering. He made himself go. If everything went according to plan, this could be the last time he'd see many of his family members. He knew Jane would force them to cut him out of their lives.

John played it cool. The big house filled with noise as brothers and sisters, cousins, aunts, and neighbors talked and played. His little brother Adam played a few church tunes on the living room piano. Others siblings fought for keyboard time. John thought about all the work that went into building the place, and all the living that had gone on there since. There were many good memories, for sure. But his mind kept going back to the bad times: the terrifying day his parents tried to leave. The afternoons he came home from school to find another sibling was gone, sent to live in a minister's home. The day he found out it was his turn to go.

He stared out the window over the wide backyard. He knew every pathway through those woods, all the hiding places where he'd built forts and played hide-and-seek with his friends. He wished he didn't have to go. Even though they'd brought him to this wretched church, John still loved his mother and father.

But after more than two decades under Jane Whaley's spell, they were too far gone. As his mother cleared the dishes from the dinner table, John excused himself. It was time to leave.

He walked outside and took one last look at the family homestead. He didn't feel melancholy. He was excited to begin his journey. He'd be gone soon to Chapel Hill, to become a doctor. All he needed was a little luck—and his car title—and he'd leave this insanity behind.

John glanced at the text message on his phone. The title was ready, just in time. It was Wednesday, July 16, 2014, just two weeks before school was to start.

He had to act fast. He jumped in his car and drove to the church office, picked up the title, and drove to the local office of the North Carolina Department of Motor Vehicles to have the registration switched over. That was it. And even better, it was Wednesday. He and Jessica could leave that very night.

That evening he and Jessica dressed for church like they always did.

"This is it!" John whispered to her. She smiled, but he could tell she was nervous, too. The plan was to leave the house, and then when everyone was in church, circle back, get their things, and head east to Charlotte. They told Jessica's parents they had to gas up the car before church.

John's heart was racing as he pulled into the BP station parking lot. He put the car in Park and called Jamey Anderson to let him know the adventure had begun.

"I'm rooting for you," Jamey said. "And just remember,

we're here. If you need us to call the police, we can. Dani-elle is here for you. I'm here. We're just a phone call away."

John and Jessica got out of the house without being seen. As they headed east, their phones started to beep and ping. The church knew they were gone.

Then Jessica began to panic. In the rearview mirror, she saw a car coming up on their tail. She worried it was church security. Her father, Randy, was on the team, and he'd be as mad as a hornet.

John could tell his wife was scared to death. But he knew there was nothing he could say that would make her feel better. So he pushed his accelerator to the floor until the car behind him disappeared.

When he felt safe, John pulled the car to the side of the road but kept the engine running. It was time to send a text to their parents and top church leaders, announcing their departure. John's hand shook as he banged out the message.

As you know, I'm starting med school this fall, so Jessica and I are heading to Chapel Hill to get an apartment and get things lined up for August. We really love you so much. We want to keep our relationship good and we will stay in touch. Love you so much. John and Jessica.

He hit Send. That was it. No turning back.

Benjamin was in the sanctuary tuning up his cello for a church orchestra performance when his phone vibrated in his pocket. He took a quick peek. It was the text.

I'll be damned. He did it, Benjamin thought.

Benjamin glanced at Peter, who was sliding his phone back into his pocket, a trombone resting on his lap. Peter gave a slight nod. It was all part of the plan. Benjamin, Peter, and Jeffrey all knew John would be leaving any day. They had asked him not to tell them when. They needed plausible deniability.

Benjamin and Peter watched the commotion unfold. Peter's wife, Amy, and Chad's wife, Lauren, were whispering. They jumped up together and raced over to Jane Whaley. The ministers soon gathered. It wasn't long before Jane was marching toward Benjamin and Peter.

"I have to tell you something," she said. "John David and Jessica just left. Did y'all know anything about this?"

"What?" Benjamin exclaimed. "No way. I had no idea."

Whaley clasped her hands. "I knew this was going to happen! I felt it in the Spirit. The college devils have taken hold of John David. We tried and tried, but he didn't receive the deliverance. God told me this was going to happen. You need to call John and tell him that he's out of the will of God. Tell him he's going to hell if he doesn't come back. And if he talks to you, you need to let me know."

By then, John and Jessica were well on their way to Charlotte, where their friends Luiz and Risa had moved after fleeing the church. They were in Brazil at the time, but had left a house key with Raul Latoni, a pastor at Calvary Church in Charlotte. All John had to do was pick it up, and he and Jessica would have a place to stay.

Sweaty and tired, John knocked on the pastor's door. Pastor Latoni opened the door and ushered them in.

John and Jessica sank into a couch in the living room. They were nervous, not accustomed to interacting with strangers.

"Luiz told me what's going on," Latoni said. "I want you to know you are not in trouble with God for leaving that place. There are a lot of people in the world who serve God—people outside of the Word of Faith. It's OK for you to do what you think is right. You don't have to be afraid of the wrath of God for leaving there."

Latoni was kind and understanding. John and Jessica wept as they recounted their escape. They were exhausted from their ordeal. "You need to get some rest," the pastor told them. They got the key and thanked him.

At Luiz's apartment they parked the car inside the garage, out of sight. While their telephones buzzed with texts and calls from Spindale, Jessica and John spent the night reassuring one another that they'd made the right decision, that this was the first day of a great adventure. They fell asleep in each other's arms.

The next few days were a blur. They drove from Charlotte to Asheville to meet Danielle Cordes and her aunt Trudi. Jeffrey and Peter slipped away and met them for a meal together.

From Asheville, John and Jessica headed to Chapel Hill, where Jamey had set them up with a hotel room. They stayed long enough to rent an apartment for the upcoming semester, then headed back to Charlotte until it was ready.

Throughout it all, they were hammered with text messages and phone calls. The only one John picked up was a particularly frantic call from his mother, Suzanne.

"John, I just don't understand why you are doing this," she said. "You are going to go to hell."

"Mom, I am not going to hell," John said. "Just Chapel Hill."

"Can you at least tell me what happened?" she asked. "Why you left?"

John told her about the violence, the beatings, and how Jane had tried to steal his dream of medical school. It didn't seem to register.

"You can still come back," she said. "Things can be better."

"I'm sorry, Mom. I have made up my mind. I have to go."

Just when things couldn't get more complicated, Jessica discovered she was pregnant. Her pregnancy lent another layer of stress. John knew they weren't emotionally or financially ready for a child. It was going to be tough enough adjusting in the outside world themselves, how were they going to do it with a baby?

And Jessica had a bigger concern: What if Jane was right? What if something terrible happened to the baby because they left? She had to fight those feelings. When things got overwhelming, she phoned Danielle and Jamey, who would talk her off the ledge.

John didn't care about Whaley's threats of damnation, cancer, and lightning bolts. He saw through that nonsense years ago. It wasn't the wrath of God that frightened him; it was the threat of losing his family.

One day the call came. It was his father, Rick.

"John, I talked to Jane. She said you are attacking the church," Rick said. "She said we're not supposed to talk to you anymore."

"But I'm your son," John snapped. "Why would you do this? Just because I want to go to medical school and make something out of myself?"

"There's more to it than that, son. The Bible says…"

"No, it doesn't," John said, interrupting his father. "For one, this whole thing about cutting me off if I attack makes no sense. And I'm not really attacking. I haven't said much to anybody, and if I did, I spoke nothing but the truth. If it's the truth, you really can't call it attacking. And two, the Bible doesn't say anything about cutting off attackers."

John was on a roll, letting out years of pent-up frustration, years of anger at the parents who had failed to protect him from harm. They'd thrown him and his siblings to the lions. He'd had enough.

"I'm your son. If I'm wrong, wouldn't it make sense to keep talking to me and try to show me what's right? Instead of just cutting me off?"

"I'm sorry, John, I can't talk to you anymore."

His father hung up the phone. John shook his head in disgust. He'd expected his dad to respond that way. Maybe one day his parents would see the truth and break Whaley's spell. Until then, John would move forward with his life. No matter how bad it got on the outside, he'd never go back.

26

PERSEVERANCE AND REDEMPTION

Matthew Fenner did everything right but was still getting nowhere. And time was running out.

He attended local political events in an attempt to talk to candidates and officials about the threat of Word of Faith Fellowship. They responded with blank faces. He called the sheriff's office to talk to Chris Francis. He did the same with Brad Greenway. They did nothing.

Matthew had been accepted at the University of North Carolina, and was set to start classes in the fall of 2014. But the clock was ticking on his case. In North Carolina, the statute of limitations for assault cases was usually two years. By August 2014, he had only six months left to get police moving. It was clear that Rutherford County law enforcement was content to run out the clock.

So Matthew's grandfather stepped in. The Reverend Robert Rape, Sr., was a kind, forgiving man. For nearly thirty years he had led small local congregations, teaching them about the gospel. Now in his late sixties, his occupation was caring for his flock of grandchildren and great-grandchildren, all of whom affectionately called him Papaw.

Rape loved Matthew. Yes, he was homosexual, and in the evangelical community, that was considered a sin. But Rape believed Jesus came to save sinners, not just saints. His grandson was a good and gentle soul, as much a beloved child of God as all the rest. He had supported his grandson's efforts to get justice, but the time had come, he felt, to make a few calls himself.

Sheriff Francis called Matthew and asked for a meeting in his office.

In late August, Matthew and his grandfather walked into the sand-colored brick building in downtown Rutherfordton. Francis was cordial. Rape got down to business.

"Matthew has a few questions he wants to ask about this deal that's been going on for about a year with him. We are all concerned about it," he said.

"Why isn't law enforcement pursuing any serious charges on my case?" Matthew asked. "I just need understanding, because I know what happened to me."

Francis jumped in. There was nothing else he could do, he said, because Greenway wasn't willing to prosecute. Greenway makes those kinds of decisions.

"I have not looked at one thing in your case file," Francis said. "Yesterday I talked to the district attorney. I didn't agree with him wholeheartedly, but we're doing what he suggests because he's the one who prosecutes the case."

Matthew felt like he was being blasted again.

And just as he expected, Francis suggested that Matthew file misdemeanor charges with the magistrate. "I'll walk you over there right now," he said.

But Matthew was prepared. He said he had studied the law

and knew that what church members did to him were not misdemeanors. They were felonies.

"I was getting to the point where my airway was blocked off and I was blacking out. It was getting to the point where I really thought I was going to die. Should I have just died right then to convince you that something really wrong was happening?

"It's not just a religious thing. They did it because I am gay. And that makes it a hate crime."

Then he posed an insightful question: "The problem is Brad Greenway throws it on you, then you throw it back on him. So who is going to step up and do what they need to do?"

"I can't believe he's thrown it on me," Francis said.

He never did answer Matthew's question. And by that point in the meeting, Matthew knew the sheriff wasn't going to do a thing.

Despite everything he had done in his quest for justice, Matthew was right back where he started.

After more than two decades in the Word of Faith Fellowship, it was time for Rick and Suzanne Cooper to make up their minds.

After John left in July, Rick followed orders. He tried to cut ties with his son, but he just couldn't follow it through.

Every time Rick called, John made it clear his mind was made up. Jane Whaley could go to hell. What she did to him and his brothers and sisters and every other person inside that cult was wrong.

By October 2014, three more Cooper children left the church. First it was Benjamin and Micah. Then Peter, though his wife, Amy, had refused to go with him. Jeffrey and his family left, too.

Jeffrey's moment of truth came after he had warned Whaley the violence had to stop.

"You do realize this physical abuse has to stop or you will get in trouble?" he said. "It stops, or I leave." She promised him it would. But at a church service three days later, Jane told the congregation that an earlier case of abuse—a young man who was thrown through a wall during deliverance—had never happened. Instead, she said the boy tripped and fell into the wall. It was an accident.

Jeffrey knew otherwise, and so did everyone who'd been there that day. He was fed up with her lies. Jeffrey and his wife stood up in the middle of the sermon and walked out. This was not the way he wanted to live his life.

Jeffrey left the church with a warning: don't mess with the Coopers, or you'll regret it deeply. Whaley knew Jeffrey had years of solid inside evidence he could use against the church.

Now Jeffrey, Benjamin, and Peter just needed to get their parents free.

They decided Jeffrey would make the case. So he sat down with his parents and explained exactly why he'd left. He knew going in it was going to be a hard sell. His parents were hard-core true believers. They had been so for two decades. So he approached the conversation from a legal perspective. He'd seen the bookkeeping, he'd attended the coaching sessions and strategic plans. He'd witnessed what he believed were crimes, everything from tampering and obstruction of justice to felony fraud. He believed that the church's actions were criminal.

"What kind of church beats its congregants and breaks the law?" Jeffrey asked his parents. "Jane abuses children. She destroys families. Is she really channeling a loving God? Who benefits from her rules? It damn sure isn't her followers."

With his wife, Natalie, by his side, he revealed how the church hurt him and his family. How they tried to break up his marriage. How they beat him, isolated him without any justification.

Jeffrey, always meticulous, made his case. Going into the meeting, he didn't think they would leave. He just wanted to plant the seeds of doubt. But he could tell, his parents were stunned.

At first they didn't know what to say. Everything Jeffrey said made sense. The conversation eventually reestablished lines of communication, and over time Rick and Suzanne began to question their beliefs. Suzanne even admitted to Rick that she'd been pressured to lie in court, falsely testifying that Shana had abused her children.

"They told me that if I ever told you, or anybody, I'd be a Judas," she said, tears welling in her eyes.

She told him how horrible she felt when their children were moved from their home, and the bitter humiliation she suffered at the hands of Whaley and other ministers. She'd taken it all out on Rick and her family, watching their every move and turning them in when they stepped out of line.

"How did we end up here?" she asked.

She already knew the answer. They were both vulnerable, flawed people looking for a supportive community where they could fit in. And there she was, Jane Whaley, promising an easy road to salvation. All they had to do was follow her edicts, walk and talk her way, and they'd be among the chosen, living forever in the Kingdom of Heaven.

They'd bought it. But now, after years in the church, they finally realized it was nothing but lies. Now they had to find the strength to leave.

The Coopers realized that they'd come to Word of Faith Fellowship for the sake of their children. And now their children were leading them back to freedom.

There was a good chance Chad would stay behind, and

probably Lena, too, since she was in Brazil. But the youngest three—Blair, Adam, and Jacklyn—would leave with them.

For Rick, the revelations from Suzanne and Jeffrey were almost too much to take. He had placed his faith in this church, and it had made a mockery of his relationship with God. Word of Faith Fellowship had ruined his relationship with his wife and children. It had ruined his whole damn life.

Rick set up a meeting with Jane and all the key church leaders: the Covingtons, Caulders, Websters, Karel Reynolds. The so-called pillars of the church. He wanted them all there.

Rick had been a loyal follower for twenty-one years. He never complained. He didn't protest when Whaley forced his sons to live with ministers. He didn't say a word when he wasted a year of his life imprisoned in the Lower Building. He had endured everything because he thought his family was living in the will of God. He trusted the church leadership. When things went wrong, he blamed himself. Not anymore.

"It ends now," Rick told Suzanne.

When they walked into Jane's office the following day, the righteous and holy were already gathered. Rick thanked them for meeting with them, then he confronted Jane about her lies. He described in detail what Suzanne had told him about the scheme to take Shana's children and give them to the Covingtons. Rick had never talked so frankly to the church leaders. For the first time in years, he felt empowered. He heard his old voice again.

"You like to talk about things being wicked. That's wicked," Rick said. "You caused my wife to perjure herself. So if it ever comes back, who's going to take the fall?"

Whaley was stone-faced.

"Suzanne will, of course," she said.

Rick could feel his blood pressure rising. It took everything he had not to snatch her up and slap her. Kent Covington could see things were on the verge of boiling over.

"Rick, you're getting upset," Kent said.

"Oh, yeah," Rick said. "I'm definitely upset. But that doesn't mean what I'm telling you is not true. What you've done is extremely wrong. It's beyond wrong. It's illegal. And it's immoral."

"Well, Rick, you just don't understand what we were going through," Brooke said. "You don't understand everything that was at stake."

Rick glared at her. It was the same old, worn-out Word of Faith response. How could the church leaders be wrong? They were God's hands, doing the work of Jesus.

Suzanne signaled for them to go. She could see they weren't getting anywhere. Rick nodded. He had said what he needed to say.

For the first time in two decades, his mind was clear of Jane Whaley. He was no longer afraid of her. He had reality on his side. And he wasn't afraid of retaliation. Everyone in that room knew the Coopers could expose everything about the church. "We're not going to put up with it anymore," Rick said. "We're done."

And with that, Rick and Suzanne got up from the couch and walked out of Jane's office, into a new life. They had seen the truth. The truth had set them free.

When Matthew Fenner started classes at the University of North Carolina in Chapel Hill, he thought he could put the beating business behind him. He made friends and blended in with the other students on the sprawling campus. It was a liberal, public university. No one judged him for being gay.

He did well academically, but that was never an issue. Mat-

thew was bright. And now that he was out of Rutherford
County he could take seriously his goal of becoming a doctor.

During the day it was easy to bury everything that happened to him at Word of Faith Fellowship. Rushing from
class to class, studying and socializing, there was no time for
memories. Maybe that was why the images returned at night.

He had no closure. He couldn't overcome the injustice. The
images came back at night, and wrecked his sleep.

Matthew's grandparents and his aunt Lynn called to see
how he was doing. Danielle called, too, offering news and
encouragement.

Patrick was still out of the church, but Matthew knew
his friend was troubled. Patrick's mother, Shana Muse, had
been trying to help him adjust, but Patrick missed his siblings
keenly. Now he was "self-medicating" to cope with the stress.

Matthew understood Patrick's struggle. The church was
especially brutal if you were gay. Matthew and Patrick had
been attracted to each other, but they had both moved on.
Matthew still cared deeply for his friend.

Matthew's cell phone rang.

"How are you, Matthew?" his aunt asked.

"I'm doing fine," he said.

"Are you still coming home for fall break?"

"I was planning to. I miss you guys."

"Good. I was thinking. We need to make another run at
filing charges."

Matthew sighed. "I don't know."

Lynn knew she had to pitch the idea quickly. She reminded
her nephew that Brad Greenway had refused to meet with
him. He refused to return telephone messages. No one could
get an answer from him. Well, when Matthew came home,
Lynn said, she would get a group of people together and they'd
all head to his office. And they'd camp outside until he saw

them. They were willing to stay there for days, even if it meant being arrested. That would generate publicity, just before voters went to the polls. Greenway was up for reelection. He wouldn't want any negative publicity.

Matthew thought about it. This was probably his last hope. If no charges were filed by January 27, 2015, nothing would ever happen.

He thought of the kids who were still inside the church, subject to daily abuse. He couldn't let Whaley and her ministers keep getting away with it.

"Let's do it," he told his aunt.

On the afternoon of October 16, when a law enforcement source told them Greenway was in his office, Matthew, his grandparents, his aunt Lynn, Nancy, Huddle, and Christina Bryant went to Greenway's office. The receptionist said Greenway was inside, but he was busy.

"Well, you can tell him we're not going to leave until he sees us," Lynn said.

Inside, Greenway was frustrated. It was only a few weeks before the November election, and these people just wouldn't go away. Matthew was just as relentless as Whaley, and Greenway was caught in the middle.

He decided to get it over with.

Greenway greeted the group and led them into his office. He was clearly uncomfortable, Nancy remembered.

"What do you want to talk about?" he asked.

Matthew was firm. "I've tried calling. I've tried to meet with you." Then he recounted everything that happened to him in the church that night in January 2013. And when he finished, he asked Greenway why he wouldn't file charges. "I just want justice," he said.

What Greenway said next shocked everyone in the room.

"I didn't know anything about your case," he said. "Not one detail. I have never seen an incident report."

Nancy was livid. Sheriff Francis had told Matthew in August that Greenway was the one who declined to prosecute the case. Sisk had said the same thing. Now Greenway was saying that he never saw the incident report—and wouldn't take action without one.

Nancy took a deep breath. "If you got the incident report, would you read it?"

Greenway said yes. But they had to hurry. He was leaving soon.

Matthew and the others went straight to the sheriff's office across the street. Up the steps, and into the main lobby, they went to a window.

"I need to get a copy of an incident report," Matthew said. He explained he had talked to Joey Sisk in April 2013. The deputy searched. He couldn't find a report.

"We don't have one," he said.

"What do you mean? Are they purged from the system after a period of time?"

The deputy shook his head.

At that moment, Matthew and the others realized that Sisk had never created a report. All that talk by Francis and Sisk of Greenway deciding not to prosecute was nonsense. They had never intended to investigate Matthew's allegations.

While Matthew was trying to get the report, Nancy found Wayne Guffey, a deputy she knew could help. She knocked on his office door.

"Wayne, I need a favor," she said.

Guffey knew what was going on inside the church, as well as the office's "unwritten rule" to stay away from Word of Faith cases. But Guffey was a by-the-book lawman. And he was no fan of Chris Francis. Not because of his hands-off approach to the church. He felt Francis was ill equipped to handle the job.

Guffey looked up from his desk. "Yeah?"

"I need you to take a report from Matthew Fenner."

Nancy said she didn't have time to explain everything, but she went into enough detail so he'd know it was important.

"Bring him in," Guffey said.

Nancy grabbed Matthew in the hallway. "Follow me." He could tell by her look he had to hurry.

She sat him down in Guffey's office. "Tell me what happened, son," the deputy said.

Once again, Matthew shared every detail of his abuse. As he was finishing, Greenway passed through the lobby. When he spotted the group, he turned white.

"We'll have the report for you in a few minutes," Nancy informed him.

Greenway stammered. "Um… OK…" He disappeared into an office. When Guffey finished, he printed out a copy of the incident report and handed it to Matthew.

"Thank you, Deputy," he said.

The group found Greenway. "Here you go," Matthew said as he handed the paper to the district attorney.

"Now you have a copy. I hope you read it this time," Nancy said.

Lynn added, "We're not going away."

Matthew returned to Chapel Hill. A week later—and just a few days before the general election—he got a call from Greenway, asking him to testify before a grand jury. It would be up to them to decide whether to move forward with charges.

But what Greenway didn't tell Matthew was that he wouldn't be the only one testifying at the presentment hearing—the same rare legal proceeding Greenway used in the

Michael Lowry case. Even though the proceedings are secret, he had shared the information with Whaley, who summoned church members to testify, including Matthew's mother, Linda Addington.

Josh Farmer invited Greenway to his office to discuss the Matthew Fenner case. When Greenway got there, he was greeted by Whaley and several congregants, including Addington. They told him that Matthew wasn't gay, and nothing happened that night in the sanctuary.

"It's a big made-up story," Addington told Greenway. "He did it to get attention. He's a liar. He's been a liar his whole life."

Greenway sat quietly in his chair. He didn't ask any questions.

A few days later, Greenway told Farmer he'd allow Matthew's mother and other church members to testify before the grand jury.

Whaley then had a series of meetings with congregants who had witnessed the attack. She wanted to make sure their stories matched her narrative, that Matthew was a liar and nothing happened. As with Michael, they were to say no one in the church knew Matthew was gay. After all, he had a girlfriend, Danielle Cordes.

The meetings were attended by the church's attorneys, including Webster and Chris Back. At one session, several former members would later recall that Back sat in a chair, pretending to be Matthew. They said members had to demonstrate what they had done to Matthew the night of the incident. When one man pointed to Back's head and said, "I put my hand on him right here," Whaley started screaming: "NO, NO, NO, NO! YOU DID NOT DO THAT! YOUR HAND WAS NOT ON HIS HEAD. THAT IS WITCHCRAFT!" The participant quickly changed his story. And that sent a warn-

ing to the others: watch what you say. Meanwhile, Webster
and Back went along with the proceedings—even though all
North Carolina prosecutors have a duty to report any mis-
conduct.

Matthew had no coaching. He only knew that he had to
show up at the Rutherford County Courthouse at 9:00 a.m.

The night before the hearing, he drove from Chapel Hill
to his grandparents' house. His friends and family gathered
around. They wouldn't be allowed inside the courtroom, but
they promised to go with him and wait outside the chambers.

Matthew sat on the same bench that Michael Lowry had
occupied two years earlier. He was more determined than
nervous. He had waited two years for this moment.

When his name was called, Matthew didn't hesitate. In
a quiet but firm voice, he recounted everything—from the
time his mother joined the church to the beating that almost
took his life. He didn't waver. By the time he finished, he was
emotionally drained, but relieved. And when he was excused,
Matthew bounded out of the courtroom.

"How did it go?" his aunt asked.

He shrugged. "I just told them the truth."

Over the next few hours, a steady parade of church members marched into the courtroom. They took the same oath
as Matthew, but several lied.

Addington took the stand and glanced at the grand jurors.
She spotted a woman she used to work with. The woman
knew about Addington's troubles at home, her gay son. But
then she recognized another familiar face: Kirstin Santos, a
Word of Faith Fellowship member. Addington didn't know
how she could've ended up on the jury panel. She didn't
think members would be allowed to participate, but somehow, Santos was on the jury. Santos was only one vote. A
majority would still decide whether the case moved forward.

Still, Addington knew it only took one strong-willed juror to sway the others.

Addington took a deep breath to calm her nerves, then began her testimony. She said she wasn't there the night her son was allegedly beaten. She said she didn't believe it had happened. "Matthew exaggerates," she said.

She said her son wasn't gay—even though Matthew had told her years earlier, and that was one of the reasons they had joined the church. Addington knew that Whaley and Brooke were aware of her son's sexual orientation—her son had "opened his heart" to them after they became members. Whaley believed Matthew could change, and that was why he was subjected to so many blasting sessions. (At one point, Whaley even bragged to others that it had worked, and to keep Matthew "straight," she set him up with Danielle.)

Addington didn't know how long she testified, but as she continued to undermine her son's credibility, something strange happened. For the first time, she was overcome by a wave of guilt. She realized that the church had turned her against her boy. She loved him. She didn't want to hurt him. Now she felt "sick as a dog."

When she got home, Addington was summoned to Whaley's office. Kirstin Santos had just reported to Whaley the conversations between jurors. Apparently, a few members of the panel thought little of Addington for picking the church over her son.

"They didn't believe you," Whaley snapped.

Now Addington had to make it right. Whaley ordered her to return to the courthouse and find the judge and Greenway and once again tell them that her son was a liar. Addington was appalled, but she did what she was told. Whaley had this uncanny ability to get people to do her bidding—even when they knew it was wrong. And so it was with Addington. She was so loyal to Whaley that she betrayed her own son.

Matthew drove back to school and prepared for his final exams. He was at peace now. He'd had his day in court. Now it was out of his hands. Over the next few weeks, events began to break his way.

First, election day came, and Greenway was defeated.

Then, even with a Word of Faith Fellowship member on the panel, the grand jury voted that there was enough evidence for Greenway's office to file charges.

In early December, a real grand jury convened. It handed up indictments against five members of the church, including Brooke Covington. She was charged with assault and kidnapping, along with Justin Covington, his sister Sarah Covington, Robert Walker, Jr., and Adam Bartley.

Matthew was flooded with congratulations from family and friends. He made sure he thanked them all. He was interviewed by journalists from all over the country. But Matthew really didn't have time to talk or celebrate. In a few days, he'd start taking finals. If he was going to be a doctor, he'd better make straight As. So that night, alone in his dorm room, he tried to study. But it was difficult. How could he focus on books when he knew the church would come after him? He knew they'd use all their money and influence to try to discredit his character. Feeling a little anxious, he closed his textbooks, picked up his cell phone, and called Nancy. She had been there for him all along, like a surrogate mother. And that night, for an hour or so, they recounted their journey.

"I'm still stunned it got this far," Matthew said.

"They thought we were going to go away," Nancy said.

"They don't know us, do they?"

They both laughed, but then Nancy got serious. "It's going to get rough," she said. "But I want you to know one thing,

Matthew. No matter what they do, no matter what they say, I'll always be here for you. I'm just a phone call away. You know that."

"I know," Matthew whispered. "I know."

That night, Matthew knew the case was far from over. Whaley and the church would work hard to manipulate the system. So while Matthew didn't know what would happen next, he was sure of one thing: whatever they threw at him, he'd take it.

27

THE REUNION

Three months after leaving the Word of Faith Fellowship, the Coopers were trying their best to adapt to life on the outside. It was a daily struggle. The more they learned about the outside world, the more they realized how much of life they had missed.

John David Cooper threw himself into medical school. Without the pressure of work projects and church services, he was able to focus on his classes. He excelled. In between, he doted on Jessica. Her parents were constantly pressuring her to come home. She was pregnant and lonely, and he knew she was vulnerable.

John took out student loans to help pay for school, and looked into enlisting in a special US Navy program that would pay for his medical school in return for service. He ran it past his brothers, who thought it was a good idea. To his classmates and others on campus, he looked like the typical college student. He got along well with everyone, but he was guarded about his past. He felt ashamed and embarrassed to admit that he had grown up in a fundamentalist cult. At times he felt like he was from another planet. When people talked about a movie or television show, he could only sit and listen. He'd missed out.

Benjamin had an easier time. He had graduated law school and passed the bar. His recycling business was thriving. His wife gave birth to a son. Their only regret was not leaving the church sooner. Jeffrey and his wife were enjoying a similar upward trajectory.

Peter was applying to medical schools. Despite his best efforts, his wife stayed behind in the church. He learned his arranged marriage was over when he was served with divorce papers.

The brothers reached out to Chad and Lena, but they had stopped taking their calls. In time, they told one another, they'd break free, too.

The brothers had rough days, but leaned on each other for support. They had heard about the indictments being handed up in the Matthew Fenner case. Five people were charged, including Brooke Covington. But Sarah and Justin, two of Shana's children, were also indicted. It was bittersweet. Yes, Brooke was in trouble. But their cousins were, too.

Everyone knew and liked Matthew. John hadn't been there that night in January 2013, and if he had, he couldn't say he would have stopped the attack.

He knew something had to be done to stop the church. He had been wrestling with the idea of going after them himself someday. Maybe he'd offer a hand to the people who'd helped Matthew, but right now everything was still too fresh. He needed time. He needed to focus on school and Jessica and eventually his new baby.

Meanwhile, Rick tried to keep his children engaged in a more measured and kindly form of Christianity. He invited them to visit different churches in the area, and sent them information about dynamic preachers, but his children resisted. It was frustrating, but he reminded himself he would still be in the Word of Faith Fellowship if it weren't for them.

His relationship with Suzanne remained distant. They struggled to shed the strict teachings about music, television, and proper Christian behavior. They bought a big-screen television, but they often felt guilty or embarrassed for watching certain shows or movies.

They joined some family members for vacation to Hilton Head Island, South Carolina, a plush resort town, but were embarrassed to bare their skin in public. Suzanne wore capri pants all week.

At home, the Coopers felt besieged in what was supposed to have been their dream home. Church members kept them under constant surveillance. They avoided their front yard, because former friends who lived across the street often took videos on their cell phones.

Suzanne knew they'd have to leave Rutherford County if they ever hoped to live normal lives, but right now she had planning to do. Her mother was coming to visit for the first time since 2001, when Rick and Suzanne had tried to escape. Suzanne wanted to make it special, a real homecoming.

It was early December 2014. Suzanne's younger children had never celebrated Christmas, or a birthday. In the old days, before Jane Whaley banned Christmas, Rick and Suzanne went all out for holidays. Suzanne collected Christmas ornaments during their travels in the military. Now she didn't have a single one. The church had made her sell them at its annual yard sales.

Her youngest son, Adam, was sitting at the piano in the living room, practicing "O Holy Night." Adam was musically gifted, and now he was free to learn songs that weren't on the church's playlist. He'd been talking to Mama-Gail on the phone, and discovered that "O Holy Night" was her favorite. He was four years old the last time she had visited. He wanted to surprise her. He spent hours at the keyboard, practicing.

Suzanne laid her hand on Adam's shoulder. She had an idea.

"You know what time it is?" she asked him, her voice full of smiles.

Adam turned to look at his mom.

"It's time to go Christmas shopping!" she said. "I'm going to get a tree and all the decorations. When Mama-Gail gets here, she won't believe it," she said.

Adam glanced at the clock. It was 11:30 p.m.

"I want to go with you!" he said. "I've never had a Christmas tree."

The words stung Suzanne. Adam was eighteen years old.

"Well, you're going to have one this year," she said. "And it's about time."

Suzanne and Adam were giddy on the way to the all-night big-box discount store, laughing and blasting Christmas carols on the car radio.

In the past, Rick and Suzanne tried to keep their kids away from stores during the holiday season. If they had to let the children tag along, they'd tell them to look down, or look away from the Christmas decorations.

Even driving around town, the children in the Word of Faith Fellowship were told to turn away from houses decked for the holiday. Their only knowledge of Santa Claus was from Jane Whaley's rambling sermons that derided him as an evil, pagan symbol.

Adam walked slowly down the store aisles, studying every figurine. A Santa and his elves, Rudolph the reindeer, an inflatable snowman, nativity scenes, candy canes, and candles. Adam picked up a snow globe and shook it, then watched the white flakes settle to the bottom.

He was interacting with these symbols for the first time. He was overwhelmed. "There's so much stuff," he said.

Suzanne couldn't remember seeing her son so enthralled. In that moment, everything became clear to her. In the Word of Faith Fellowship, people are trained not to feel, not to care. The endless blastings, the battering, the isolation—*none of that expels demons*, she thought. It extinguishes hope. It suffocates joy. Everything about Jane Whaley and the church was a lie. Every action was meant to erase her followers' will and make them dependent.

Suzanne and Adam filled their cart with strands of colored lights, red and green ornaments, and shiny gold and silver tinsel. They picked out greenery for the mantel, a wreath to hang above the fireplace, and stockings for the children.

A resident from the county noticed their joyful, fascinated shopping spree.

"Did y'all leave the Word of Faith?" the woman asked, recognizing Suzanne.

"Yeah!" Adam said, beaming.

"This is Adam's first time celebrating Christmas," Suzanne said.

"Well, praise the Lord. I'm happy for you two. I hope you have a great Christmas," the woman said.

"We surely will," Suzanne said.

The woman smiled and walked away. Suzanne turned back to Adam. "We need something to put on top of the tree."

"What goes up there?" Adam asked.

"Well, it could be a star, or an angel," Suzanne said.

"Let's get an angel. That would drive Jane crazy!" Adam said. He sifted through the tree toppers and found a frilly golden angel. He felt like a rebel.

"It's perfect," Suzanne said.

"If Jane saw this we'd be dealt with, you know?"

"We don't have to worry about her now," Suzanne said.

They paid for the ornaments and went back to pick out a tree. Suzanne wanted a real tree, the biggest one they had.

They went to the garden section of the store, out in the cold. Adam couldn't believe there were so many shapes and sizes of evergreens. He walked along the rows, feeling the branches. They picked one that was more than six feet tall.

Before they hauled it all home, there was one more purchase Suzanne had to make.

She felt consumed with guilt for what she'd let happen to her family. She was horrified at how she had treated her relatives on the outside, especially her mother. The screaming, the slammed-down telephone calls, and finally cutting her off completely, it was unforgivable. She had robbed her mother of so many milestones in her grandchildren's lives, and Mama-Gail had never stopped loving them, waiting and hoping and praying... Now her mother was coming back.

Suzanne recalled a Top 40 radio hit from her childhood: "Tie a Yellow Ribbon Round the Ole Oak Tree." It was a story song about a man returning home after three years at war, looking anxiously for an agreed-upon sign that the woman he loves would welcome his return.

The music and lyrics played in Suzanne's head as she picked up a spool of yellow ribbon and dropped it in the shopping cart. Soon, she was humming the song, the lyrics stuck in her head: "tie a yellow ribbon round the ole oak tree."

Suzanne realized a handful of yellow ribbons wouldn't be enough. She grabbed another bundle. *Mom deserves more, she thought. She deserves a hundred yellow ribbons, and a big yellow banner that says Welcome Home, Mom.*

It was nearly 5:00 a.m. by the time Suzanne and Adam finished shopping. There was a light fog and a chill in the air as they strapped the tree to the top of the black Toyota. When they got home, they put on some music and placed the big tree against the back wall of the living room. The deep green of the branches and the red base were vibrant against the white carpet and walls. They hung the ornaments and strung up the lights, arranged red poinsettias across the mantel and hung a wreath above the fireplace. Adam built a fire. His mother killed the overhead lights.

"Are you ready?" Adam asked.

"I'm ready!" Suzanne said.

Adam plugged in the Christmas lights. The tree glowed. The shadows from the fire danced against the walls. Christmas music and pine-tree scent filled the room.

"I think it's beautiful," Suzanne said.

"Me, too, Mom."

Suzanne and Adam sank into the couch. They sat in silence, fascinated by the magic they had created. There was no need for words.

Wanda had been on the road for nine hours, through a stretch of Florida, all of Georgia, and South Carolina. Now she had just a little bit of Rutherford County left to do. She could have stopped, spent the night, and got up fresh in the morning, but she didn't want to waste another second. She had lost too much time already.

After her grandsons left the church, they started calling her, asking her to visit. Wanda jumped at the chance to spend Christmas with her grandchildren, and meet her new great-grandson. The Cooper family was growing, and this time Wanda would be around to enjoy the little ones.

Wanda's heart raced in anticipation as she turned onto Old Stonecutter Road. As her car approached Suzanne's driveway, she saw a big yellow banner hanging on the house. She peered to make out the letters: Welcome Home, Mom. She saw all the ribbons tied to the trees. She knew exactly what they meant.

She put the car in Park, turned off the headlights, and broke into sobs. She cried and cried—tears of joy—until she was certain she looked like a mess. But she didn't give a damn. It had been years since she'd been here. She deserved a good cry.

The front door burst open and everyone ran outside to greet her. She could hear them calling her name: Mama-Gail! Mama-Gail! They opened up the car door, grabbed her suitcase, hugged her, and kissed her. Little Blair and Adam had grown up. She had never met Jacklyn, and she was a sweet, delightful girl. The rest of the brood would be there that night, for a special dinner.

Suzanne smiled at her teary-eyed mother from the back of the crowd. "Come inside, Mom."

The house was full of light, all decked out in Christmas. That was when Wanda knew they had truly broken away from the church.

That evening Suzanne scrambled around the house, putting the final touches on the table. The rest of her children and other guests would arrive soon. The dining table was packed with food from end to end: turkey, black-eyed peas, butter beans, and pies and cakes. All the fixings of a Southern feast, and Mama-Gail's famous sweet potato balls—yams mixed with pineapple, then rolled in shredded coconut, and topped with a cherry. The kids had loved them when they were little. It was set up like a smorgasbord. Everyone would fill a plate, find a place to sit, and eat.

Rick's mother, Cora, who lived next door and had left the church weeks after the Coopers, was the first to arrive. Adam was helping in the kitchen, listening to Bruno Mars's new hit "Uptown Funk" and singing along: "I'm too hot, hot damn! Called a police and a fireman."

Cora was aghast. "Adam, that music is ungodly!" she said.

Adam just kept dancing. Cora persisted, raising her voice. "You are bringing profanity into the house."

"Well, this isn't your house," Adam snapped.

Rick shot him a dirty look. Adam knew his father was angry. He didn't care. They were assimilating at different paces. The family was going to have to live through awkward moments.

"Mom," Suzanne said to Wanda. "John David and Jessica just pulled up."

Wanda raced to the door and wrapped her arms around John, squeezing him tight. Then she glanced at Jessica's baby bump and smiled.

Soon the house was packed. The family feasted, then gathered around the piano to sing along as Adam played the songs he had learned for Wanda. He'd learned a lineup of Christmas songs, tunes he had never heard before, and mastered in a couple of weeks' time.

For the first time in anyone's memory, the house was filled with music and laughter. But no matter what they did, no matter how much they tried to steer the conversation away from the church, the shadows were inescapable.

There were reminders everywhere. The neighbors across the street were church members, and no doubt were sending reports of their ungodly merriment back to Jane. The town was lined with businesses owned by congregants, where they all had worked endless hours. The courthouse, where Shana so desperately fought to get her children back, loomed nearby.

The Cooper children had few life experiences outside the Word of Faith Fellowship. They never went fishing or hunting, things most boys do growing up in rural North Carolina. They never played team sports, not like normal high school kids. They weren't even allowed to watch them. They had family members still inside Word of Faith Fellowship. It was inevitable their stories returned to the church. The harshest experiences were spoken of in a matter-of-fact tone: the Lower Building, droning out the same praise chorus for twenty minutes straight, being pulled out of math class and blasted for giggling.

Suzanne's children recounted their experiences without malice, bitterness, or blame, but it hurt her to listen. Even though she had left the church, she could not escape.

Surrounded as she was by joy, Suzanne was overwhelmed by guilt. The last time this many of her children had been together in the house was the Sunday before John fled.

Suzanne was always on the move, the ultimate hostess, refilling drinks and checking food in the kitchen, so most of her family didn't notice when she slipped outside. She didn't want her family to see her cry.

But Wanda saw her struggling. She followed her daughter out to the deck.

In the distance, a sliver of the Blue Ridge Mountains cut into the evening sky. A tree-lined creek meandered through the property, fallen leaves rustled in the breeze. There was so much beauty in these foothills. How could something so ugly sprout up here? On the next hill, Suzanne could see the lights of her sister Cindy's house. How different their lives were now. They were so close by, but they lived in different worlds.

"I can't believe I let this happen," Suzanne said.

"Suzanne, it's OK," Wanda said, wrapping her arms around her oldest daughter. "We're together now. That's the important thing. And we're going to get through this."

"But, Mom, the stories they've told me about things that happened to them in that place," Suzanne said. "It makes me so mad. Sometimes I can't stand myself for what I have done.

Chad and Lena are still in there. And Cindy and her kids. And Shana's kids."

"Suzanne, they will come back to us," Wanda said. "Just like you came back to me. We don't know what tomorrow will bring."

"I just can't understand how all this happened. How I didn't see it, right in front of me."

"Honey, we can't live in the past. If you do, that woman will control your life forever."

"It's just overwhelming," Suzanne said. "You don't feel love in the Word of Faith. You don't feel emotion. You really learn not to feel."

Wanda stroked her daughter's hair.

"In the church, they say don't feel this or don't feel that, because it's not right. It's evil. And after a while, you just start to be unloving, uncaring, inhuman. I guess I'm starting to feel human again. And that hurts."

As Wanda hugged her, music emanated from inside. Adam was playing "O Holy Night" on the piano, and doing a beautiful job. The family was singing.

EPILOGUE

John David Cooper gathered up his courage and read the telephone number on the slip of paper.

So many positive things had happened to him since he left the Word of Faith Fellowship. Did he really want to make the call, and open up a new can of worms? Why not just walk away, leave the nightmares in the past?

By the summer of 2015, John had wrapped up his first year of medical school at UNC Chapel Hill. He was the happy father of a baby boy. His parents and most of his eight siblings had left the Word of Faith Fellowship. They were all at different stages of moving on with their lives.

So was John—until he took a class that threw his past in his face.

He was taking a block of psychiatry courses, including one on domestic violence. As a doctor, he'd have to learn to recognize the signs of abuse, and how to respond.

The lectures described how abusive people manipulate and control their family members, and how victims often blame themselves or hide behind a wall of shame. The lectures triggered horrific memories of Word of Faith Fellowship. A string of nightmares sent John to his professors for help. He met three different instructors in private and recounted his life inside the church. All three responded the same way: he had to report the child abuse to authorities.

"But the authorities won't do anything," he told them.

He explained the 2005 church lawsuit against the Rutherford County Department of Social Services that left law enforcement toothless when it came to investigating children in the church.

That didn't matter, the doctors said. John still had a moral and legal obligation to report the abuse.

John told Rutherford County DSS officials he'd seen children beaten by teachers and ministers in the church's K–12 school. He had seen children assaulted in the sanctuary and other places on church grounds. The abuse grew worse over time, he said. He listed the names of victims and their abusers.

The agency investigated, but soon closed the probe, saying his allegations were unfounded.

John knew his professors were right. Doctors help people. How could he continue in his career while ignoring everything that happened to him? What could he do now?

John decided to call an investigative reporter. Maybe a journalist could expose the church.

His older brothers were lukewarm about the idea. If John wanted to do it, fine, but they weren't going to get involved. They knew Jane Whaley would brand them as "attackers," and cut off what little contact remained with loved ones still in the church.

John understood. He finally found the ally he needed in Jamey Anderson, who'd grown up with him in the church. The men had reconnected after John fled in the summer of 2014. Jamey lived in Chapel Hill, where he was finishing his last year at the University of North Carolina School of Law.

Their friendship led them to reestablish contacts with Matthew Fenner, another UNC student, and Nancy Burnette, who had worked in the past as a source for the *Associated Press*. John recalled his cousins, nephews, and nieces who were still in the Word of Faith Fellowship, as well as many other children. They were undergoing the same abusive practices he'd endured for two decades. Unless somebody spoke up, nothing would ever change.

John took a deep breath and dialed. It was the beginning of John's journey—one that would not only expose the church's practices, but eventually lead to a federal investigation of the Word of Faith Fellowship.

Mitch Weiss, an investigative reporter, was driving home from work when he answered his mobile phone. John Cooper introduced himself, and made an important request. "I don't want us to be exploited. And I don't want the story to be sensationalized. I just want the truth to be told," he said.

Mitch didn't hesitate: "That's not a problem."

John wanted to meet in person. Mitch was anxious to meet John, too. For years, Nancy and John Huddle had tried to get journalists interested in investigating the church. Mitch was one of the few who'd taken them seriously.

He'd been following developments in the church since 2012, when Michael Lowry said church leaders tried to beat "gay demons" out of his body. Mitch had written that story, and was working on a follow-up about the church when he learned that Michael Lowry had gone missing. Mitch had walked unannounced into the church in February 2013, was given a personal tour by Jane Whaley herself, and found the missing man in the church basement. Whaley allowed an interview, but only if she and several other church leaders could stay in the room.

Michael recanted his story, saying he had never been beaten. Mitch found Michael was subdued, groggy, like he was medicated, using stiff, repeated phrases that indicated he'd been coached. Mitch had no way of proving that, but he never forgot the blank look on Michael's face, a marked change from the man he'd met a few weeks earlier.

In December 2014, five church members were indicted on charges of assaulting Matthew Fenner. Mitch was determined to take a deeper look at the Word of Faith Fellowship.

But it wasn't easy. There were few documents or newspaper stories. What he did find were custody cases, old filings from the mid-1990s in the wake of the *Inside Edition* episode.

Mitch turned to Nancy and Huddle for help. They had a network of nearly thirty survivors, but most weren't ready to go public. Some were afraid of Whaley's revenge. Others were embarrassed: they had been caught up in a cult. What would their new friends think?

Nancy and Huddle encouraged them to talk. Authorities had let them down, they said, and ongoing public pressure might finally force law enforcement to do something.

John Cooper didn't know any of that. He didn't know Nancy or Huddle well. He only knew that Mitch was driving five hours from Greenville, South Carolina, to Chapel Hill to talk to him.

He wondered if Mitch would believe him. Parts of his story sounded outrageous, like crime fiction. Jamey said he'd sit in, too. They could even meet up at his apartment.

Jamey understood John's trepidation. He had never talked to a journalist about the church, either. But they could do it together.

For five hours that day in August 2015, John and Jamey talked about their years in the church. They discussed their earliest memories—being blasted as babies, the beatings and isolation as they grew older. Jamey went into detail about the persecution of the Five Boys. John explained how Jane Whaley had arranged his marriage. They discussed the church's draconian rules regarding sex.

It was story after story of emotional and physical abuse—how children suffered, and how parents stood by and let it happen. And how parents became victims, too.

"They try to reframe the abuse as the love of God—they're doing it for God," John David Cooper said.

Mitch listened and asked follow-up questions. As day turned to night, Mitch asked one last question: "What made you decide to talk?"

"The children," John said. "They need to be saved."

Jamey nodded. "I don't want any other child in Word of Faith to suffer like I did," he said. "Nobody ever helped us. People just walked away. I don't want to be that person."

It was a good start, but Mitch knew he needed more people to talk. If the allegations were true, there would be strength in numbers. If dozens of people came forward, how could Whaley deny them all without seeming detached from reality?

What other material was out there that could substantiate the allegations? Tapes? John and Jamey said they had some. Videos? They weren't sure there were any. Any documents? They didn't know.

Mitch took their stories to his editors. They had an obligation to look into the more serious allegations, because they involved children.

The editors agreed and added *AP* investigator Holbrook Mohr to the project. Together they went to work tracking down former members scattered all over the world.

Over the course of two years, the team interviewed one hundred former members—most of whom had never spoken to a journalist. Many suffered the symptoms of post-traumatic stress disorder: flashbacks, nightmares, and depression. Some turned to drugs, alcohol, or other addictive or self-destructive behaviors.

Not surprisingly, they found that many former members struggled in their relationships with God and the church. After living lives so intensely dedicated to "pleasing the Lord," some had walked away from religion entirely.

"For me, I still have not been able to go back to any church," said Theresa Dodrill, who left in 2008 after twenty years. "It got so bad that I remember saying that either God is mean, or these people are evil."

John Blanton, one of the Five Boys, said he no longer believes in God. He has found a new use for pages in his Bible. "I use them to roll joints," he said.

The investigative team scoured local, state, and federal courts, and found all kinds of documents, police reports, incident slips, and full investigations buried by law enforcement agencies. They uncovered depositions, family court rulings, child welfare files. They found more than one hundred cassette tapes of sermons conducted by Jane Whaley, her husband, Sam, and other church leaders, as well as audio of family and criminal court hearings and videos of church services.

The documents helped corroborate the victims' allegations of systemic corruption and abuse. But the journalists knew the believers—and their pain—were the heart of the story.

Survivors of Word of Faith Fellowship continue to struggle long after they leave. Most will never fully recover. Many of their marriages fail; after years of regimented morality, outbursts of enthusiasm and attempts to "make up for lost time" usually backfire. Some end up homeless, addicted to alcohol or drugs, or mired in unhealthy exploitative situations.

Loneliness can be suffocating for those who've never spent time unaccompanied. Young people who leave the church have missed a lifetime of movies and music, which can make it difficult to fit in with peers. They don't always catch references to Americana or pop culture, which stirs feelings of isolation even in a crowd. Some find their night terrors interfere with intimate relationships.

In February 2017, the *AP* ran the first in a yearlong series of investigative stories that exposed extensive abuse in the Word of Faith Fellowship. Violations include brutal beatings, children routinely wrested from their families, and a pipeline of young laborers brought from Brazil and forced into virtual slavery in North Carolina—all perpetrated in the name of Jesus Christ. The *AP* disclosed how businesses owned by church leaders came up with a fraudulent unemployment scheme to pay workers—and keep their tithes flowing in—during a major economic downturn.

These stories revealed widespread institutional corruption and incompetence that allowed the church to escape serious charges. At least six times over two decades, authorities investigated reports that church members were being beaten. And every time, orders came down from Jane Whaley: witnesses must lie to protect the sect.

The *AP* investigation showed that lawyers Frank Webster and Chris Back were among the Word of Faith Fellowship members who coached congregants and their children on what to say to investigators. Webster and Back—assistant prosecutors for three counties nearby the church—provided legal advice, helped at strategy sessions, and participated in a mock trial for four congregants charged with harassing a former member.

After the stories ran, Webster and Back were forced to leave their jobs. No criminal charges were filed against them.

The *AP* reports brought to light several other criminal actions and enterprises.

Three church leaders, including Kent Covington, entered guilty pleas in May 2018 for their roles in the unemployment scheme that lasted between 2008 and 2013. The charges carry a maximum penalty of thirty years in prison and a $1 million fine. A fourth pleaded guilty a year later.

And in late April 2019, Covington was sentenced to thirty-four months in prison and ordered to pay $466,960 in restitution for his role in an unemployment fraud scheme.

Before sentencing Covington, US District Court Judge Martin Reidinger said he wouldn't recuse himself from the case as some former Word of Faith Fellowship members had suggested. He said he could be fair and balanced even though he acknowledged in court that a Word of Faith Fellowship member had clerked in his office, and that he had been to several events at the church. (What the judge didn't disclose from the bench was that at the request of a church leader, he had discussed the Nuremberg Trials at a community college. Mitch was there that night in October 2015. So were nearly two hundred people—most of whom were Word of Faith members.) At Covington's sentencing, nearly one hundred and fifty people—mostly Word of Faith Fellowship members— packed just about every row of seats in Reidinger's courtroom.

Even though the *AP* had published numerous stories about Word of Faith Fellowship, the judge either didn't read them, or simply ignored them. That was because as he stared at the men and women dressed up in their Sunday best, Reidinger said he just couldn't understand how such a wonderful, beloved, and respected man in the community could take such a wrong turn.

"This is a case that just baffles me. I've seen hundreds of cases and I think I have a pretty good grasp of the psychological pathology that underpins these cases. This one I don't understand," he said.

But Reidinger said one thing was clear: he "needed to send a message to the community as a whole. You can't do things like that. You can't use any kind of government program as a personal piggy bank."

Still, Reidinger missed the point. Covington wasn't a guy who lived an exemplary life and made an honest mistake. He wasn't a businessman who tried to keep his businesses afloat so he could keep his employees working during tough economic times, as his attorney had claimed. No, Covington was carrying out a carefully planned scheme approved by the top leadership of the church.

Jane Whaley was not charged in the case, but survivors considered it a promising development when court records named her as a coconspirator, someone who "promoted" the illegal activity.

As of October 2019, the Word of Faith Fellowship was still in business. In fact, even with the arrests, trials, and dirty laundry, the sect seems to thrive. Jane Whaley has not been charged with a crime, even after years of proof and accusations.

"When will it end? When will the church be held account-able?" Jamey Anderson asked.

Anderson has failed to erase his memories of the church. The church continues to erase him from its own history. They banned him from the funeral of his beloved grandfather Dr. Pat Pagter in February 2015, and even omitted him from the list of family members in the obituary.

After leaving the church, Jamey largely made it on his own. He reconnected with his biological father and a few family members on the outside. He graduated from law school and landed a job with a respected Charlotte firm.

His future seemed bright. Then, in October 2016, police arrested him for trespassing on his brother's property.

His brother, Nick Anderson, who remained in the church, had sworn to a magistrate that Jamey had been spotted outside his house. Jamey presented overwhelming evidence he was nowhere near his brother's home. At the time, he was actually sixty miles east in a Charlotte restaurant with a group of fellow lawyers.

Jamey had restaurant receipts and affidavits from the at-torneys.

The charges were dropped, but Jamey was humiliated. He had to explain to his bosses what happened—and that he'd grown up in a religious cult. A few months later, his contract with the law firm wasn't renewed.

There were no consequences for Nick Anderson, or the other Word of Faith Fellowship member who helped him file the charges.

"It was meant to send a message," he said softly.

Jamey is a smart, funny man with a sarcastic sense of humor. His mood changes when he talks about the church. He becomes sullen. Sometimes, his memories transport him to a dark, damp storage room with green carpet, the place where he was beaten and left alone for days. It was the room where he prayed to die. He stays up at night talking to other former members. The person he talks to most is Nancy Burnette, who has become an ad hoc cult-recovery therapist as the years pass.

Nancy is one of the first people escapees seek out when they leave the church. She was one of the advocates who introduced us to many people harmed by the church, including Keela Blanton, a mother with a tale of tragic loss.

Not everyone joined the church willingly, or was brought there as a child. Other people crossed paths with the church by the worst sort of happenstance, and saw their lives torn apart.

In the summer of 2008, Blanton, who knew little about the church, was pregnant and facing a jail sentence when court clerk and church member Laura Bridges made her an irresistible offer: Bridges and her husband would care for the baby until Blanton was out of jail and back on her feet. This way, the child would be in an intact family, and not end up in foster care, Bridges told her. Blanton thought her prayers had been answered. So, in July 2008, when the boy was five days old, Blanton signed an agreement granting Bridges temporary guardianship until her release from jail, when she would resume "full responsibility for my child."

Blanton served time for various charges, including attempting to obtain controlled substances by fraud. When she was released, the foster mother, Bridges, told Blanton that she had fallen in love with the boy and wanted to help care for him.

The baby continued to spend much of his time with the couple, which Blanton said seemed like a blessing. Until he began seeming anxious, and came home with bruises on his face. In August 2012, Blanton refused to send the boy back to the Bridgeses' home. She filed child abuse reports with the sheriff's office and social services authorities.

A clinical assessment said the boy showed "signs of being coerced and brainwashed," but Blanton's struggle was just beginning. Bridges and her husband, and the Word of Faith team of lawyers, were determined to make the child their own.

That was when Nancy Burnette got involved. She did all she could to help, getting advice from Robynn Spence, the clerk of courts, on how to file court motions on Blanton's behalf. But they could not match the church's team of lawyers, led in the custody case by Mark Morris.

Blanton said members of the church followed her and snapped photos of her and her family. In October 2012, Blanton had enough. She swallowed a handful of pills. She recovered from the suicide attempt, but the Bridgeses eventually won sole custody of the boy.

In the fall of 2017, Keela Blanton said she had one message for her child, now sealed away inside the sect: "Mama didn't do it. Mama didn't walk away," Blanton said, weeping. "I love you with all my heart, everything that's in me. I love you."

Nancy Burnette has dedicated her life to helping people like Blanton, and helping former members leave the church and rebuild their lives.

Stealing time away from her job and family, Nancy has been a constant presence at court hearings. She has opened her home and her wallet to people caught in the church's tentacles. If someone needs clothes for a job interview, or a ride, or a place to stay, they call Nancy.

Her investment of emotion and time are incalculable. Still, she lives by the vow she made to herself and the survivors: she will not quit until every child in the Word of Faith Fellowship can live free of abuse.

John Huddle's childhood was the antithesis of Nancy's. He came from the storybook middle-class family, but in his search for spiritual certainty, he was ensnared by Jane Whaley's twisted take on the Bible and its promises for believers.

He now spends his free time counseling former members and updating his popular blog. He's become a bit of an expert on American cults over the years, and the burning question remains: Why would anyone join a cult?

"I didn't know the Word of Faith Fellowship was a cult," John said. "Nobody looks to join a cult."

People join the Word of Faith Fellowship for a variety of reasons: to save troubled marriages, to kick alcohol or drug or gambling addictions, or to become part of a dynamic community of God's chosen people. Huddle and others say they became members because the church's charismatic leader, Jane Whaley, offered them hope in a world full of confusion and heartbreak. In Whaley's world, they believed, they had found a special place, safe from the mad world outside, with opportunities for American-style upward mobility.

"She had a way of making vulnerable people feel special," Huddle said. "She took a page out of the cult playbook."

Whaley was a godlike figure who professed to have all the answers. Members were usually isolated from the outside world as their leader took control over every aspect of their lives. People who stepped out of line or questioned authority were threatened with violence or expulsion. All of these are classic cult behaviors, Huddle said. The longer he stayed at Spindale, the more he realized he was a victim.

"We couldn't do anything without Whaley's permission. We were told not to have contact with family or friends who weren't church members," he said.

One of the experts Huddle turned to was Lorna Goldberg,

who has a master's degree in social work from New York University and is an expert on cults.

Goldberg said cults like Word of Faith appear to be legitimate at the outset.

"Over time, there's a whole belief system that they buy into. Their only route to salvation is by continuing to be a true believer in this group, that if they leave they will be doomed to hell, and there will be terrible consequences for them and it could even impact their family," she said.

Time and again, the former members told Mitch and Holbrook that Whaley warned them that terrible things would happen to them and their families if they questioned her authority or even thought about leaving the church.

Bad things happened to Huddle when he left. "But it wasn't because of God," he said. "And my worst days outside the church are better than my best days inside."

One day, Huddle hopes that his family will be free. When he closes his eyes, he pictures himself surrounded by his children and grandchildren. Until then, he stays up at night, working on his next post, fielding more phone calls.

Other survivors' stories play out like Greek tragedies. Take sisters Suzanne Cooper and Shana Muse.

Suzanne was responsible for recruiting Shana and another sister, Cindy Cordes, to the Word of Faith Fellowship. Suzanne turned on her sister in 2002, and her legal testimony resulted in Shana's four children being taken from her to live with the Covingtons.

The six-year custody battle destroyed Shana Muse; she once again turned to drugs and landed in prison.

Shana has put that life behind her. Three of her children—Patrick, Sarah, and Rachel—left the church since 2013, and are reunited with their mother. Her son Justin remains inside. She keeps his picture at her bedside.

In 2014, when Shana learned Suzanne had left the church,

she was thrilled. It didn't take long to repair their broken bond. In the middle of their first embrace, Suzanne whispered, "I'm sorry."

She didn't have to say anything else. "We're family. In the end, that's what matters," Shana said.

Now the sisters are inseparable. They both spend most of their free time babysitting their grandchildren. They pray for the day that Shana's last child, Justin, leaves the church, as well as their sister, Cindy, and her family.

Suzanne and Rick Cooper divorced in 2016. Suzanne works as a teacher in Charlotte. In Spindale her house was always filled with more than a dozen children, her own and others. She didn't have a moment to herself. She's learning to live on her own, she said, and learning to embrace peace and quiet.

Rick Cooper said Word of Faith Fellowship was the biggest mistake of his life. It cost him everything but his faith, and even that is still a work in progress.

"In life, the past is the past. You can only move forward," he said.

That's a philosophy his children are trying to embrace.

The Cooper brood is getting their lives together. Chad Cooper, an attorney, left the church in late 2015. The last sibling, Lena, left in the summer of 2018.

John David Cooper is an officer in the US Navy, serving his residency at Walter Reed National Military Medical Center in Washington, DC. He and his wife, Jessica, have separated. The baggage from all the years inside the church caught up with them.

Peter Cooper is finishing medical school at the University of South Carolina.

Jeffrey Cooper, an estate planner, is still married to Natalie, the woman he met inside the church all those years ago. They are raising a daughter, and his business is thriving. Jeffrey kept his promise: once the church began "messing with his family," he helped Benjamin and John and the others fight back. As soon as the fraud investigation began, he turned over his clutch of church business and accounting documents to state and federal authorities. He helped his brothers navigate the North Carolina State Bar, the agency that handles ethics complaints.

Their complaint disclosed the actions of Frank Webster, Chris Back, Josh Farmer, Mark Morris, and other attorneys in the church to obstruct the Matthew Fenner investigation.

"Over the course of time, Mrs. Whaley held several meetings with every possible witness she could get her hands on. Notably, these meetings were all generally attended and conducted by attorneys who are members of Word of Faith Fellowship.

"Under the nose of the attorneys present, Mrs. Whaley told several witnesses to change their story or that they were 'in witchcraft' if the witnesses did not recount the story exactly how Mrs. Whaley wanted it to be said," the complaint said.

The complaint also said that Farmer and Morris "flagrantly participated" with Whaley by drafting the affidavits of a large number of witnesses—affidavits that contained inaccurate information.

The state bar agreed to investigate in 2016. But to this day, the agency hasn't disclosed what became of the complaint.

"There was nothing about any of this that was normal," Jeffrey Cooper said.

When he was inside, he knew he was helping Jane Whaley and leadership. He hoped that somehow, if he pointed out the errors of their actions, they'd change, or that maybe they just didn't know the law. But over time he realized church leaders not only knew they were breaking the law, they didn't care. The hypocrisy was clear. It was time to go.

Benjamin Cooper has turned into the family pit bull. He and his wife live in Charlotte with their two children and run a successful recycling business, but much of his time is dedicated to exposing Jane Whaley and her church. Both attorneys, Benjamin and Micah have offered legal advice to former members and urge other survivors to tell their stories.

The church has learned that Benjamin Cooper should not be underestimated. He is a driving force in keeping this story alive, pressing authorities to act and helping organize former members to participate in an A&E Network documentary about the church.

Initially scheduled to premiere in November 2018, the six-part TV series was put on hold. The Word of Faith Fellowship hired a law firm with ties to the Church of Scientology to block the broadcast.

Josh Farmer has publicly taken credit for the postponement, saying the network buckled under pressure when the Word of Faith Fellowship questioned payments to former church members. A&E denied the church's threats were the reason for postponing the six-part series, instead saying the network needed time to put some finishing touches on the show.

Danielle Cordes has graduated from the University of Florida and works in the insurance business, but she struggles to overcome the memories of abuse. She remains in close contact with Matthew Fenner.

She has kept her past a secret from most of her new friends, but she doesn't hesitate to talk to journalists.

A few years after she left, she said she visited her old house, just to see if her family would speak to her. Her father closed the door in her face.

"You don't understand what that's like," she said. "There are times I want to pick up the phone and call my mother, share something that happened to me. But I can't," she said.

Meanwhile, Matthew Fenner works as an emergency medical technician, and still dreams of becoming a doctor. He has spent years fighting for justice.

More than six years after Matthew was beaten in the sanctuary, Brooke Covington was the first person to face trial in the case on May 30, 2017. It should have been an easy decision for a jury.

One of the other defendants, Shana Muse's daughter Sarah Anderson, testified on Matthew's behalf. Even though she knew it would be detrimental to her own case, Sarah admitted that she had participated in the brutal attack and testified that it was orchestrated by Brooke Covington.

On June 6, 2017, a juror brought unauthorized documents into deliberations. He was arrested. The judge declared a mistrial. It was another blow for Matthew. But nothing like what was coming.

Less than two weeks after the mistrial, Matthew's beloved grandfather Robert Rape was found dead in his yard from a shotgun blast to the chest. Matthew was broken. His grandfather was the most important male figure in his life, the one who had given him a place to live after he escaped the Word of Faith Fellowship.

Authorities said Rape committed suicide. But the manner of death left many people wondering if he had been killed.

Meantime, charges against Brooke Covington and the others are still pending. At the time of this writing, no court date has been set.

As for Michael Lowry, his life has gone from bad to worse. After he recanted, the sect arranged to have him marry a woman in one of the Brazilian churches. He refused, and fled again. He moved to Michigan to live with his aunt.

He moved out on his own, and he fell in with a group of "bad people" in Detroit, his aunt said. He lives now in a group home.

"I don't have much hope," Michael said. "I need help, I know. But where am I going to get it?"

His aunt said all the years of abuse inside the church have taken a toll. She worries for Michael's safety. At times he roams the streets. When he closes his eyes, he said, it all comes back to him: the nightmares, the brutality. He still doesn't know if he's gay. That doesn't matter, anyway.

"I don't think I'll ever escape," he said, predicting that "I'm going to end up dead. I know it. Maybe that's the only way it will ever stop."

The victims' stories are only part of the *AP* series. The investigative team was likewise disturbed by the way law enforcement and social services have handled allegations about the sect.

The documents and interviews show that government agencies and public officials charged with enforcing the law seemed to look the other way when Word of Faith Fellowship was involved in a case. For years, the church was allowed to operate with impunity.

When the church officials needed help, they were quick to call in the Rutherford County Sheriff's Department. For decades, they had a pipeline to law enforcement. In one email to Sheriff Chris Francis in 2013, Josh Farmer summoned the sheriff to meet with him and two other church officials to discuss a member who had escaped.

Mr. Sheriff:
I hope you are doing good. If you have some time on Thursday or Friday, I would appreciate a brief meeting to discuss something of concern to me and my church. It is regarding an ex-inmate from the Spindale prison who recently left the church. Douglas MacDonald and DeWitt Prince and my father would likely come with me. I realize that this is likely a very busy time of the year for you. If you can make time for us briefly, I would appreciate it.

Best Regards,
Joshua B. Farmer

It was written on Christmas Eve.

When the investigative team knocked on Brad Greenway's door, they didn't know if the former prosecutor would talk to them. To their surprise, Greenway invited Mitch and an *AP* videographer inside.

Some former members said they had talked to Greenway before the grand jury hearings in the Lowry and Fenner cases. One member said the church leaked critical information to the district attorney. Grand jury hearings are supposed to be secret. Greenway said yes, he had met with church leaders before the hearings. While he couldn't recall specifics of the conversations, he denied supplying them with "inside information."

Sitting in his living room that day, Greenway said he "grew tired" of dealing with the Word of Faith Fellowship. "Outsiders just don't understand what it's like trying to make a case against the church." If minors make accusations, he said, some might change their stories. And then, he said, "You're going to have twenty people who come in, who are former Navy pilots, schoolteachers, principals, and they're dressed to the nines, and they're going to say these kids are lying. And if you look back, the people they take in come from prison, are drug addicts, they're alcoholics, so when they come and make these allegations, they're not believable or there's something that can impugn their character. So you don't have the ideal witnesses."

When reminded that both Lowry and Fenner were raised in the church with no criminal records, Greenway shifted course, saying, "I'm not talking about them."

He didn't say who he was talking about.

Cult leader Jim Jones had 1,500 followers at the height of his power. David Koresh had close to 800. Word of Faith Fellowship has thousands of members spread out all over the world. When current members were questioned about the church's brutal practices, the response was nearly always the same: "I have never seen anyone abused in our church."

That is the conundrum.

Jane Whaley's followers cannot grasp that what they're doing, and seeing, is abusive. They don't see "blasting," punching, shoving, kicking, and screaming at a fellow believer— even a child—as abuse. They believe it is the only way to break free from the devil that stands between them and holiness. How can these things be wrong when Jane Whaley says it is directed by the Lord himself?

Law enforcement and social workers know better. Pinning a child to the floor and hitting and punching him to expel invisible devils is child abuse. Just ask Jeffrey Cooper.

One day at the Covingtons' house, Jeffrey heard a loud shriek, like a wounded animal. He followed the sound to a bathroom. When he opened the door he saw his cousin pinned down while a minister repeatedly whacked him with a paddle.

Jeffrey turned his head and left the room. "I knew what I saw: felony child abuse," he said. But he was too afraid to stop it, too afraid to report it to police.

While journalists lift the veil on the Word of Faith Fellowship, the full scope of abuse may never be known. Many secrets have been buried for decades. Under public pressure in the wake of the *Inside Edition* piece, Rutherford County Sheriff Dan Good and District Attorney Jeff Hunt asked the North Carolina State Bureau of Investigation to look into allegations of abuse in the church. State investigators compiled a damning, 315-page report in 1995 with detailed allegations of brainwashing, sexual abuse, physical attacks, and people being restrained by church leaders.

But local authorities declined to prosecute, even though some of the people named in the report said they were willing to press charges. The report was never released to the public.

When the *AP* obtained a copy, the journalists discovered that not only was the abuse widespread, but most of the church's leadership was still in place nearly two decades later.

The church has been able to survive, in part, because of the way its leaders shape the narrative. Jane Whaley claims it has been persecuted because of its religious beliefs.

It was like that in 1995. It's like that in 2019.

The tactics are the same. The church has lashed out at its former congregants. People like Jamey Anderson's mother, John Huddle's ex-wife and children, and Shana Muse's son Justin have released videos online calling their relatives liars.

Since December 2017, the church has bought airtime on a local radio station. Three days a week, Whaley's followers go on the air to sing the praises of the church or criticize those who have chosen to speak out. By early 2019, one hundred and fifty followers had given their "testimony." The videos are posted online.

The Word of Faith Fellowship has not faded into the shadows. Church leaders actively support conservative political candidates and appear at events for the Freedom Caucus, an archconservative Republican group.

In July 2017, the Whaleys' daughter, Robin Webster, attended a fund-raiser for Republican Lieutenant Governor Dan Forest. The same month, political operative and Word of Faith associate Bryson Smith sent an email to Sheriff Chris Francis containing a guest list for a fund-raiser for US Congressman Mark Meadows, R–North Carolina.

Sam and Jane Whaley were among the numerous Word of Faith Fellowship members on the list. So was their daughter, along with others, like Todd and Karel Reynolds and several members of the Caulder family.

Whaley and her followers supported Donald J. Trump in his 2016 presidential campaign, and some attended his inauguration. When the president held a rally in Charlotte in October 2018, numerous members of the church sat in the front row wearing volunteer passes, including Robin Webster and Leigh Valentine. In fact, Valentine has been one of Trump's biggest supporters. Her Facebook page is filled with her at 2016 Trump campaign events. And right there, on her page, she has several photos of her with Trump, just the two of them. After his election, Valentine claimed she was a member of a little-known presidential group promoting religious outreach. It's unclear whether she is. But in May 2019, for a black-tie event, she touted her close relationship with the president. Valentine was of the featured speakers at a Washington "gala" for Constitutional Millennials, a group that says it's "working to restore our country back to its biblical foundations." In her bio, she says she "currently serves as a leader under President Trump for faith leadership outreach."

Now in her late seventies, Jane Whaley is still in charge, and shows no signs of slowing down. Over the years, the investigative team had tried to interview Whaley and other church leaders, including the Covingtons. They couldn't visit the church because it's on private property. But before the *AP* stories ran, the team either knocked on the front doors of key Word of Faith Fellowship leaders or visited them at their businesses. The reporters were told by church members to talk to Whaley, or had doors slammed in their faces. So the investigative team sent questions via emails to Josh Farmer, who acted as the church spokesman, or to Whaley's Charlotte-based attorney, Noell Tin. Farmer and Tin denied any allegations put to them. As for Whaley, she tried to spin the *AP* series, saying no abuse has ever taken place inside the church.

"I would never hurt anyone—especially children," she said.

But Whaley's own words and deeds have exposed her dark side. It's hard to say you don't abuse congregants when you can hear Whaley screaming at members during blasting sessions that sound like outtakes from a horror movie. Audio tapes of her sermons from the mid-1990s reveal her philosophy of devils and deliverance.

The Word of Faith Fellowship might not be as big as the

Church of Scientology. And Jane Whaley might not have the following of televangelists like Joel Osteen, Creflo Dollar, or other prosperity gospel preachers. But Jane Whaley—the woman who was once shunned by televangelists' wives—has amassed millions.

And while some of her contemporaries, like Robert Tilton, have faded, Whaley keeps going.

What makes Jane Whaley tick? What makes her unique among her kind?

One aspect is her undying focus on the "unclean," a code word for anything sexual. Outer appearances say Jane Whaley came from a normal background and lived an ordinary life. She went to college, competed on the swim team, taught high school math, married, and had a daughter. But something happened in her life that made her believe that sex is evil and demonic, and should be avoided whenever possible.

At some point in her life, she started believing that men were mostly to blame for the uncleanness in her world.

Her confidantes were women. They were the first "true believers." When the hammer came down on the "unclean" and the Lower Building filled up, all the inmates were men and boys. Yes, women were accused of "giving in to the unclean," but their punishment was not nearly so severe. Men were blasted and isolated. Women are, for the most part, humiliated and shamed. Their blastings appear much more mild.

Only Whaley knows what shapes her strict doctrine. Other practices are easier to see: Jane Whaley is materialistic. Those who knew her well say she bragged about her secret shopping sprees. Randy Fields, a former security team member, said once the offerings were counted up in her office after services, Jane "took the cash and headed out the door." No one in the congregation ever saw the books. They were too afraid to ask.

In August 2014, Whaley and her daughter sued the US government, claiming members of the Transportation Security

Administration lost or stole a leather satchel they were carrying on a flight from Charlotte to Israel. Whaley said the bag contained $74,000 worth of jewelry.

In a sworn deposition in a child custody case in April 2017, Whaley spoke of "love offerings"—gifts and cash people give to her out of the goodness of their hearts.

She said she has a steady stream of "love offerings" coming in from congregants in the United States as well as Brazil and Ghana.

But that wasn't enough. Jane Whaley evidently hoped to build a spectacular new sanctuary, and pay for it with a boulder-sized emerald-encrusted stone that might or might not have been stolen. It's a caper worthy of an international crime thriller.

It began in 2014, when a member of the Brazilian church, a gem dealer, asked his minister to watch the rock for him while he was in the hospital—it was worth millions, he said. When the man was released, his rock was gone. The preacher wouldn't say where it was.

The gem dealer's daughter, Rebeca Melo, was a teacher in the Word of Faith Fellowship school in Spindale. Her dad told her his stone was missing. She confronted Jane Whaley.

Jane told her she and all the Brazilian pastors knew where the rock was, but that it wasn't worth much. The security team escorted Melo off church grounds.

What they didn't know was that Melo had recorded the conversation. The investigative team drilled down and found more details and documents regarding the rock.

The rock was in the custody of FreightWorks, a trucking company owned by Josh Farmer and his father, Ray, as recently as December 2015. It was stored in a North Carolina warehouse.

Two companies that specialize in precious stones analyzed the rock or parts of it. One of them, EGL USA, noted that it

was the largest emerald-encrusted stone of its kind the group
had ever seen.

It's unclear how the rock got to the United States. Once
there, Mark Morris and other church leaders went to a gem
show in Arizona to meet Dwayne Hall, a reality TV character
known as the gem hunter on the show *Prospectors*.

Hall said Josh Farmer asked him to clean the gem and prepare it. Farmer said he was a preacher who wanted to use the
proceeds to build a church and school in a poor village in
Brazil. Farmer, Morris, and other church leaders prayed with
Hall, and he decided to do the job.

In early 2016, Hall said that Farmer had come for the rock
and told him it was worthless. The gem hunter was never
paid. He said he worked more than a year on the rock because
he thought it was for a charitable cause—he had no idea that
Farmer was not a preacher. And after it left his house, that's
where the trail goes cold. No one—except the church—knows
what happened to the emerald-studded stone.

The reporters discovered that the US Department of Home-
land Security is looking into the alleged theft on behalf of
the Brazilian government. Brazil is one of the most resource-
rich nations in the world, and a gem like this is considered
national patrimony.

Meanwhile, Josh Farmer continues to promote his trucking company. In February 2017, he announced the "exciting
news" in a press release that FreightWorks had been certified under the International Cyanide Management Code to
transport sodium cyanide, a deadly poisonous chemical used
in the mining industry.

Some former members find that troubling. If authorities take
action to shut down the church, will they arrest more members? And if they do, will it be peaceful? No one wants another
Jonestown—where over nine hundred cult members drank a
cyanide-laced drink when faced with an end to their church.

One thing is clear: Jane Whaley cannot hide any longer. She has used the right of religious freedom, a cornerstone of American democracy, to shroud her activities long enough.

John David Cooper started this story with his telephone call. He knows he made the right decision. "The end is near for Jane Whaley," he said.

Like the others, he doesn't know how it will end. It has gone on for so long that many have lost hope. But John Cooper is keeping the faith, believing that good people will do the right thing, and justice will come to Rutherford County, North Carolina.

★ ★ ★ ★ ★

ACKNOWLEDGMENTS

This book has been years in the making and we'd like to thank a number of people who helped us along the way. We'd like to thank John David Cooper, who made the phone call in the summer of 2015 that led to the *Associated Press* investigation that revealed widespread abuse inside the Word of Faith Fellowship. A special thanks to Ben Cooper, who was tireless in helping us, and to Rick and Suzanne and the rest of the Cooper family for allowing us to tell their story. Former congregants Jamey Anderson, Christina Bryant, Danielle Cordes, Matthew Fenner, John Huddle, Michael Lowry, Shana Muse and her children, Jeanna Powell, and too many others to name spent hours reliving painful memories to pull back the curtains on the Word of Faith Fellowship. We'd also like to thank Nancy Burnette, who never hesitated to help gather court and police reports, or to act as a liaison to people harmed by the church.

None of this would have been possible without the support of the *Associated Press* and numerous people who helped us along the way, including editors Rick Pienciak and Kristin

Gazlay. Peter Prengaman gathered documents and poignant stories in Brazil. Alex Sanz guided video coverage.

We'd also like to thank our agent, Frank Weimann, at Folio Literary Management, and John Glynn, our editor at Hanover Square Press, for believing in this project and in us.

Most important, we'd like to thank our families, the people who picked up the slack at home while we traveled for interviews and spent long nights and weekends researching and writing this book.

GLOSSARY

Giving In to the Unclean: A catchall term used for a wide variety of sins, such as having erotic thoughts.

Locked In: Phrase used to remind congregants they needed to get permission from Jane Whaley or others in church leadership before making any decisions, including buying a car or having sex with their spouses.

Open Your Heart: Phrase used by ministers to encourage congregants to disclose their deepest—and often darkest—secrets.

Take Hold: An expression used to warn congregants to shape up, obey what they've been told by church leadership.

Under Authority: A term used to warn congregants to follow Jane Whaley's strict rules and edicts.

Work Projects: Congregants are expected to "volunteer" on their weekends or after work to help with the church's construction projects. It could mean working as a handyman helping to renovate a congregant's home or property owned by church ministers.

Walking Out a Friendship or Walking Out a Relationship:
Terms used to signal when a couple has been paired and are now exclusive. They can sit together at church and have lunch together, but their actions are closely watched and they must refrain from anything the church considers unclean.

NOTES ON SOURCES

PROLOGUE

Our account of John David Cooper and his wife fleeing the Word of Faith Fellowship on July 16, 2014, is based on numerous interviews with former members, including John David Cooper; his parents, Rick and Suzanne Cooper; and brothers Benjamin, Jeffrey, and Peter. They said John David Cooper was beaten to expel demons in a practice called "blasting."

For information about the church's practices, including blasting and discipleship, we conducted interviews of nearly one hundred former members, including John David Cooper, Rick and Suzanne Cooper, Danielle Cordes, Matthew Fenner, John Huddle, Jamey Anderson, Rachel Bryant, and Sarah Anderson. The former members described how they and others were rebuked from the pulpit, isolated from the outside world, and prohibited from watching television, listening to the radio, reading newspapers, and watching movies. Nearly two dozen former members talked about how they were removed from their families and forced to live with ministers who became their de facto parents.

We also drew on numerous tapes of Jane Whaley sermons from

the 1990s as well as court and police documents, including the 1995 State Bureau of Investigation report.

In addition, we gleaned information about the church's practices from several custody cases. They include Jane Whaley's 2017 deposition in a custody case involving Sarah Anderson, who left the Word of Faith Fellowship in 2016, and her former husband, Nick Anderson, who was still inside the church.

In her deposition, Whaley said blasting is used to "break the power of Satan. So in the name of Jesus you drive the demons out." She also acknowledged that the church has prohibitions against television, radio, and magazines.

1

We conducted extensive interviews with numerous members of the Cooper family, including Rick and Suzanne Cooper, and extended relatives.

For the section that Whaley is considered a prophet by her followers, we drew on interviews with dozens of former congregants.

For information about the church's practices, we conducted interviews with nearly one hundred former members. We also pulled from police and court documents, and reviewed transcripts of depositions from custody cases involving Word of Faith Fellowship members.

In her 2017 custody-case deposition, Jane Whaley discussed in detail her belief in strong prayer, known as blasting. When an attorney asked Whaley if a "shrill cry" comes "out of you" during blasting, she responded, "Right, it's a cry. It's a shrill cry."

Attorney: "A shrill cry?"

Whaley: "Uh-huh. To prevail against the spirit of darkness that's coming at somebody."

Our account of congregants screaming, convulsing, or vomiting into buckets during such church practices as blasting is based on interviews with numerous former members, as well as John Peter Evans, the Trinity Foundation investigator who infiltrated the church.

The estimate on church membership and physical description of the compound is based on interviews with numerous people who attended the church at various times since its founding. Jane Whaley also gave *AP* reporter Mitch Weiss a tour of the church on February 8, 2013.

Our account of Jane Whaley scolding Suzanne Cooper for her daughter's boots is based on interviews with Suzanne Cooper and her mother, Wanda Henderson.

In her 2017 custody-case deposition, Jane Whaley discussed her beliefs about how people should dress in a godly way. Her thoughts on blue jeans, for example, are that they should only be worn for work.

Whaley: "If you're a friend of the world, you're an enemy of God because everywhere you go, there's all kind of jeans."

We drew additional information about what congregants should wear from videotapes of Jane Whaley's sermons, as well as numerous tape-recorded services from the mid-1990s.

Our account in which Whaley sells shoes and other items from the pulpit is based on interviews with Suzanne Cooper and her mother, Wanda Henderson.

The offering plate being passed around multiple times during services is corroborated by dozens of former members of the Word of Faith Fellowship.

2

We conducted interviews with numerous members of the Cooper family and extended relatives as well as dozens of other former members of the Word of Faith Fellowship.

The historical information on Brooke McFadden Covington comes from interviews of people who know her, news articles, the 1995 State Bureau of Investigation report, and Whaley's 2017 deposition.

Dozens of former congregants described what they considered Whaley's obsession with the "'unclean' demons," often focused on thoughts of a sexual nature or natural functions of the body, such as erections.

The information about "blasting" and how the ritual is practiced in the church is based on countless hours of interviews with dozens of former members of the church. Most said the sessions often devolved into violence that would include shaking, pushing, slapping, or punching. They said that congregants were often restrained, pinned to the floor, during the violent attacks.

The 1995 State Bureau of Investigation report makes numerous references to blasting, including one witness who described it as "when adults scream in children's faces for hours at a time."

In her 2017 child custody deposition, Whaley said blasting means "any strong demonstration of the power of God." Whaley elaborated that it is used to "break the power of Satan. So in the name of Jesus you drive the demons out." But rather than characterize it as screaming, she said it's "a sound of the Holy Spirit that comes up out of you."

The longtime affiliation of Karel Reynolds and Brooke Covington is based on dozens of interviews, Jane Whaley's 2017 deposition, and the 1995 SBI report. One witness in the report described Reynolds and Covington as the number two and three top leaders, respectively, just below Jane Whaley in rank. The same witness stated that "Sam Whaley was an ordained minister, but he was merely a front." Another witness noted that Covington, Reynolds, and Jayne Caulder held leadership responsibilities while "Sam Whaley slowly lost any authority that he had over time."

The role of Covington and Reynolds in counseling the Coopers is based on interviews with Rick and Suzanne Cooper.

3

We conducted interviews with John Peter Evans and numerous former members of the Word of Faith Fellowship and reviewed dozens of pages of documents collected by Evans during the Trinity Foundation investigation. His presence in the church was corroborated by multiple people who were members at the time.

The information about Robert Tilton and Leigh Valentine is based on interviews and news accounts. Part of Valentine's biography comes from her June 13, 2018, appearance on WCAB—a Rutherfordton, North Carolina–based radio station. In December 2017, the Word of Faith Fellowship began purchasing airtime at the station to counter what it called the *AP*'s "negative news stories" about the church. Since then, more than one hundred and seventy church members, including Valentine, have given glowing "testimonies" about their experiences in the congregation.

The information about "blasting" and how the ritual is practiced is based on hours of interviews with dozens of former members of the church, with most saying the sessions often devolved into violence.

Information that Jane Whaley publicly called out her husband, Sam Whaley, and singled him out for blasting was corroborated by John Peter Evans and multiple former members of the church. In the 1995 SBI report, one witness noted that "Jane Whaley publicly belittles her husband."

For the sections on Joe and Dayle English, we drew on news stories, interviews with John Peter Evans, and numerous former church members, as well as the couple's own accounts broadcasted on WCAB and posted on YouTube.com. Information about Ray Nenow came from his appearance on WCAB.

Our account that John Peter Evans was mentored by Sam Whaley and Douglas MacDonald is based on interviews with Evans. Mac-Donald's long association with the church is confirmed by accounts in the 1995 SBI report and his presence on the Word of Faith Fellowship website, where he is listed as a minister.

Information that Evans witnessed a six-month-old baby being blasted is based on Evans's account. But numerous former members also recounted seeing babies and their own children being blasted at the church.

4

We interviewed John Peter Evans and numerous former members of the Word of Faith Fellowship and reviewed documents collected by Evans during the Trinity Foundation investigation.

We also reviewed footage of 1995 episodes of *Inside Edition* and a televised news conference Jane Whaley called in response to the negative television reports.

Documents and letters attributed to Jane Whaley or the church were recovered by the Trinity Foundation from a dumpster on the grounds of the Word of Faith Fellowship.

For the section about Leigh Valentine, the information came from news reports, interviews with former church members, a biography posted on Valentine's business website, and her June 13, 2018, appearance on WCAB.

The biographical information on Sam and Jane Whaley and their daughter, Robin, came from dozens of interviews, published material, yearbooks from Jane Whaley's time at Appalachian State, as well as police and legal documents, including the 1995 State Bureau of Investigation report and Whaley's 2017 child custody deposition. We also drew on numerous tape-recorded Word of Faith Fellowship sermons from the mid-1990s.

For the section on the history of the Prosperity Gospel and Kenneth Hagin, Sr., we relied on numerous interviews with former Word of Faith Fellowship members who went to Rhema Bible College and knew Jane Whaley in Tulsa, Oklahoma, friends and colleagues of Kenneth Hagin, Sr., religion experts, historical documents, and published material.

The information about the church's beginning in a steak house in 1979 is noted in the 1995 SBI report and its growth was described in interviews with multiple former members, as well as by some current members who appeared on WCAB. We also pulled from documents, including the church's incorporation papers.

For our section about "blasting" and how the ritual is practiced in the church, we interviewed numerous former members. All of them were blasted. Most of them said the sessions often devolved into violence that included shaking, pushing, slapping, or punching. Many said they were pinned to the floor while others screamed and punched them.

We also drew on court documents. North Carolina Superior Court Judge Randy Pool, on December 8, 2000, issued a ruling in a custody case in which he described blasting.

"This Court finds that blasting is a high-pitched, shrill, piercing, nonverbal scream. The purpose of blasting was described by witnesses for both the Plaintiff and Defendant as for use in driving out devils. Children are said by WOFF authority figures, staff, and school personnel to be 'given to the control of devils which necessitates blasting.'

"Blasting has been and is used on children from birth and will occur from within one foot of a child. Frequently, more than one person engages in blasting at one time. Children are blasted repeatedly for hours. Children and adults are sometimes physically restrained while being subjected to blasting."

Pool said blasting was dangerous to children.

"Certain practices of Word of Faith, including blasting prayer, had an adverse effect on the health, safety, and welfare of children[,]" and "pose a potential harm."

The case involved a father who left the church and his wife who stayed behind. They had three children. Pool ordered that the parents have joint custody but warned: "Neither parent shall allow the children to be permitted to engage in blasting."

The information that Jane Whaley suspected John Peter Evans was a plant is based on interviews with Suzanne Cooper, who recalled being in the meeting in which it was discussed. Whaley's interaction in confronting Evans is based on multiple interviews with Evans.

5

Whaley's anticipation of, preparation for, and reaction to the 1995 *Inside Edition* episodes are based on interviews with multiple former members of the Word of Faith Fellowship as well as statements she made in the media.

In the 1995 SBI report, Jane Whaley's lawyer, James H. Atkins, expressed "concerns regarding *Inside Edition* being in town and stirring up controversy." In the same document, it is noted that church leaders contacted some former members, telling them not to get involved with *Inside Edition.*

We reviewed the footage of the 1995 episodes of *Inside Edition,* a televised news conference Jane Whaley called in response to the negative television reports, numerous newspaper accounts, and the 1995 State Bureau of Investigation report.

The church's support of Sheriff Dan Good is noted in the 1995 SBI report.

The biographical information for Stephen and Cindy Cordes comes from interviews with relatives as well as the couple's appearances on WCAB.

Passages about the church's regard for communal living is based on dozens of interviews with former members, including those who lived in shared homes, including Rick and Suzanne Cooper and Jamey Anderson.

The information about the death of Harold Lloyd is based on his son's appearance on *Inside Edition* and the 1995 SBI report.

For the section on Crystal Taylor, we interviewed Taylor and numerous former members of the Word of Faith Fellowship, and reviewed law enforcement documents and the 1995 State Bureau of Investigation report.

The information that Jane Whaley acknowledged that she was aware of several instances of sexual abuse at Word of Faith Fellowship is based on a three-hour recording of Whaley secretly made in October 2012 by former congregant Christina Bryant, who was trying to gather information to expose the church's abuses.

6

Whaley's reaction to the 1995 *Inside Edition* episodes is based on interviews with multiple former members of the Word of Faith Fellowship as well as statements she made to the media. Rick and Suzanne Cooper recalled being prepped on what to say if questioned by investigators.

In the 1995 SBI report, Jane Whaley's lawyer, James H. Atkins, expressed "concerns regarding *Inside Edition* being in town and stirring up controversy." In the same report, it is noted that church leaders contacted some former members, telling them not to get involved with *Inside Edition*.

We conducted interviews with John Peter Evans and numerous former members of the Word of Faith Fellowship. We also reviewed internal church documents, footage of the 1995 episodes of *Inside Edition*, the 1995 State Bureau of Investigation report, and court records related to an investigation by the Rutherford County Department of Social Services.

The information about the waiver and release agreements is based on a review of a copy of one of the agreements and interviews with former members.

We talked at length with John Huddle for his biography and account of being drawn into the Word of Faith Fellowship.

The information on the death of Harold Lloyd and allegations of abuse made by others noted in the 315-page SBI report is based on reviews of the report, which was obtained by the authors unredacted and in its entirety.

The biographical information on Brooke Covington is based on interviews with multiple former members, including Sheri Nolan, Sarah Anderson, and Shana Muse.

7

We conducted interviews with numerous former members of the Word of Faith Fellowship, various members of the Cooper family, including Suzanne Cooper's mother, Wanda Henderson, and Suzanne's sister Shana Muse.

Biographical information on Robin Whaley Webster comes from interviews with numerous former members, including Jay Plummer, Sr.; his wife, Susie; Suzanne Cooper; and Whaley's 2017 deposition. When Whaley's family moved a few doors down from him in the early 1980s, Plummer and Robin became close friends.

The section on Suzanne Cooper's pregnancy is based primarily on interviews with Rick and Suzanne Cooper and Wanda Henderson, Suzanne's mother. Multiple former members have corroborated that Jane Whaley tried to control her congregants' sex lives, including when they could have children. In the 1995 SBI report, one witness "stated Jane Whaley disapproves of married couples having sex and refers to it as 'lustful devils.'"

Our account about Whaley's "move of God" is based on interviews with Jeffrey Cooper and his mother, Suzanne Cooper. Numerous former members corroborated Jane Whaley's ongoing insistence that members of her congregation confess their sins to her.

For the section on Crystal Taylor, we interviewed Taylor and numerous former members of the Word of Faith Fellowship, reviewed law enforcement documents, and obtained a lengthy audio recording of Jane Whaley discussing the case. Allegations that Taylor had been sexually abused are also found in the 1995 SBI report, Rutherford County Department of Social Services records, and court documents.

8

For the section on Sam Whaley opening with a prayer before the US House of Representatives, we relied on the July 14, 1999, edition of the Congressional Record and a C-Span video of the prayer.

The information that Congressman Charles Taylor's office provided computers to the church is based on a December 2000 article by the *Charlotte Observer*.

The information that Laura Bridges landed a job in the Ruther-ford County court clerk's office in 1997 is based on a lawsuit filed by congregant Ramona Hall.

Our account that Sam Whaley had become an "afterthought" in the Word of Faith Fellowship is based on dozens of interviews in which former members said Jane Whaley was the ultimate leader of the church. In the 1995 SBI report, one witness noted that "Jane Whaley publicly belittles her husband."

Whaley acknowledged in her 2017 custody-case deposition that Word of Faith Fellowship has ties to churches in Brazil and Ghana.

The section on Shana Muse is based on numerous police and court records and interviews with Muse, her relatives, and other former members of the church, including Suzanne Cooper, Wanda Hen-derson, and Muse's children: Patrick Covington, Sarah Anderson, and Rachel Bryant.

The section on Rick Cooper's concern about his children being forced to work is based on interviews with Cooper, his wife, Suzanne, and his children. Dozens of former members corroborated during interviews that congregants, including children, are forced to work.

The scene about the Coopers' attempt to leave the church in 2001 is based on interviews with Rick and Suzanne Cooper, their chil-dren, including Benjamin and Jeffrey, as well as Shana Muse and her mother, Wanda Henderson.

9

The section on Shana Muse is based on police and court records and interviews with Muse, her relatives, and other former members of the church, including Suzanne Cooper, Wanda Henderson, and Muse's children: Patrick Covington, Sarah Anderson, and Rachel Bryant.

In her 2017 deposition, Whaley acknowledged that the church teaches against television, radio, and magazines.

For our section about the church's strict rules involving sex and holidays, we drew on dozens of interviews with numerous former members, including Rick and Suzanne Cooper. In her 2017 child custody deposition, Whaley said Christmas is a "pagan holiday." When an attorney challenged that it was a celebration of the birth of Jesus Christ, Whaley said he was "ignorant."

For Whaley's views on holidays and other Word of Faith Fellowship practices, we also pulled from tape-recorded sermons from the mid-1990s.

10

We conducted multiple interviews with Jamey Anderson, three of the so-called Five Boys, and other witnesses who were in the sanctuary when Jane Whaley designated them with the name. Nearly two dozen former members recounted witnessing Anderson being beaten, locked up, or humiliated from the pulpit during his life in the church.

Other members of the Five Boys, including John Blanton and Peter Cooper, corroborated the way they were isolated and abused. Multiple other former members of the church recounted the Five Boys being isolated from their peers and shamed by church leaders.

For the section on Mark Doyle, we pulled from numerous interviews of former church members as well as Doyle's appearance on WCAB, which is posted on YouTube.com. His treatment of children in the church is based on interviews with multiple former members, including Jamey Anderson and Benjamin and Peter Cooper. We also reviewed police and court documents related to Doyle's criminal case. He was charged but later acquitted of beating a teenager in the church.

We conducted numerous interviews with John Huddle for our account of his time inside the church, including his 2002 move to Spindale, North Carolina, from Greenville, South Carolina.

11

We talked at length with John David Cooper, his relatives, and numerous former members about the Word of Faith Christian School and the church's practices.

In the 1995 SBI report, Jane Whaley acknowledged that she and others paddled children. Whaley stated that "the number of strikes a student received from a paddle was determined by the spirit of God." Some, she said, may have received "five or six strikes from the paddle."

Dozens of former members, however, said it was common for children to be hit much more than that. Many, like Danielle Cordes, said the beatings could last for hours, leaving deep, painful bruises.

12

We conducted numerous interviews with Benjamin Cooper, his relatives, and former members.

For the part on the violence that had gotten worse over the years, we drew on dozens of interviews with multiple former members. All said shaming and abuse were a way of life and primarily revolved around blasting. Information about "blasting" and how the ritual is practiced in the church is based on hours of interviews with dozens of former members of the church, with most saying the sessions often devolved into violence such as shaking, pushing, slapping, or punching.

We also drew on court documents, including North Carolina Superior Court Judge Randy Pool's December 8, 2000, ruling that said blasting had "an adverse effect on the health, safety, and welfare of children."

Mark Doyle's biographical information is based on numerous interviews with former members as well as his appearance on the church's radio show on WCAB. Our account of his treatment of children in the church was based on interviews with multiple former members, including Jamey Anderson, Benjamin Cooper, and his brother Peter Cooper, as well as court records in which he was charged and acquitted of assault. We also interviewed Benjamin Talley, the man who filed assault charges against Doyle.

13

The information about Shana Muse's fight for her children is based on interviews with Muse, her children Sarah, Rachel, and Patrick, as well as numerous others, including Rick and Suzanne Cooper and Wanda Henderson. We also reviewed court records and published material that followed Muse's journey.

Our account that violence inside the church had gotten worse with time is based on interviews with multiple former members. All said shaming and abuse were a way of life and primarily revolved around blasting. Information about "blasting" and how the ritual is practiced in the church is based on hours of interviews with dozens of former members, police reports, and court documents. Most said the sessions often devolved into violence such as shaking, pushing, slapping, or punching.

Our account of William Brock's role in the church is based on interviews with former members. Suzanne Cooper noted that he was the only person who could sway Jane Whaley's behavior. She recalled one incident in which he scolded Whaley for delays in the construction of the Coopers' house.

Kent Covington's biographical information is based on interviews with former members, including Sheri Nolan, Sarah Anderson, Rick and Suzanne Cooper, as well as state business documents, North Carolina criminal records, the 1995 SBI report, Jane Whaley's 2017 child custody deposition, and information from the websites of Covington's businesses.

For information about the church being a cult, we drew on interviews with former members, psychologists, and published material, including a 2002 newspaper story in which Mary Alice Chrnalogar, a cult expert, called the Word of Faith Fellowship "one of the top five most dangerous cults in America."

The section of how Brooke Covington conspired with Muse's daughter to retrieve a note that could be used against Shana in the custody case was based on interviews with Shana Muse, her daughter Sarah, who wrote the note, and Suzanne Cooper, one of the women who picked it up. Information about how Brooke Covington prepped members to lie under oath came from a number of sources, including Suzanne Cooper, Rachel Bryant and Sarah Anderson.

14

For the part about the child abuse investigation, we drew on dozens of interviews with former members, including Danielle Cordes, Rick and Suzanne Cooper, John David Cooper, and Jamey Anderson. We also relied on court documents, including a federal lawsuit filed by the church against the Rutherford County Department of Social Services.

We interviewed Danielle Cordes and numerous former members about the church's practices, including spanking. In the 1995 SBI report, Jane Whaley acknowledged that she and others paddled children, though the passage did not name specific children. Whaley stated that "the number of strikes a student received from a paddle was determined by the spirit of God." Some, she said, might have received "five or six strikes from the paddle."

In the 2003 lawsuit, the church said it "believes in the use of corporal punishment as discipline for misbehavior of children, based on religious doctrine as mandated by the Bible." But the church argued that spanking is more a spiritual act than a physical one. Therefore, the church "teaches not to apply hard pressure with the paddle." Both the child and adult performing the spanking are taught to cry out to Jesus and to mix faith with the spanking, asking God to change the child's heart. And the lawsuit said "only one to three swats are administered."

We talked to dozens of former members who disputed that account. They said it was common for children to be hit multiple times and the spankings could last for hours. Many former members, like Danielle Cordes, described the routine. At first, they'd get hit with a paddle between fifteen minutes to a half hour. Then a minister or parent would stop to see if the child had a "breakthrough." But usually the adult would deem that the child still had sin in their heart. So they would resume the spanking. Dozens of former members said spankings were so commonplace that they could take place at any time in any location—from Jane Whaley's office to their homes. We talked at length to numerous members who said they were badly hurt in the sessions.

We based Lynn Millwood's biographical information on her appearance on WCAB. For our account of her behavior inside the church, we conducted interviews with multiple former members, including Danielle Cordes. The account of Danielle Cordes's abuse at the hands of Lynn Millwood is based on interviews with Cordes and others. Danielle's brother, Stephen Cordes, confirmed her accounts. Stephen said Millwood was assigned to his family and beatings were common.

15

The information about Lacy Wien's attack and the criminal charges she filed against Jane Whaley is based on court documents and published reports, including her appearance on *Inside Edition* when she said she'd endured more than one thousand spankings during her decade in the church.

Part of Wien's allegations were that she was assaulted by Whaley for resisting blasting. We interviewed numerous former Word of Faith Fellowship members who said the violence would become more intense if they resisted blasting, or other forms of church discipline.

For the section on the settlement of the church's lawsuit, we relied on documents from the federal court and the North Carolina Department of Health and Human Services, and interviews with numerous former members of the Word of Faith Fellowship, including Danielle Cordes, Jamey Anderson, and John David Cooper.

The following language is contained in the settlement:

"Under no circumstances shall RCDSS [Rutherford County Department of Social Services] commence any investigation of any WFF member or subject child based on WFF religious beliefs or practices concerning music, television, radio, movies, dress or appearance, sports, holidays, or birthdays.

"Plaintiffs maintain that their religious practices of strong or blasting prayer, or discipleship, as practiced by WFF and WFF members cannot constitute abuse or neglect within the meaning of the laws and Constitution of the State of North Carolina, or the Constitution of the United States."

16

Our account of how Luiz Vargas and other Brazilians were treated by the church is based on interviews with numerous former members, including fifteen who belonged to the Brazilian church. They said they were forced to work, often for no pay, and subjected to physical or verbal abuse.

The history of the Brazilian churches is based on documents and dozens of interviews, including some conducted by *Associated Press* reporter Peter Prengaman in Brazil for stories subsequently published by *AP*.

For the section about Jamey Anderson, we talked at length to nearly a dozen former members, including Anderson, Jay Plummer, Sr., and his wife, Susie, and son, Jay Plummer II.

The biographical information about Todd and Karel Reynolds is based on their appearances on WCAB, as well as interviews with former members.

Our account of Jane Whaley telling her congregation a story about Joe English being thrown across the room was described by numerous former members. They said Whaley often repeated it from the pulpit—and that it was a pivotal moment in Word of Faith Fellowship's history. The former members said violence became more frequent after Whaley's announcement.

For biographical information about Rusty Millwood, we drew on his appearance on WCAB. We also conducted interviews with former members who talked about Millwood's role inside the Word of Faith Fellowship.

17

We conducted dozens of interviews of former members, including John David Cooper, Benjamin Cooper, and Luiz Vargas for information about how young people were paired off for marriage. We talked at length with John Huddle about how difficult it was for him to leave the Word of Faith Fellowship.

Our account of the unemployment scheme was based on multiple interviews with former members, including Randy Fields, Rick Cooper, and Rachel Bryant, who said they participated in "God's plan," as well as court documents that corroborated their stories.

We conducted interviews with former members about Jane Whaley's finances and "love offerings." Additional details were contained in Whaley's 2017 deposition in a child custody case involving Sarah Anderson and her former husband, Nick Anderson.

The section about the Lower Building is based on numerous interviews with multiple people who spent time there, including Michael Lowry, Rick Cooper, Patrick Covington, and Chad Cooper, as well as people like Jeffrey Cooper, who had knowledge of how the building was being used to house the church's "worst sinners." We also used police and court documents.

In her 2017 deposition, Whaley acknowledged that some people—including a young boy—lived in the former storage building, including Rick Cooper and Shana Muse's children Patrick and Justin Covington, "to get help" or to have a "heart change." She noted that at least one person was there for two years.

But in the deposition, Whaley said no one was held against their will. Over the years, she said the building was used for different purposes. When Lowry was there, Whaley said the building was being used for "Bible study."

"Then Mark Morris and Chris Hall, two of the ministers in the church—Mark's an attorney—went down there and started teaching them, and they had Bible study and prayer every night... So their lives began to change. It was more like a Baptist retreat session."

When the attorney asked, "Baptist retreat?" Whaley responded yes. "A retreat-like session at that time where men would come together, pray. I'm talking—talking about at night. They had their jobs. They had their schools in the daytime. Then along that time we had—I can think of four or five situations where parents, a wife kicked their young people out of the house. Patrick and Justin was involved in it at that time... They had nowhere to go. So they went and sent them down there to get prayer, to get in the Word, to get a heart change. One wife, which was Suzanne Cooper, kicked her husband out, and he had no place to go. And out of the kindness of my heart—they didn't have money for him to go somewhere—I told him he could live there."

We also pulled information about the building from a three-and-a-half-hour secretly taped conversation between Whaley and Christina Bryant in October 2012.

Former members said beatings and blasting were a way of life in the Lower Building. We also used court and police documents to describe the practice.

For biological information about Mark Morris, we drew on information from his appearance on WCAB. For his behavior inside

the church, we drew on nearly two dozen interviews from former
Word of Faith Fellowship members.

18

We interviewed numerous former members of the Word of Faith
Fellowship, including Michael Lowry and John Huddle, as well as
people who tried to help them, including Nancy Burnette and Brent
Childers of Faith in America.

We reviewed court documents related to the two foster boys in
Burnette's care, as well as interviewed their former foster mother.

Information about Robynn Spence is based on interviews with
her before she died and nearly a dozen people who knew her, including Michael Davis and his wife, Amanda, two former Rutherford
County law enforcement officials. The information that Spence suspected Ramona Hall of using her court position to help the church
comes from interviews with Spence, Nancy Burnette, and former
Word of Faith Fellowship members.

Our account of Michael Lowry's quest for justice is based on interviews with Lowry, his supporters, former church members, as
well as police reports and court documents that name the people allegedly involved in the violence. We conducted an interview with
former district attorney Brad Greenway.

Information about the Lower Building is based on numerous interviews with former members who spent time there. In her 2017
deposition, Jane Whaley acknowledged that some people were sent
there, but said the building was mostly used for Bible study.

Our account of the meeting between Robynn Spence and Kevin
Logan is based on *AP* interviews with Spence as well as six people she told about the plot, including Burnette, Mike and Amanda
Davis, and Jack Conner, a former Rutherford County sheriff. Later,
an *AP* reporter talked briefly to Logan, who confirmed that he had
met with Spence. But he declined to go into detail because he said
he was afraid for his life. We also pulled transcripts from a secretly
recorded tape of a conversation between Rutherford County Sheriff Chris Francis and Spence's father. On the tape, the sheriff said a
man was hired to "harass" Spence, not kill her.

19

We talked at length with members of the Cooper family, including John, Benjamin, and Peter.

John David Cooper described his beating as the worst he had experienced up to that point. Peter Cooper and other former members confirmed John's assault.

For the section about the Lower Building, we relied on dozens of interviews with former members who were in the structure or visited to minister to congregants inside the place. We also pulled information from court documents and a PowerPoint with the layout of the building created by former member Patrick Covington.

We talked at length to Rick Cooper about his time in the building.

For the section on Jerry Cooper's run-in with members of the church security team, we interviewed Jerry Cooper, Michael Lowry, and Randy Fields. Information about the criminal case is based on court records, a transcript of the trial, and eyewitness accounts by people like John Huddle.

Our account of how church leaders, including Jane Whaley, her son-in-law, Frank Webster, and others tried to derail criminal investigations is based on interviews with former members who were at the meetings, including Jeffrey Cooper.

For the section on the unemployment benefits scheme, we relied on interviews with nearly a dozen former members and court documents. Four church members, including Kent Covington, pleaded guilty for their roles in the scheme.

20

The section on Christina Bryant's conversation with Jane Whaley is based on interviews with Bryant, as well as a secret three-and-a-half-hour recording she made during the October 2012 meeting.

We interviewed numerous former members, including Michael Lowry, Jerry Cooper, Jeffrey Cooper, Nancy Burnette, and others, as well as a visit to the church by *AP* reporter Mitch Weiss.

Michael Lowry's experience in the church is based on dozens of interviews, including ones with Lowry and Jeffrey Cooper.

During interviews, Jeffrey Cooper described Whaley's attempts to derail investigations into Lowry and to hide that the Lower Building was used as a de facto prison.

Information about the Lower Building is based on interviews with multiple people who spent time there.

In her 2017 deposition, Whaley acknowledged that some people were sent there, including Rick Cooper and Shana Muse's children Patrick and Justin Covington, "to get help" or to have a "heart change."

Multiple people have noted that beatings and blasting were a way of life in the Lower Building.

Lowry's disappearance is based on interviews with Nancy Burnette, John Huddle, Brent Childers, and others.

The information about Lowry's interview with an *AP* reporter is based on Mitch's notes and recollections of the event.

21

For biographical information about Matthew Fenner and his time in the church, we drew on numerous interviews with Fenner, his family, and friends, including his mother, Linda Addington, and Danielle Cordes. Our account of Jane Whaley hitting Danielle Cordes is based on interviews with Danielle and several former members, including her brother.

The section on Fenner's travels with the Whaleys is based on multiple interviews with Fenner. His church-sanctioned relationship with Danielle Cordes and his attraction to Patrick Covington are based on interviews with Fenner, Patrick, Danielle, and others.

Our account of Matthew Fenner's assault on January 27, 2013, is based on dozens of interviews, police records, court testimony, and recordings of Fenner's meetings and phone calls with law enforcement officials, including former federal prosecutor Jill Rose and Rutherford County Sheriff Chris Francis.

Seven former members recounted the event to the authors, including Fenner, Danielle Cordes, and Sarah Anderson, who admits to taking part in the attack. Witnesses said Fenner was beaten during a blasting session. Information about "blasting" and how the ritual is practiced in the church is based on hours of interviews with dozens of former members of the church, with most saying the sessions often devolved into violence such as shaking, pushing, slapping, or punching.

22

Susanna Kokkonen's visit to the Word of Faith Fellowship is based on published material and interviews with former church members.

Our account of Danielle Cordes's escape from the church is based on interviews with multiple former members, including Cordes, Patrick Covington, Jeanna Powell, and Matthew Fenner.

The section of her return home to collect her belongings is based on interviews with Cordes, Jeanna Powell, Matthew Fenner, and Patrick Covington.

23

Our account of John David Cooper's wedding is based on numerous interviews with the Cooper family and friends, as well as a video of the entire ceremony.

24

We interviewed dozens of people for our account of Matthew Fenner's fight for justice. We also reviewed court records and multiple recordings of Fenner's meetings and phone calls with law enforcement officials. Mitch also covered Fenner's trial that ended in mistrial.

The section about the plot against Robynn Spence is based on interviews with Spence before she died as well as interviews with six people she told about the plot, including Burnette. We also have emails she exchanged with an anti-cult group saying the church had a "bounty on her head."

In one mail, she wrote: "They have endless amounts of money and power... I am about the only elected official that they cannot control. We have nowhere else to turn, no one will help."

In her last email to the group in February 2014, she wrote: "I won't let them intimidate me. I'm a well-known public figure here so they will have to be very smart on how they will succeed in killing me."

Our account of the scene about the event honoring Spence and raising awareness about child abuse is based on interviews with Nancy Burnette, Christina Bryant, Jeanna Powell, Matthew Fenner, and others, as well as a recording of the event. The section where Patrick Covington recounts the violence he faced inside the church comes from more than a dozen interviews with former members who said they witnessed the beatings.

25

For the section about Jane Whaley's insistence that John David Cooper and his brother Peter attend the same medical school, we drew on interviews with John, Peter, and Benjamin Cooper, and other former members.

The account of John David Cooper's escape from the church is based on numerous interviews with John and his relatives, as well as Jamey Anderson, Danielle Cordes, and Luiz Vargas.

26

We conducted numerous interviews with former church members and others about Matthew Fenner's fight for justice, including Fenner, Burnette, and Huddle. We also used police and court documents and recordings of his meetings and phone calls with law enforcement officials.

The interactions between Fenner and his supporters and Sheriff Chris Francis are based on numerous interviews and recordings of some of their conversations. Our account of Chris Back playing the role of Matthew Fenner during a church meeting comes from interviews with several former members who were in the room.

For the section about the exodus of most of the Cooper family from the church, we drew on numerous interviews with Rick and Suzanne Cooper, as well as their sons Benjamin, Jeffrey, and John, and other family members and friends. Our account of Jane Whaley's sermon that led to Jeffrey Cooper leaving the church comes from several former members. They say Whaley claimed a member had not been abused. They say Whaley said the young man had slipped and fallen into a wall. But Cooper and others said the member was pushed so hard he went through the drywall in the church.

We interviewed Linda Addington about her testimony before the grand jury. She has since left the church and acknowledges that she was lying when she denied her son was assaulted. Our account also drew on numerous interviews with former church members and court documents.

27

Our account of the Cooper family reunion is based on multiple interviews with their family and relatives, including Wanda Henderson.

BOOKS

The Amplified Bible. Grand Rapids, MI: The Zondervan Corporation, 1954.

Bowler, Kate. *Blessed: A History of the American Prosperity Gospel.* New York, NY: Oxford University Press, 2013.

Guinn, Jeff. *The Road to Jonestown: Jim Jones and the Peoples Temple.* New York, NY: Simon & Schuster, 2017.

Hassan, Steven. *Combating Cult Mind Control: The #1 Best-selling Guide to Protection, Rescue, and Recovery from Destructive Cults.* Newton, MA: Freedom of Mind Press, 1988.

Hill, Jenna Miscavige, and Lisa Pulitzer. *Beyond Belief: My Secret Life Inside Scientology and My Harrowing Escape.* New York, NY: HarperCollins, 2013.

Huddle, John. *Locked In: My Imprisoned Years in a Destructive Cult.* Marion, NC: Survivor Publishing, LLC, 2015.

Langone, Michael. *Recovery from Cults: Help for Victims of Psychological and Spiritual Abuse.* New York, NY: W.W. Norton, 1993.

NEWSPAPERS

Associated Press. "Head of secretive North Carolina sect named in fraud scam." October 25, 2018.

Associated Press. "'Nobody saved us': Man describes childhood in abusive 'cult.'" December 13, 2017.

Associated Press. "North Carolina steps in on child abuse cases involving sect." December 8, 2017.

Associated Press. "Ex-members say church uses power, lies to keep grip on kids." November 13, 2017.

Associated Press. "Church stoked tithing with unemployment scam, ex-members say." September 25, 2017.

Associated Press. "Brazilians funneled as 'slaves' by US church, ex-members say." July 24, 2017.

Associated Press. "AP: Authorities delayed investigating gay 'demons' case." June 26, 2017.

Associated Press. "Prosecutor: Minister 'directed' beating of gay congregant." June 1, 2017.

Associated Press. "Social worker accused of hiding religious sect abuse resigns." March 17, 2017.

ABC News 13 WLOS. "Former members of Word of Faith Fellowship hold community meeting." March 11, 2017.

Associated Press. "ADAs accused of coaching sect members out of jobs in 25th District." March 11, 2017.

Associated Press. "Ex-sect members tell AP: Prosecutors obstructed abuse cases." March 6, 2017.

Associated Press. "AP Exclusive: Ex-congregants reveal years of ungodly abuse." February 27, 2017.

Associated Press. "Church members charged with beating gay man." December 14, 2014.

Associated Press. "Man recants claim he was kidnapped by church." February 9, 2013.

Charlotte Observer. "Word of Faith Fellowship sees 'persecution' for a godly walk; critics see an abusive church." November 19, 2012.

Daily Mail. "Church 'held man, 22, for four months against his will while he was physically and emotionally abused because he is gay.'" October 22, 2012.

Daily Courier. "Former employee suing Clerk of Court." January 5, 2011.

Daily Courier. "WOFF-related custody saga continues." August 23, 2005.

Daily Courier. "WOFF prayer issue debated." March 23, 2005.

Daily Courier. "Whaley testifies during appeal." February 9, 2005.

Daily Courier. "Father claims contempt of 'blasting' order." January 28, 2005.

Daily Courier. "Children gain emancipation from mother." August 27, 2004.

Daily Courier. "Couple resolves custody dispute." April 6, 2004.

Daily Courier. "Church leader found guilty." March 4, 2004.

Spartanburg Herald-Journal. "Word of Faith Fellowship sues DSS, claims harassment." December 6, 2003.

Daily Courier. "WOFF man cleared on charges." November 22, 2003.

Daily Courier. "Aunt says 'will of God' key for kids." September 11, 2003.

Daily Courier. "Custody fight goes public." December 20, 2002.

Daily Courier. "Mother tries to get kids from WOFF." December 18, 2002.

Associated Press. "Social Services probes Word of Faith church." March 14, 1995.

Spartanburg Herald-Journal. "Convicted child molester at Word of Faith agrees to worship at another church." March 8, 1995.